Understanding Communication
in Second Language Classrooms

CAMBRIDGE LANGUAGE EDUCATION
Series Editor: Jack C. Richards

This new series draws on the best available research, theory, and educational practice to help clarify issues and resolve problems in language teaching, language teacher education, and related areas. Books in the series focus on a wide range of issues and are written in a style that is accessible to classroom teachers, teachers-in-training, and teacher educators.

In this series:

Agendas for Second Language Literacy *by Sandra Lee McKay*

Reflective Teaching in Second Language Classrooms *by Jack C. Richards and Charles Lockhart*

Educating Second Language Children: The whole child, the whole curriculum, the whole community *edited by Fred Genesee*

Understanding Communication in Second Language Classrooms *by Karen E. Johnson*

The Self-directed Teacher: Managing the learning process *by David Nunan and Clarice Lamb*

Functional English Grammar:An introduction for second language teachers *by Graham Lock*

Teachers as Course Developers *edited by Kathleen Graves*

Understanding Communication in Second Language Classrooms

Karen E. Johnson

The Pennsylvania State University

CAMBRIDGE
UNIVERSITY PRESS

Published by the Press Syndicate of the University of Cambridge
The Pitt Building, Trumpington Street, Cambridge CB2 1RP
40 West 20th Street, New York, NY 10011-4211, USA
10 Stamford Road, Oakleigh, Melbourne 3166, Australia

First published 1995
Second printing 1996

Printed in the United States of America

Library of Congress Cataloging-in-Publication Data
Johnson, Karen E.
Understanding communication in second language classrooms / Karen
E. Johnson.
p.   cm. – (Cambridge language education)
Includes bibliographical references and index.
ISBN 0-521-45355-0. – ISBN 0-521-45968-0 (pbk.)
1. Language and languages – Study and teaching.   2. Second language
acquisition.   3. Communication in education.   4. Teacher-student
relationships.   I. Title.   II. Series.
P53.J6 1995
418′.007 – dc20   94–27033
                                                              CIP

A catalog record for this book is available from the British Library

ISBN 0-521-45355-0 Hardback
ISBN 0-521-45968-0 Paperback

101483

17.88 *

To Glenn

Contents

Series editor's preface

The nature of classroom communication has long been a focus of research for scholars interested in the effects of classroom interaction on learning. From this research much has been discovered about classroom speech events and participation structures, the nature of teacher talk and student–teacher interaction, and the effects of cultural factors on classroom communication. Much less is known, however, about communication in second language classrooms, though this topic is of considerable interest to language teachers and teacher educators interested in the nature of effective second language teaching. Karen Johnson's book is therefore a welcome addition to the field of second language education, since it offers a comprehensive description of communication in second language classrooms, the factors which shape the nature of such communication, and ways in which patterns of communication can help develop or limit opportunities for students to use and learn a second language in classroom settings.

Using data from authentic classroom discourse, Johnson shows how teachers use language to control and direct second language classroom communication. The nature of this communication is viewed as resulting from the dynamics of teacher–student interaction and teachers' efforts to attain their instructional goals. Throughout the book, Johnson presents parallel accounts of classroom communication, examining it from both teacher and learner perspectives. She demonstrates that teachers' perceptions of the nature of language learning, of classroom activities, and of norms for classroom participation often differ from those of their students, and that these differences can be a cause of misunderstanding and a barrier to effective learning. Throughout, Johnson uses classroom data that present a fascinating and thought-provoking account of the nature of second language teaching as it actually occurs in the moment-to-moment processes of classroom interaction.

This book will be valuable both for teacher educators interested in developing more effective ways of preparing second language teachers, and for classroom teachers interested in examining their own teaching. Teachers can use the framework Johnson develops to examine interactions in their own classrooms as well as the assumptions they bring to teaching. Both teachers and teacher educators will also find this book a useful source of strategies that can be used to promote more effective second language classroom communication.

Jack C. Richards

Preface

Understanding Communication in Second Language Classrooms focuses on communication as the central feature in teaching and learning within second language classrooms. It examines the classroom as a unique communication context with highly regulated patterns of communicative behavior that are actively negotiated between teachers and students. It explores how and why these patterns of communication are established and maintained so that teachers can come to understand the ways in which the nature of classroom communication ultimately determines how and what second language students learn.

The conceptual framework presented in this book views the dynamics of classroom communication as being shaped by the moment-to-moment actions and interactions that occur during face-to-face communication between teachers and students, and by what resides within teachers and students that shapes, in part, how they communicate with one another in classrooms. The framework is designed to enable teachers to recognize how the patterns of communication are established and maintained in second language classrooms, the effect these patterns have on how second language students participate in classroom activities, and how their participation shapes both the ways in which they use language for learning and their opportunities for second language acquisition.

Understanding Communication in Second Language Classrooms provides readers with a clear account of the dynamics of classroom communication. It also provides multiple opportunities for readers to examine specific aspects of classroom communication in terms of their potential impact on student learning and second language acquisition. Finally, it illustrates ways of promoting effective patterns of classroom communicative competence.

This book would not have been possible without the insight and support of numerous students, colleagues, and friends. I am grateful to my many former M.A. TESL students whose personal and professional insights are included in this book. Their interest in and commitment to improving the quality of classroom communication has helped advance my own understandings of the ideas presented in this book. I also would like to thank

Paula Golombek and David Shipp for their comments on the earliest drafts of this book and for providing their critical insights as practicing second language teachers. I am indebted to my colleague Donald Freeman for his incisive comments, which enabled me to clearly articulate the residual message that undergirds the conceptual framework presented in this book. I am also grateful to Patricia Dunkel and Dennis Gouran for supporting me with both time and encouragement throughout the writing of this book. A special thanks goes to Jack Richards for his personal and professional support and to Mary Vaughn, Jane Mairs, and Sandra Graham for their help in the publishing process. Finally, my deepest gratitude goes to my best friend and husband, Glenn, for his unwavering support and encouragement.

Karen E. Johnson

Note on transcriptions

The following conventions are used in the transcriptions of language lessons:

Italics indicates emphasis.
Ellipses (. . .) indicate pauses.
Brackets [   ] indicate overlapped speech.
Parentheses (   ) indicate actions.

Unattributed quotations come from unpublished research; the names of the informants have been changed.

PART I:
A FRAMEWORK FOR UNDERSTANDING COMMUNICATION IN SECOND LANGUAGE CLASSROOMS

1 *Communication in second language classrooms*

In second language classrooms, the language, whether it is English or another language, is the medium through which teachers teach, and students demonstrate what they have learned. Acquiring that language is the ultimate instructional goal of second language education. Yet, how teachers and students use language to communicate in second language classrooms mediates between teaching, learning, and second language acquisition. Therefore, understanding the dynamics of classroom communication is essential for all those involved in second language education. However, understanding communication in second language classrooms is not a simple task. Classroom communication in general has been described as a "problematic medium" (Cazden 1986: 432), since differences in how, when, where, and to whom things are communicated can not only create slight misunderstandings, but can also seriously impair effective teaching and learning. Moreover, if that classroom is filled with students from a wide variety of linguistic and cultural backgrounds who possess a range of second language proficiency levels, then teachers cannot assume that their second language students will learn, talk, act, or interact in predictable ways. On the other hand, if teachers understand how the dynamics of classroom communication influence second language students' perceptions of and participation in classroom activities, they may be better able to monitor and adjust the patterns of classroom communication in order to create an environment that is conducive to both classroom learning and second language acquisition.

The overall goal of this book is to enable teachers to recognize how the patterns of communication are established and maintained in second language classrooms, the effect these patterns have on how second language students participate in classroom activities, and how their participation shapes the ways in which they use language for classroom learning and their opportunities for second language acquisition. This book puts forth an integrated view of classroom communication, by acknowledging that what makes up the whole of classroom communication is the interrelationship between what teachers and second language students bring to classrooms and what actually occurs during face-to-face communication within classrooms. The framework for understanding communication in second language classrooms presented in this book represents a lens through which teachers can begin to recognize this interrelationship and how it shapes the dynamics of communication in second language classrooms.

The classroom as a communication context

All communication occurs in a context. For example, on the surface, Excerpts 1.1 and 1.2 appear similar.

Excerpt 1.1
What time is it?
It's ten o'clock.
Oh, OK, thanks.

Excerpt 1.2
What time is it?
It's ten o'clock.
Right! Very good. *It's* ten o'clock.

In both excerpts, the participants alternate turns speaking, appear to understand each other's intentions, and frame their responses accordingly. However, it is obvious that these exchanges take place in different contexts. In Excerpt 1.1, the first speaker is genuinely seeking information about the time, and the second speaker provides an acceptable answer. In Excerpt 1.2, the first speaker is interested not in the actual time but in whether the second speaker could correctly produce the contracted form of "it is." Hence, the meanings communicated between the speakers in each excerpt are determined, in large part, by the context within which they occurred.

The communication context can also determine the rules that govern how speakers communicate, or the structure of communication. In classrooms, the structure of communication is easily recognizable. Teachers tend to control the topic of discussion, what counts as relevant to the topic, and who may participate and when. Students tend to respond to teacher-directed questions, direct their talk to teachers, and wait their turn before speaking. Teachers can ignore students who talk off-topic, or listen patiently and then direct them back on-topic. They can allow students to call out during a lesson, or insist that they wait to be called on before speaking. Teachers can place their students in small groups so they have more opportunities to control their own talk, to select which topics to talk about, and to direct their talk to whomever they wish. At any point, however, teachers retain the right to regain control over the structure of classroom communication. Thus, teachers, by virtue of the status they hold in their classrooms, play a dominant role in determining the structure of classroom communication.

Differences in the meaning and structure of communication are also determined by the ways in which participants perceive themselves in a particular context (Barker 1982). Such perceptions include a lifelong accumulation of experiences through which people interpret and construct their own representations of the world (Britton 1970; Bruner 1983; Piaget 1957). These experiences have been described as the basis of knowledge, or the frames of reference through which people are able to construct new and unique understandings of what they experience by relating it to what they already know. Learning, therefore, is a matter of changing, expanding, and/ or reconstructing the frames of reference through which people interpret new experiences.

In second language classrooms, how teachers perceive their students and how students perceive their teachers can shape both the meaning and structure of classroom communication. Differences in these perceptions tend to result from differences in prior formal-schooling experiences, or the norms and expectations that in the past governed how to talk and act in classrooms. In one of my own graduate seminars, I was reminded of the subtle nature of these differences during a discussion on the topic of class participation. A Chinese student explained that it took her several semesters to figure out why a certain percentage of her course grade was allocated to something called "class participation." She admitted that before coming to the United States to study she thought if she listened quietly and took notes she *was* participating in class. Of course, this surprised the American students, since their conception of class participation was to raise questions or share their ideas during class discussions. Clearly, this Chinese student held a very different understanding of the concept – an understanding based on years of formal schooling according to norms and expectations different from those of the American students.

Throughout this book, the classroom is viewed as a unique communication context, one in which the meaning being communicated and the structure of that communication are shaped by the perceptions of those who participate in classroom activities. Differences in teachers' and students' perceptions of the classroom context can lead to different interpretations of and participation in classroom activities.

Classroom communicative competence

Understanding the dynamics of classroom communication is essential since how students talk and act in classrooms greatly influences what they learn. Mehan (1979: 33) suggests that "students need to know with whom, when, and where they can speak and act, they must have speech and behavior that are appropriate for classroom situations and they must be able to interpret implicit classroom rules." Full participation in classroom activities requires competence in both the social and interactional aspects of classroom language – in other words, classroom communicative competence (Wilkinson 1982). Just as communicative competence is considered to be essential for second language learners to participate in the target language culture (Canale & Swain 1980; Hymes 1974), classroom communicative competence is essential for second language students to participate in and learn from their second language classroom experiences.

Differences in students' linguistic and cultural backgrounds inevitably influence how, when, where, and why they communicate in second language classrooms. If students are unaware of the social and interactional norms that regulate participation in classroom activities, they may learn little from their classroom experiences (Cook-Gumperz & Gumperz 1982; Wilkinson 1982). Hence, knowledge of and competence in the social and interactional norms that govern classroom communication are essential components of successful participation in second language instruction.

For students operating in a second language, classroom communicative competence is also believed to be an essential component in the process of second language acquisition. Recent classroom-based research suggests that "the processes of classroom interaction determine what language learning opportunities become available to be learned from" (Allwright 1984: 156); therefore, "any second language learning that takes place must in some way result from the process of interaction the learner takes part in" (Ellis 1990: 91). For second language students, classroom communicative competence means not only successfully participating in classroom activities, but also becoming communicatively competent in the second language. To understand the communicative demands placed on their second language students, teachers must recognize that the dynamics of classroom communication are shaped by the classroom context and the norms for participation in that context.

Introducing the framework

The framework for understanding communication in second language classrooms used throughout this book has been adapted from a model of communication and learning put forth by British researcher Douglas Barnes (1976). Barnes characterizes the patterns of classroom communication established and maintained by teachers as determining not only the ways in which students use language but also what students ultimately learn. He disagrees with the notion that students are passive receivers of knowledge and claims this to be an inadequate account of what actually occurs in classrooms. He challenges educators to examine classroom communication in its entirety, including the role students play as active participants in the creation of knowledge.

Barnes supports the notion that teachers and students interpret classroom activities through their own frames of reference. Moreover, since these frames of reference tend to be different, teachers and students are likely to have different interpretations of the activities in which they participate. Therefore, Barnes believes that classroom learning is a negotiation between teachers' meanings and students' understandings – a sort of give-and-take between teachers and students as they construct shared understandings through face-to-face communication. Barnes argues that classroom learning is based primarily on the relationship between what students know and what teachers offer them in classrooms. Ultimately, he recognizes the patterns of communication in classrooms as representing a crucial aspect in the learning process in that they constrain, to a greater or lesser degree, students' participation in learning and in the construction of knowledge.

In this book, Barnes's model of communication and learning acts as a point of departure for explorations into the dynamics of communication in second language classrooms. Thus, classroom communication is examined not only in terms of what actually occurs in second language classrooms, but also in terms of what teachers and students bring to second language classrooms, and how that shapes what occurs there. To do this, it is necessary to acknowledge that there are two dimensions to how teachers and students talk, act, and interact in second language classrooms. The first represents the moment-to-moment actions and interactions that constitute what actually occurs in second language classrooms. The second represents what teachers and students bring to the second language classroom. The interrelatedness of these two dimensions implies that what resides within teachers and their students (who they are, what they know, and how they act and interact) shapes how they will communicate with one another in second language classrooms. The challenge set before teachers is to recognize both the obvious in their classrooms and the not so obvious within themselves and their students. Put another way, understanding the dynamics of communication in second language classrooms means recognizing how that which is hidden merges with and shapes that which is public.[1]

The framework for understanding communication in second language classrooms is presented in Figure 1.1; it is adapted from Barnes's original model. The box at the left acknowledges that second language students possess knowledge and use of language, both their native language and what they have acquired of their second language; these guide how they understand the world around them, participate in social interactions, and organize their learning. This knowledge is acquired within the linguistic, social, and cultural contexts of their real-life experiences and, thus, represents an important aspect of the frames of reference through which students

---

1 I acknowledge Donald Freeman for recognizing this point and helping to launch my own thinking on the dynamics of classroom communication.

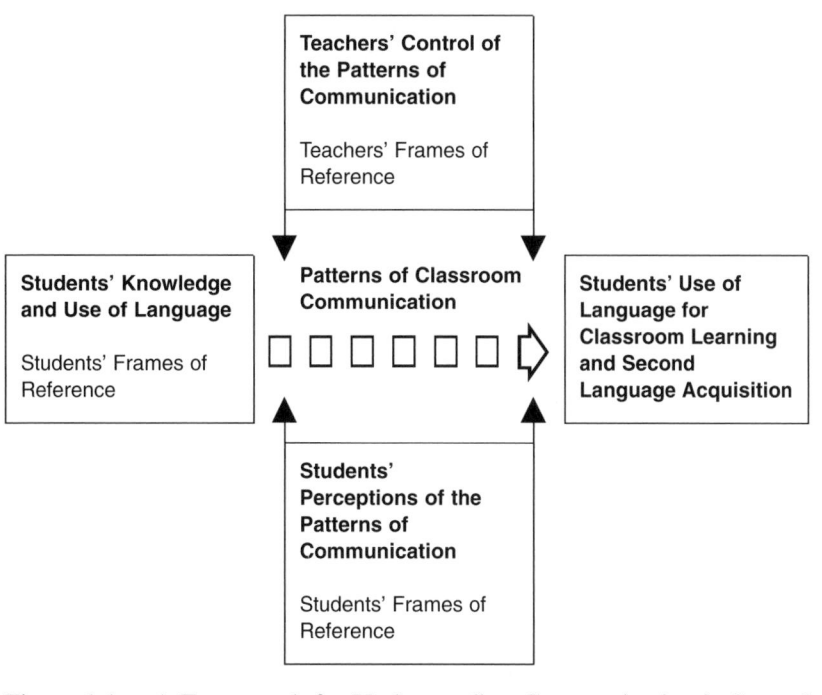

Figure 1.1:   A Framework for Understanding Communication in Second Language Classrooms. (Adapted with permission from Douglas Barnes, *From Communication to Curriculum,* 2nd ed., Portsmouth, NH: Boynton/ Cook Publishers, 1992.)

use language to make sense of and interact with the world around them. However, the extent to which second language students are willing or able to demonstrate this knowledge can be constrained, to a greater or lesser degree, by the patterns of communication that are established and maintained in second language classrooms.

Thus, the central area of the framework represents the patterns of classroom communication, or shared understandings of how, when, where, and with whom language is to be used during second language instruction. These patterns are not permanent, but are continually constructed and reconstructed by teachers as they control the patterns of classroom communication (represented by the downward-pointing arrows) and by students as they interpret and respond to what their teachers say and do (represented by the upward-pointing arrows). Teachers' control of the patterns of communication is shaped, in part, by their frames of reference – that is, by aspects of their professional and practical knowledge that shape how they interpret and understand their own and their students' communicative behavior within the classroom context. In addition, students' perceptions of the patterns of communication are shaped by another aspect of their frames of reference: the norms and expectations they hold for their own and their teachers' communicative behavior based on their prior experiences as students in classrooms. Finally, as indicated by the box at the right, the patterns of classroom communication that are established between teachers and students can work to either foster or constrain the ways in which students use language for classroom learning and their opportunities for second language acquisition.

Throughout this book, this framework can be used as a lens through which to cultivate an integrated view of classroom communication, one that helps to converge the obvious with the obscure and alter the way in which teachers understand the dynamics of communication in second language classrooms.

An overview of the framework

An overview of the framework for understanding communication in second language classrooms follows. Specifically, each component of the framework is defined, and its contribution toward the dynamics of communication in second language classrooms is evaluated.

Teachers' control of the patterns of classroom communication

Probably the most important component of the framework for understanding communication in second language classrooms is teachers' control of the patterns of classroom communication. Teachers control what goes on in classrooms primarily through the ways in which they use language. Typically, they retain this control through a question–answer mode of interaction. Belleck et al. (1966) describe the language of the classroom as a game with rules, both implicit and explicit, that direct the nature of classroom communication. The object of the game, they explain, is to carry on talk about subject matter, and success is based on the amount of learning displayed by students after a given period of play. The teacher sets up the rules of the game, is the most active player, and acts as the solicitor while students act as respondents.

The underlying structure of classroom language has been characterized as following a pattern of acts: an initiation act (teacher), a response act (student), and an evaluation act (teacher), commonly referred to as IRE (Mehan 1979; Sinclair & Coulthard 1975). Notice the IRE pattern in Excerpt 1.3, taken from an actual second language classroom, in which the teacher was conducting a lesson on preposition usage with Yung, a third grade student.

Excerpt 1.3
Teacher: Where is the cup?

Yung: On top of the box.
Teacher: Right, the cup is on top of the box. (T moves cup)
          Now, where is the cup?
Yung: In the box.
Teacher: The cup is . . . ?
Yung: In the box.
Teacher: The cup is in . . . ?
Yung: The cup is in the box.
Teacher: Right, very good, the cup is in the box.

In this excerpt, the teacher's initiation, "Where is the cup?" indicates to Yung that she is to name the location of the cup using the correct preposition. Yung's response, "On the box," contains the correct preposition, as indicated by the teacher's evaluation, "Right," but the teacher continues with a complete sentence to cue Yung as to the desired structure of her answer. As the exchange continues, the teacher enforces her request for a complete sentence by restating part of the sentence using rising intonation. Yung appears to miss this cue and instead merely responds, "In the box." After the teacher's prompt of, "The cup is in . . . ?" Yung correctly interprets what the teacher wants and produces a complete sentence. The exchange ends as the teacher evaluates Yung's response and repeats the sentence for emphasis.

As Excerpt 1.3 illustrates, the IRE pattern allows teachers to maintain control over the structure of classroom communication; at the same time, however, students must be able to recognize that structure and learn to speak within it. Hence, knowledge of the rules of the language game and the underlying structure of classroom communication are essential components of classroom communicative competence.

Teachers also use language in the classroom to control the content that is learned during instruction. They can exert this control by using conventionalized language that is specific to a content area but that may act as a barrier for students who do not know its specialized meaning. Notice, in Excerpt 1.4, how the teacher's use of grammar terminology for the comparative and superlative form of adjectives confuses Anna as she attempts to produce the correct answer.

Excerpt 1.4
Teacher: Why did Mr. Smith choose this car? Which form of the adjective should we use? Why did he choose this car?
Anna: It cheap.
Teacher: Can you make a sentence, . . . Do we use the comparative or superlative? What do you think? Why did he buy this car?
Anna: That car, car cheap. He no have much money, so that car cheap, he buy.

Teacher: Right, but, remember we studied the comparative and superlative of adjectives . . . OK, we said to make them we use "er"
and "est," remember?

Anna: Yeah.

Teacher: So, which is it, the comparative or superlative?

Anna: Comparative?

Teacher: Comparative?

Anna: Superlative?

Teacher: Right, the superlative, cheapest, it's the cheapest one.

In this exchange, Anna's response focuses on the meaning of the teacher's questions as opposed to the correct grammatical form of the adjective. Her attempts to use more exploratory language are rejected in favor of the conventionalized grammar terminology. In fact, it is not clear if Anna understood this terminology, since she identifies "superlative" only after her first guess was questioned by the teacher. It may be that this teacher's pedagogical purpose was to enable Anna to use grammar terminology as a shared way of talking about this particular linguistic feature of the language. It remains unclear, however, whether the use of such conventionalized language inhibited or enhanced Anna's opportunity to acquire this feature of the language.

TEACHERS' FRAMES OF REFERENCE

The ways in which teachers organize the patterns of classroom communication can be understood, in part, by their frames of reference. These include aspects of teachers' professional and practical knowledge that, to some extent, shape how they interpret and understand their own and their students' communicative behavior. Thus, teachers' frames of reference encompass the range of their prior experiences as students and as second language learners, the nature of their professional knowledge and how that knowledge develops over time, the theoretical beliefs they hold about how second languages are learned and how they should be taught, and the ways in which they make sense of their own teaching experiences. By exploring these aspects of teachers' frames of reference, we can begin to come to terms with what it is that teachers bring to classrooms and how their frames of reference contribute to the dynamics of communication within second language classrooms.

Students' perceptions of the patterns of classroom communication

A second important component of the framework for understanding communication in second language classrooms is students' perceptions of the patterns of classroom communication. If we consider teaching and learning to be an interactive process, or as Barnes (1976) claims, a give-and-take between teachers' and students' shared understandings, then how students interpret what teachers say and do will also shape the patterns of classroom communication. Students' perceptions of the patterns of classroom communication can be examined in terms of how students perceive and respond to what their teachers say and do during second language instruction. For example, in Excerpt 1.5, notice Pavel's attempts to participate in a teacher-directed substitution drill on the formation of plural nouns.

Excerpt 1.5
Teacher: Let's try some more things, let's talk about . . . one desk . . .
Pavel: One desk, two desks.
Teacher: Desks, good, that sounds so much better.
Pavel: Dancing, one dancing . . .
Teacher: I'm not talking about dancing, let's talk about the flag . . . one
         flag, two . . . ?
Pavel: Two flags.

In this excerpt, Pavel appears to understand how to construct plural nouns, in fact, his contribution of "Dancing, one dancing . . ." appears to be an attempt to offer a new word that might fit into the substitution drill. However, given that Pavel's contribution is a verb and not a noun, the teacher interprets his suggestion as off-task, or incorrect, and responds, "I'm not talking about dancing . . . let's talk about the flag . . . one flag, two . . . ?" Pavel's answer, "Two flags," demonstrates that he can fit his communicative behavior into the structure of this instructional activity. The teacher's reprimand may also have been the result of Pavel's unsolicited initiation, since besides being incorrect, it also represented a violation of the IRE sequence.

As Excerpt 1.5 illustrates, difficulties arise when students participate in ways that do not match their teachers' norms and expectations for appropriate communicative behavior. Such differences are likely to be accentuated for second language students whose expectations about appropriate classroom behavior are largely based on formal schooling experiences within a different linguistic, social, and cultural context. Thus, ways of acting and interacting that may have been perfectly acceptable in their prior classroom experiences may no longer be acceptable, or at least may seem strange, within second language classrooms.

Most students eventually learn the norms of appropriate communicative behavior based on what they experience with their teachers. Barnes (1976: 33) states, "his [the teacher's] questions, his tone of voice, gestures and stance, the way he receives pupils' replies – the whole of his behavior – will be affirming and reaffirming what uses of language he expects from pupils." However, since the norms of communicative behavior in classrooms are generally not explicitly taught, but instead tend to be implicitly enforced through the teachers' use of language, it may be difficult for second language students to infer the kinds of communicative behaviors that their teachers expect during second language instruction.

STUDENTS' FRAMES OF REFERENCE

The ways in which second language students perceive and respond to their teachers are also based, in part, on their frames of reference. As mentioned previously, these encompass students' expectations about the norms of appropriate communicative behavior in classrooms based on their prior schooling experiences. In this component of the framework, the discussion of students' frames of reference is limited to students' culturally acquired expectations about the norms of how to talk and act in classrooms and the discrepancies that may exist between their expectations and those of their second language teachers. By exploring this aspect of students' frames of reference, teachers can begin to recognize students' preconceived notions about classrooms and classroom communication and how second language students themselves contribute to the dynamics of communication in second language classrooms.

Students' knowledge and use of language

The third component of the framework for understanding communication in second language classrooms also focuses on students' frames of reference. Second language students enter classrooms with an accumulation of prior experiences and knowledge through which they interpret the world around them. Embedded in this knowledge is their use of language, the medium through which they represent their experiences to themselves and to others. When students are forced to operate in a second language, they must acquire a new means of encoding and representing their experiences. This involves much more than grammatical competence in the linguistic structures of the language (Hymes 1972). It also encompasses competence in appropriate language uses within a range of sociolinguistic contexts, competence in initiating and sustaining unified interaction with others, and competence in the verbal and nonverbal communication strategies needed for effective communication or to compensate for communication breakdown (Canale & Swain 1980). Furthermore, communicative competence is measured by the extent to which second language students can comply with the norms that regulate communication within any given sociolinguistic context.

When these students enter second language classrooms, they may continue to rely on ways of knowing, communicating, participating, and learning acquired through their native language. If the patterns of communication that are established and maintained in second language classrooms inhibit students' opportunities to demonstrate their knowledge and use of language, teachers may erroneously assess students' academic abilities and achievements. Once again, as teachers develop an appreciation for the wide range of knowledge and uses of language that second language students bring to classrooms, they may be better able to monitor and adjust the patterns of communication so as to maximize students' competencies within the second language classroom.

Students' use of language for classroom learning and second language acquisition

The final component of the framework for understanding communication in second language classrooms concerns the extent to which the patterns of classroom communication lead to, or at the very least foster, students' use of language for classroom learning and second language acquisition. Fillmore (1982) claims that the language in second language classrooms has two roles: to convey the content of what is to be learned and to provide input in order to acquire that language. She further suggests that language input shapes second language acquisition only when it is placed within concrete, meaningful contexts in which learners can understand the message even if they do not understand all of the language. If language use in meaningful contexts aids comprehension and is essential for the process of second language acquisition, then the patterns of communication that exist in second language classrooms will likely influence the amount and quality of exposure students have to the second language.

Researchers interested in the relationship between classroom interaction and second language acquisition have proposed various hypotheses that acknowledge the role of both learner input and output as shaping the language learning experiences available to second language students (Ellis 1990). By coming to understand the patterns of communication that exist in second language classrooms, teachers can recognize the extent to which the dynamics of classroom communication can influence the complex processes of both classroom learning and second language acquisition.

An overview of the book

This book has three distinct sections. Part I, "A Framework for Understanding Communication in Second Language Classrooms," presents an in-depth discussion of each component of the framework and evaluates the contributions each makes toward the dynamics of communication in second language classrooms. Chapter 1 presents an overview of the framework for understanding communication in second language classrooms. It recognizes the classroom as a unique communication context and illustrates the communicative demands placed on teachers and students in that context. Chapter 2 focuses on teachers' control of and contributions toward the patterns of communication in second language classrooms. It illustrates how teachers use language to control the structure and content of classroom activities and the ways in which teachers' frames of reference contribute to what and how they teach. Chapter 3 examines second language students' perceptions of and contributions toward the patterns of communication in second language classrooms. It demonstrates how students attempt to fit their communicative behavior into the patterns of classroom communication and how their perceptions of classroom activities shape the ways in which they participate in and learn from such activities. Chapter 4 reviews how students' culturally acquired knowledge and use of language shape their ways of talking, acting, interacting, and learning. In addition, it explores how discontinuities between students' ways of using language at home and the ways language is expected to be used in second language classrooms can create social and educational obstacles for second language students. Finally, Chapter 5 focuses on how the patterns of classroom communication that are established and maintained in classrooms can either foster or constrain class participation by second language students, their use of language for classroom learning, and their opportunities for second language acquisition.

Part II, "Examining Patterns of Communication in Second Language Classrooms," uses the framework presented in Part I to take a holistic view of the dynamics of communication in second language classrooms. Chapters 6 and 7 examine teacher–student and student–student interactions and explore the possible impact that the nature of these interactions has on students' use of language for classroom learning and second language acquisition. Chapter 8 places the framework for understanding communication in second language classrooms within broader social contexts by examining how both community- and school-based issues affect what goes on inside second language classrooms.

The book concludes with Part III, "Promoting Communication in Second Language Classrooms." Chapter 9 focuses on how teachers can vary the patterns of classroom communication so as to maximize second language students' linguistic and interactional competencies. It also examines how altering the patterns of classroom communication can increase students' opportunities to use language for classroom learning and second language acquisition. Finally, Chapter 10 deals with defining, establishing, and extending second language students' classroom communicative competence.

2 Teachers' control of the patterns of classroom communication

Teachers are generally characterized as controlling most of what is said and done in classrooms. Part of this control comes from the special status of teachers. When I enter my graduate seminars, my students turn their attention toward me, open their notebooks, and wait for class to begin. This always surprises me, especially since I design my seminars in such a way that groups of students know they are responsible for organizing and leading each class session. When I ask them why they do this, they simply reply that I am the teacher. In second language classrooms, the teacher's status may be even more elevated, in that the teacher is the only native, or near-native, speaker of the language and therefore is seen as an invaluable source for second language students.

Beyond their status, teachers' control over the patterns of classroom communication is generally maintained through the ways in which they use language. In fact, teachers' control of the patterns of communication determines, to a large extent, how, when, where, and with whom language is to be used in the classroom. Of course, this will also depend on how students interpret and respond to what teachers say and do.

This chapter focuses on the ways in which teachers use language to control the patterns of communication in second language classrooms. Excerpts from actual language lessons are examined in order to determine who talks, when, and for what purposes; this will shed light on the interactional strategies that teachers and students use to participate in classroom activities. The chapter also examines the subtle ways that teachers use language to control the structure of classroom communication, how students are expected to fit their communicative behavior into that structure, and the ways in which teachers use language to control the content that is to be learned.

The chapter concludes with a consideration of the frames of reference through which teachers interpret and understand their own and their students' communicative behavior in classrooms. Using excerpts from the journals and narratives of actual second language teachers, I explore teachers' prior experiences as students and second language learners, the nature of their professional knowledge, their theoretical beliefs about second language learning and teaching, and how they make sense of their own teaching experiences.

It should be noted that teachers' language in this chapter is not viewed within the traditional body of research known as "teacher talk." Such research deals primarily with the observable characteristics of teachers' language, that is, the structural adjustments that teachers make in their language when speaking to second language students, the ways in which they correct or repair student errors, and the functional aspects of their language during second language instruction (for comprehensive reviews, see Chaudron 1988 and Ellis 1990). While such research does provide insight into the type of linguistic input second language students receive from their teachers and the extent to which, if at all, this input aids second language acquisition, it tends to view teachers' language in isolation, separate from the interactive nature of classroom communication as a whole. In this chapter teachers' language is viewed within the contexts in which it is used, and as contributing to the overall dynamics of classroom communication. Finally, it is important to bear in mind that teachers' control of the patterns of communication represents only one component of the framework for understanding communication in second language classrooms. However, it is probably the most important, since it may be one of the only components of the framework that teachers themselves actually have the freedom and ability to change as they see fit.

Teachers' use of language during classroom lessons

Cazden (1986) describes classroom lessons as classroom speech events, with specialized rules and expectations concerning the appropriateness of teachers' and students' communicative behaviors. The underlying structure of classroom lessons generally consists of a sequence of acts, namely, an initiation act, a response act, and an evaluation act (IRE) (Mehan 1979; Sinclair & Coulthard 1975). The IRE sequence, briefly explained in Chapter 1, represents the most basic interactional sequence of classroom lessons. That is, the teacher initiates a question, a student responds, and the teacher provides an evaluation. These sequences are easily recognizable in classroom discourse. The IRE sequence exists within three broader phases that make up the overall structure of classroom lessons (Mehan 1979). These include an opening phase, which serves to orient the students to the content to be taught, as well as provide procedural information about how they will be expected to participate in the lesson; an instructional phase, which contains *topically related sets,* or instructional activities that focus on specific aspects of the content being taught; and, finally, the closing phase, which provides both informative and procedural information about what students will be expected to do with what they have learned.

Transcripts of language lessons can illustrate the ways in which teachers use language to control the patterns of communication in second language classrooms. The two excerpts that follow are taken from two different second language classrooms; they are deliberately long so as to provide a broad context within which teachers' and students' communicative behavior can be understood. These excerpts feature two different teachers, teaching very different lessons to very different groups of second language students. The purpose is not to make comparisons between teachers, or to evaluate the effectiveness of their instruction, but to illustrate the ways in which these teachers use language to control the patterns of communication in second language classrooms.

Excerpt 2.1: Structure versus meaning

In Excerpt 2.1, the teacher is leading an intermediate English as a second language (ESL) class in a substitution drill designed to teach the correct usage and form of comparative and superlative adjectives. The setting is a secondary school. The teacher's stated goal for this lesson is to enable his students to recognize the grammatical forms of comparative and superlative adjectives and to be able to use them correctly to complete a substitution drill. Two students, Bin and Tomo, are attempting to complete the following drill by inserting the underlined words based on cues given in the textbook.

It's warm this evening.
Yes, the evenings are getting warmer.
I think it's the warmest it has ever been.

As you read the transcript, take note of the underlying structure of the patterns of communication: who talks, when, to whom, and what is said. Second, note how the teacher uses language to control the content that is communicated during the lesson. Notice also the ways in which the teacher informs students of how they are to talk and act during the lesson. Finally, note the language Bin and Tomo use to complete the task – especially Bin, as he attempts to give the correct answer.

Excerpt 2.1
1. T: OK, let's try number one.
Bin? Yes, why don't you start
and Tomo will follow. Go ahead,
try it . . . Number one.

2.	Bin: It warm this evening.
3.	Tomo: Yes, the evenings are getting warmer.

4.

5. T: OK, . . . How could we change that a little bit?

6.

7.

8. T: Let's take out "getting." Let's not use the verb "get," all right?

9.

10. T: Let's just say . . . let's take out "getting," let's say, "It's the warmest it's ever been" . . . , "It's the warmest spring." How does that sound?

11.

12. T: Let me write that down . . . (T writes on board: The evenings are getting warmer.) Well, let's see what you get.

13.

14. T: Now, maybe we can look at this sentence and see how we can change it to make it better. . . . OK, let's take out the word "get," OK, because remember in the second sentence of our dialogue, we use "getting" with the comparative, so for example, . .

15.

16. T: The evenings are getting warmer.

17.

18. T: OK, warmer . . . Is that the comparative or the superlative?

19.

20. T: Comparative, OK? All right, "getting" is the verb, what does that "getting" mean?

21.

22. T: What does getting mean?

23.

Bin: I think, it get warmest this evening.

Bin: Getting warmest?
Tomo: The warmest?

Bin: It get warmest.

Bin: OK.

Bin: Getting warmer.

Bin: Getting warmest.

Bin: Getting warmer.

Ss: Comparative.

Bin: Getting warmer.

Tomo: Starting.

24. T: Starting, maybe becoming.
25.   Vinny: Beginning to.
26. T: Beginning to, all right, so they are in the process of becoming, they're changing to the point of being warmer . . . they are becoming warmer.
27.   Bin: Evenings getting warmer.
28. T: OK, evenings, all right . . . now, let's put in the superlative here. . . . We'll go from this one, "The evenings are getting warmer" . . . to this one, "It's the warmest it's ever been."
29.   Bin: Evenings getting warmer . . .
30.   Tomo: It's the warmest it's ever been.
31.   Bin: It the warmest.
32. T: Right, here we get the superlative, right? So, what is the meaning of this sentence with the superlative?
33.   Bin: Warm
34. T: What does "it's" stand for? Or, "it has"?
35.   Bin: Warmest
36.   Tomo: Evening
37. T: OK the evening, this particular evening, that we are talking about is the warmest ever, it's ever been before, it's one hundred ten degrees, so it's the warmest it has ever been,
38.   Tomo: It's the warmest it's ever been.
39.   Bin: Wow! One hundred ten? No here, one hundred ten! Too hot!
40. T: Bin?
41.   Bin: It the warmest, warmest it ever been.
42. T: All right, good . . . let's go on . . . look at number two.

THE STRUCTURE OF CLASSROOM COMMUNICATION

Clearly, the teacher–student exchanges in Excerpt 2.1 follow the IRE sequence. In almost every exchange the teacher provides an initiation, a student responds, and the teacher evaluates that response. However, embedded in these interactional sequences are options, usually signaled by the teacher, for altering the IRE pattern. For example, in several instances Bin's responses, which were incorrect, were not evaluated but were instead followed by a second initiation. In turn 20, the teacher asks, "What does that 'getting' mean?" to which Bin responds incorrectly, "Getting warmer." Ignoring Bin's incorrect response, the teacher repeats his question in turn 22. This behavior, on the part of the teacher, seems to indicate to the other students that they are free to respond, for in turns 23 and 25, both Tomo and Vinny call out answers. Thus, this appears to be one acceptable alteration of the IRE sequence.

Recognizing that there is variability in the structure of the IRE interactional sequence, Mehan (1979) maintains that it becomes the responsibility of the students to learn to speak within the structures that teachers establish. This is evident in turn 37, where the teacher uses the example of "one hundred ten degrees" to elaborate on the meaning of the adjective "warmest." Bin, who throughout the entire exchange has been unable to produce the correct grammatical form of the adjective, responds in turn 39, "Wow!, One hundred ten? No here, One hundred ten! too hot!" It appears that Bin did understand the meaning of "warmest"; in fact, he relates this extreme temperature to the weather conditions outside when he claims, "No here." However, the teacher appears to be more concerned with the grammatical correctness of Bin's response than with his interpretation of the meaning of "warmest" and, therefore, responds in turn 40 with, "Bin?" This signal of nominating Bin with a question intonation serves to elicit the correct answer from Bin within the established structure; he responds in turn 41: "It the warmest, warmest it ever been."

Lemke (1985) characterizes this sort of response from teachers as exerting *interactional control* versus *thematic control* over the patterns of classroom communication. In this case, the teacher was willing to sacrifice Bin's understanding of the adjective "warmest" in order to maintain control over the structure of the interactional patterns. Moreover, by ignoring Bin's reference to the weather conditions outside the classroom, the teacher sent a subtle message to Bin that he only values the answer he is looking for: in this case, grammatical correctness.

Acknowledging that this teacher was using language in this lesson to control the structure of communication, the question becomes what, if anything, did Bin learn from this exchange? Eventually, he was able to produce the correct answer, but did he actually learn the form and function of the comparative and superlative adjectives? Caution must be taken when addressing this question. Cazden (1988) suggests that we cannot assume that there is a one-to-one relationship between the teacher question and student answer as evidence of student learning. She claims "there is a critical difference between helping a child somehow produce a particular answer and helping a child gain some conceptual understanding at a future time" (p. 108). What can be assumed, however, is that this teacher enforced interactional control as a means of getting the answer he was looking for, with less regard for Bin's understanding of the content. In this excerpt, the teacher insisted that Bin conform his communicative behavior to the interactional patterns that were established for this activity, and eventually Bin complied.

CONTROL OF THE CONTENT OF THE LESSON

There are several instances in Excerpt 2.1 in which this teacher used conventionalized language to control the content of the lesson. Both Barnes (1976) and Lemke (1989) describe teachers' use of conventionalized language as a matter of initiating students into specific ways of communicating in the classroom community. In Excerpt 2.1, this teacher not only used a great deal of grammar terminology, but he also expected his students to use this terminology. For example, in turn 14, the teacher explains, "OK, because remember in the second sentence of our dialogue, we use 'getting' with the comparative, so for example, ..." Bin continues to answer incorrectly. The teacher asks in turn 18, "Is that the comparative or the superlative?" and several students respond in turn 19, "Comparative." Nowhere in this excerpt does Bin actually use the words "comparative" and "superlative," and given that almost every attempt he made was incorrect, it seems doubtful that he actually understood the meaning of the grammar terminology.

This teacher also controlled the content of this lesson through the types of questions he asked. MacLure and French (1980) have defined two interactive strategies commonly used by teachers to indicate to students the answers they want. In the first strategy, *preformulation* (p. 35), the teacher's question serves to orient the students to the context of the question and provide some indication of how it should be answered. For example, in turn 32, the teacher asks a preformulated question: "Right, here we get the superlative, right? So, what is the meaning of this sentence with the superlative?" This question acts as a cue for Bin to answer using the superlative form of the adjective; however, he misses this cue and instead answers in turn 33, "Warm." Since Bin's answer was not what the teacher was looking for, the teacher uses a second strategy, *reformulation* (p. 38), which involves rephrasing the question so that it is less complex and more specific. In turn 34, the teacher's reformulated question, "What does 'it's' stand for? Or, 'it has'?" is an attempt to help Bin produce the correct answer. Although

Bin's response is still incorrect, Tomo appears to understand the reformulated question and answers in turn 36, "Evening."

Overall, Excerpt 2.1 illustrates the ways in which this teacher used language to control the structure and content of this lesson. Now consider a second excerpt, in which a different teacher paid more instructional attention to the meaning that was communicated and less to the structure of that communication.

Excerpt 2.2: Meaning vs. structure

In Excerpt 2.2, the context is a beginning ESL listening and speaking class in a secondary school. They have just finished reading a newspaper article about the making of a new Hollywood movie, and the teacher is asking the class to talk about their favorite movies. The teacher's purpose in this lesson was to allow the students to share their ideas and possibly generate some new vocabulary words within the context of the discussion.

Once again, as you read the transcript, take note of the underlying structure of the interaction: who talks, when, to whom, and what is said. Second, note how the teacher sustains the exchange of ideas even when students' linguistic expressions are unclear. Notice how the teacher allows the students to use more exploratory language to communicate their ideas, and her various attempts to understand what her students are trying to communicate. Finally, note the nature of the language that these students use to communicate with the teacher.

Excerpt 2.2

1. T: Vin, have you ever been to the movies? What's your favorite movie?

2.   Vin: *Big.*

3. T: *Big,* OK, that's a good movie, that was about a little boy inside a big man, wasn't it?

4.   Vin: Yeah, boy get surprise all the time.

5. T: Yes, he was surprised, wasn't he? Usually little boys don't do the things that men do, do they?

6.   Vin: No, little boy no drink.

7. T: That's right, little boys don't drink.

8.   Wang: *Kung Fu.*

9. T: *Kung Fu?* You like the movie *Kung Fu?*

10.

11. T: That was about a great fighter? . . . A man who knows how to fight with his hands.

12.

13. T: You know how to fight with your hands?

14.

15. T: Do you know karate?

16.

17. T: Watch out guys, Wang knows karate.

18.

19. T: Scary movies? *Nightmare on Elm St.*? You liked that one? You guys like scary movies?

20.

21. T: There's a theater near school? There is?

22.

23. T: You watched the *Hero* and the . . . where, and the where?

24.

25. T: And the weirdo . . . *Hero and the Weirdo* . . . I've never heard of that movie . . . Is it scary?

26.

27. T: Tan? Did you want to say something? Is there a movie that you like?

28.

29. T: You like scary movies? I think everyone likes scary movies.

30.

31. T: No, I don't like them, but, I can only watch a couple, I get nightmares, I'm a baby.

Wang: Yeah . . . fight.

Wang: I fight . . . my hand.

Wang: I fight with my hand.

Wang: I know karate.

Keiko: A scary movie . . . nightmare, yeah.

Keiko: You know, you know, you do up there . . . they have a theater? It near school.

Keiko: Yeah, I watch the *Hero* is, and where.

Keiko: Weirdo.

Keiko: Yeah, scary . . . You like?

Tan: Scary movie.

Keiko: Oh, you like?

32.   Keiko: I know, I know, when you
                                           saw them, you scared when you
                                           sleep and then you scared they
                                           coming and they beat you up.

33. T: That's right, that's right
. . . Sometimes I get scared after
watching a scary movie . . . I
have nightmares.

THE STRUCTURE OF CLASSROOM COMMUNICATION

The underlying structure of Excerpt 2.2 also follows the IRE interactional
sequence. However, there appear to be more acceptable variations to the
IRE sequence in Excerpt 2.2 than we found in Excerpt 2.1. First, in turn 8,
Wang initiates "*Kung Fu*" as his favorite movie, and later, in turn 18, Keiko
initiates, "A scary movie . . . nightmare, yeah." In both instances, the
students offered contributions without waiting for a teacher initiation. This
appears to be an acceptable variation to the IRE sequence, since the teacher
acknowledges their contributions, probably because each was related to the
topically related set of favorite movies.

   Second, this teacher appears to be more concerned with understanding
what her students are trying to say than with the grammatical accuracy of
their responses. She accepts whatever they produce and, in turn, provides a
model of the correct linguistic construction to express their ideas. For
example, in turn 6, Vin describes an episode in the movie *Big* as, "No, little
boy no drink." Instead of correcting Vin's ungrammatical response, the
teacher responds with a positive evaluation in turn 7, and then constructs a
grammatically correct version of the sentence: "That's right, little boys
don't drink." This occurs again in an exchange with Wang about the movie
Kung Fu. In turn 12, Wang proclaims, "I fight . . . my hand," to which the
teacher responds, "You know how to fight with your hands?"

   Despite the fact that much of the teacher–student interaction follows the
IRE sequence, this teacher's evaluations, which seem more like rephrases
and/or paraphrases of students' responses, act as a means of sustaining and
expanding students' responses. Such expansions are somewhat similar to
the expansions that Anglo-American mothers provide for their very young
children (Brown & Bellugi 1964; French & Woll 1981). For example, a
mother will respond to her child's one-word utterance, such as "Cookie,"
with an expanded version of what she believes the child intended: "Do you
want a cookie?" This teacher's use of expansions enabled the exchange of
ideas to continue regardless of the linguistic limitations of her students. For
example, in turns 4 and 5, Vin says, "Yeah, boy get surprise all the time,"
and the teacher provides an expansion, "Yes, he was surprised, wasn't he?"
This happens again in turns 6 and 7, and with Wang in turns 12 through 16.

This teacher's expansions also acted as models of accurate linguistic input, since the expanded sentences represented grammatically accurate representations of the students' responses. Researchers in both first and second language education have yet to determine the actual role such expansions play in the natural process of second language acquisition; we will return to this issue and various other theories of instructed second language acquisition in Chapter 5.

CONTROL OF THE CONTENT OF THE LESSON

Throughout Excerpt 2.2, there is little evidence that this teacher was concerned with requiring her students to use conventionalized language to express their ideas. On the contrary, she allowed her students to select what to talk about, within the topically related set of favorite movies, and accepted their use of more exploratory language. For example, in turn 22, Keiko describes going to a theater to watch a scary movie, "Yeah, I watch the *Hero* is, and where"; the teacher in turn 23 rephrases the title thus: "You watched the *Hero* and the . . . where, and the where?" While the teacher did not recognize this title, she was willing to accept Keiko's answer anyway, thus implying that she was willing to accept any student contribution on this topic.

This teacher was also willing to forego the strict IRE pattern and allowed her students to initiate their own questions. Not only was Keiko allowed to inquire about the teacher's taste in movies, as in turn 30, "Oh, you like?", but she was also allowed to speculate on why the teacher might not like scary movies, as in turn 32: "I know, I know, when you saw them, you scared when you sleep and then you scared they coming and they beat you up." Once again, the teacher confirms Keiko's response and then rephrases that response as a grammatically correct statement in turn 33: "That's right, that's right . . . Sometimes I get scared after watching a scary movie . . . I have nightmares."

Teachers' control of the patterns of communication

Obviously, there are striking differences in the patterns of communication found in these two excerpts. One reason for such differences, however, may be the pedagogical purpose of each lesson. In Excerpt 2.1, the teacher was attempting to teach a specific grammatical rule using a substitution drill; therefore, his language controlled not only the content being communicated, but also the structure of that communication. In Excerpt 2.2, the teacher was providing opportunities for her students to talk about their favorite movies as a way for them to use language in a meaningful context. Therefore, her language allowed the students to participate in meaning-focused interaction, and consequently there was more variability in the structure of that communication.

Each teacher used language to control the patterns of communication in ways appropriate to their pedagogical purpose. The teacher in Excerpt 2.1 acted as an informant, providing specific information about the language that he felt his students needed to complete the instructional task, while at the same time restricting their use of that information to an established structure. To maintain the informant role, he chose to exert a greater amount of control over the patterns of communication during the lesson. The teacher in Excerpt 2.2, on the other hand, acted more as a facilitator, allowing self-selected student initiations and expanding student contributions to sustain meaningful communication. To maintain the facilitator role, she gave up some control of the patterns of communication, which in turn were taken over by the students.

Differences in these teachers' control of the patterns of communication also appeared to influence the extent to which students used language during these lessons. In Excerpt 2.1, the students' language was limited to one- or two-word responses, and generally vocabulary was taken directly from the drill. In fact, there are only two instances in which the students' responses varied from the vocabulary given in the drill. The first occurs in turn 20, when the teacher asks, ". . . what does that 'getting mean'?" and Tomo and Vinny offer, "Starting" and "Beginning to." The second occurs in turn 39, where Bin offers, "Wow! One hundred ten? No here, one hundred ten! Too hot!", which is followed by a negative evaluation from the teacher. In Excerpt 2.2, however, the students' language tends to be in the form of phrases or sentences that express ideas not previously initiated by the teacher. The teacher expands the students' responses, which encourages further communicative exchanges, as in turns 13 and 14, where the teacher asks, "You know how to fight with your hands?", and Wang replies, "I fight with my hand."

Thus, differences in teachers' pedagogical purpose may lead to differences in how they use language to control the patterns of communication, which may in turn influence how students use language during second language instruction. Remember, the intent is not to judge which excerpt represents a better model of second language instruction. On the contrary, we can, and should, expect that individual teachers will vary in the ways in which they control the patterns of classroom communication. Instead, these excerpts illustrate how teachers can use language to control the patterns of classroom communication and how these patterns can shape students' use of language during second language instruction.

Teachers' frames of reference

Think for a moment about your own teachers and/or teaching experiences. Do you recall a particular teacher you had as a student? What was it about that teacher that impressed you then and continues to impress you now? What images come to mind when you think about teaching? Do you recall a particular learning experience you had in school? What was it about that experience that enabled you to learn?

Now, think for a moment about your own second language learning experiences. Did these take place inside a classroom or in a naturalistic environment? Think about your experiences thus far as a teacher of second language students. How do you decide what to do and say during your language lessons? How do you know if your students are actually learning what you are trying to teach them? What kinds of language learning experiences do you create in your classroom? If you are new to teaching, what kind of teacher do you want to be? What kind of language learning experiences do you hope to create for your students?

The remainder of this chapter addresses these questions by examining aspects of teachers' frames of reference that shape how teachers make sense of what and how they teach. Excerpts from selected research in both first and second language teacher education are used to explore the nature of teachers' professional knowledge, their theoretical beliefs about learning and teaching, and the ways in which they make sense of their own teaching experiences.

Teachers' professional knowledge

Teachers' written journals are a valuable source of insight into what teachers know about teaching and how they acquire that knowledge. The following journal entry was written by Kent (alias), a preservice ESL teacher early in his practicum teaching experience:

When I think of a teacher I think of someone who knows the answers; the one who stands up in front of the class and tells the students what they need to know. That's what I experienced as a student. But in this class [the practicum placement], she [the cooperating teacher] doesn't act like a teacher. She never stands in front of the class, she just asks them [the students] questions and they tell her what they think. Sometimes they talk more than she does. This doesn't seem like teaching to me. It's more like *talking* than teaching.

Kent's journal entry conjures up a traditional image of the teacher as a transmitter of knowledge. It is a conception of teaching probably shared by many people, but where does Kent's conception of teaching come from? In part, it comes from his own experiences as a student, from years of watching teachers teach. Lortie (1975) refers to this as the *apprenticeship of observation*. That is, preservice teachers' images of teachers and teaching come from their own memories as students. These memories may include a repertoire of teaching strategies with which they felt comfortable as students, assumptions about how students learn based on their own learning styles and strategies, and a bias toward certain types of instructional materials with which they became familiar as students. For second language teachers, such memories may also include their own experiences as second language learners outside the walls of the language classroom (K. E. Johnson 1994).

Lortie (1975) claims these memories are asymmetrical, since they formulate a conception of teaching based on perceptions as students, not as teachers. Moreover, the imprint of such memories may be difficult for new teachers to overcome and, in fact, promotes conservatism in teaching, since new teachers tend to teach the way they were taught. During an interview, Kent spoke of his memories as a student and how these memories continue to shape his conception of second language teaching:

I remember learning more from the textbook than the teacher. In fact, the teacher just went through the textbook stuff, that's how I learned French. But that didn't matter because I loved that book. I'd do the exercises over and over . . . I thought they were really interesting. If this [the practicum placement] were my class, I'd use a different book. I'd use something like the book I had, with lots of different exercises and lots of extra practice. I think that would help the students get more out of the class.

While Kent's comments give us some insights into how he understands and thinks about teachers and teaching, what does Kent need to learn in order to become an effective second language teacher? In educational research the answer to this question depends on whether or not teachers' knowledge (what teachers know about teaching and how they acquire that knowledge) is viewed as external or internal to the teacher.

The external view is scientifically derived and tries to define what teachers need to know based on empirical investigations of what "expert" teachers do in practice (Berliner 1988; Gage 1978). Both the Holmes Group and the Carnegie Forum on Education and the Economy represent groups who seek to legitimize the teaching profession by promoting the establishment of a scientific knowledge base in teaching (Beyer 1987). This view assumes that the more research-driven knowledge teachers have, the better their teaching performances will be. For Kent, this would mean acquiring the skills and competencies of "effective" second language teachers. As part of his teacher education program, Kent would complete a range of required courses in, for example, second language acquisition, applied linguistics, and methodology, and then be expected to transfer that knowledge into effective classroom practices. In fact, most second language teacher education programs assume that there is a quantifiable amount of knowledge that will lead to effective second language instruction. The problem is that most programs operate without a theoretically grounded

definition of what effective second language teaching is or a clearly articulated rationale for how to teach second language teachers to teach (Freeman
1989; K. E. Johnson 1992b; Richards & Crookes 1988).

There are many who oppose the scientifically derived view of teachers'
knowledge. Some argue it creates an abstract, decontextualized body of
research that is both inappropriate and ineffectual in actual classrooms
(Woods 1987). Others criticize this view as being based on ideal classroom
conditions, devoid of context, denying the complexities of human interaction, and reducing teaching to a quantifiable set of behaviors (Elbaz 1983).

Clearly, Kent's reflections suggest that he possesses a great deal of
knowledge about what he believes should and should not happen in second
language classrooms. An alternative view of teachers' knowledge, known
as the experiential view, argues that teachers' knowledge resides within the
teacher. Teachers' personal values and purposes relate to and inform their
professional knowledge; therefore, what teachers know and believe about
teaching cannot be separated from who they are as people and what they do
in their classrooms (Connelly & Clandinin 1988; Elbaz 1983). Connelly
and Clandinin (1988) capture this view in their definition of the term
"personal practical knowledge":

a term designed to capture the idea of experience in a way that allows us to
talk about teachers as knowledgeable and knowing persons. Personal practical knowledge is in the teacher's past experience, in the teacher's present
mind and body, and in the future plans and actions. Personal practical
knowledge is found in the teacher's practice. (p. 25)

Using teachers' narratives from autobiographies, journals, and interviews,
Connelly and Clandinin claim that personal practical knowledge is embedded in and inseparable from teachers' practice since it aids teachers in
responding to new situations, and that it is reformulated through experience
and reflection.

Others have also emphasized the importance of teachers' experiential
knowledge. Schon (1983, 1987) argues that teachers' knowledge is tacitly
embodied in their practice. Using the term "knowing-in-action" (1987: 26),
he claims that teachers bring their own experiential knowledge to the
classroom, although it may not be articulated, and use it to make sense of
both their own and their students' behaviors. "Knowing-in-action" is
dynamic in that teachers respond to each action with adjustments made in
response to the context of that moment. Schon also stresses the importance
of reflection in the development of teachers' knowledge, since teachers can
reflect on an action in order to evaluate how their "knowing-in-action" has
contributed to the success of that action. Moreover, such reflection can
occur during the act of teaching, otherwise known as "reflection-in-action"
(1987: 26), in which teachers use their tacit knowledge to make sense of

and respond to an instructional situation spontaneously. Thus, knowing-in-action and reflection-in-action represent tacit aspects of teachers' knowledge and reflect how that knowledge becomes realized during actual classroom teaching.

Teachers who reflect on their teaching, either through journals or more formal reflective experiences as part of their teacher education program, often become more aware of not only how they teach, but why they teach the way they do (K. E. Johnson 1992c). After watching his own videotaped lesson, Kent recalled:

I guess the lesson went well, but there I am, up in front of the class, talking away . . . I sure do a lot of the talking. . . . I didn't realize this while I was teaching, but now I see that I talked most of the time and the students only got a chance when I asked a question. . . . I remember being really frustrated by this sort of thing when I was learning French. I always wanted to try things out, but the teacher rarely gave us the chance, and now I see I'm doing the same thing to my students.

By reflecting on his own classroom practices, Kent is becoming more aware of what he actually does during classroom instruction and how that may affect his students. His reflections also suggest that he may wish to change his teaching practices based on the deficiencies he experienced in his own foreign language instruction. The challenge set before Kent, one that most new teachers struggle with, is to transfer this awareness into actual classroom practices.

Other researchers have argued that teachers' knowledge represents a combination of personal and professional knowledge about teaching, learning, and the classroom context. Lee Shulman and his colleagues at Stanford University in the Knowledge Growth in Teaching Project (Shulman 1986) propose a model of teachers' professional knowledge that includes four general areas: subject matter knowledge, general pedagogical knowledge, pedagogical content knowledge, and knowledge of context. These areas of teachers' professional knowledge are believed to have a direct impact on how teachers represent their subject area: that is, what and how they teach (Kerr 1981; Shulman & Grossman 1987; Wilson & Wineburg 1988).

Subject matter knowledge includes knowledge of the major facts and concepts in a subject area as well as its major paradigms; how the area is organized; its fundamental theories, claims, and truths; and central questions of further inquiry (Grossman, Wilson, & Shulman 1989). *General pedagogical knowledge* represents general knowledge about teaching that cuts across subject areas, including beliefs and skills related to general principles of curriculum and instruction, learners and learning, and classroom management (Shulman 1987). By combining subject matter knowledge and general pedagogical knowledge, Shulman characterizes an additional component of teachers' professional knowledge, *pedagogical content knowledge*. He describes pedagogical content knowledge as "the blending of content and pedagogy into an understanding of how particular topics, problems, or issues are organized, represented, and adapted to the diverse interests and abilities of learners, and presented for instruction" (1987: 8). This concept includes a combination of knowledge related to the purposes for teaching a particular topic, students' understandings or misunderstandings of the topic, a host of curricular materials available to teach the topic, and specific strategies and representations that teachers use to make the topic comprehensible to students (Grossman 1990). Finally, *knowledge of context* includes the ecology of learning in the classroom: that is, the context-specific (Lampert 1985) knowledge that teachers use to adapt their instruction to the demands of the specific school setting and/or the needs of individual students within the unique context of their classrooms.

Applying Shulman's model of teachers' professional knowledge to Kent's experience during his TESOL practicum, we can assume that he entered the practicum with a great deal of knowledge about the language he was supposed to teach. This subject matter knowledge may consist of his tacit knowledge of his native language, as well as any explicit knowledge he may have learned about his native language through both formal and informal study. In addition, we can assume that Kent holds certain assumptions about the nature of the language learning process and of second language learners. This general pedagogical knowledge may be based on a combination of his own experiences as a second language learner, his experiences with his own teachers, and knowledge from his professional coursework on theories of second language acquisition, methods of second language instruction, language learners' styles and strategies, and so on. We can also assume that Kent has, or will eventually learn, a variety of ways in which he can represent the language so that it is comprehensible to his second language students. Again, this pedagogical content knowledge will likely be a combination of his own experiences as a student and a second language learner, as well as what he knows about how second languages are learned and how they should be taught. Finally, we can assume that Kent will enter the classroom with some knowledge of the ecology of learning in second language classrooms, as well as the unique culture of classrooms based on his prior experiences as a student and memories of his own teachers.

If we view teachers' professional knowledge as internal to the teacher, then we can assume that teachers enter classrooms with a great deal of knowledge about teachers, teaching, learning, and students. Of course, the configuration of this knowledge will be idiosyncratic for individual teachers. That is, differences in teachers' apprenticeship of observation, language learning experiences, teacher education programs, and even prior teaching experiences contribute to differences in their knowledge about teaching. Furthermore, this knowledge is likely to change over time. Freeman (1990) suggests that learning to teach can be likened to the developmental stages of learning a second language. He extends the metaphor of interlanguage (Selinker, 1974) to *InterTeaching,* suggesting that:

Teaching has phases, each of which is internally coherent as a phase of InterTeaching, and these phases are linked together by a developmental logic, a continuum of InterTeaching. As with interlanguage, each phase of InterTeaching seems to be systematic and rule-governed for the teacher who is in it; it makes sense to the teacher at some level. And those phases develop according to a pattern which has both predictable and idiosyncratic aspects to it. (Freeman 1990:14)

Returning to Kent, at the end of his practicum he began to make sense of this teaching experience based on both his prior experiences and his current practices. In his last journal entry, Kent wrote:

This experience [the practicum placement] has opened my eyes to some very different ways of teaching. I used to think that there must be one right way to teach and all I had to do was figure out that right way and then do it. I now see that there are lots of right ways. What makes it right depends on what the students want and need, and that is always different. I used to think if it worked for me, it should work for them. But I'm finding that's not always the case either. It depends on a lot of things and I'm just starting to figure out what those things are.

Teachers' theoretical beliefs

The theoretical beliefs that teachers hold about learning and teaching are another important aspect of teachers' frames of reference. Viewed as the philosophical principles, or belief systems, that guide teachers' expectations and decisions (Harste & Burke 1977), teachers' theoretical beliefs are thought to act as filters through which teachers make instructional judgments and decisions (Nisbett & Ross 1980; Shavelson 1983; Shavelson & Stern 1981). Therefore, if we understand the nature of teachers' theoretical beliefs, then we might also understand, at least in part, the filter through which they make decisions while teaching.

However, a mutually agreed upon definition of teachers' beliefs is far from realized. Pajares (1992) proposes some fundamental assumptions about the origin, structure, and role of teachers' beliefs. He proposes that, in general, beliefs are formed early in life through a process of cultural transmission, and they help shape the ways in which we construct an understanding of ourselves and the world. Belief systems, therefore, have a filtering effect on thinking and information processing and play a critical role in shaping people's perceptions and behaviors. Teachers' theoretical beliefs represent a belief substructure, and do not operate in isolation but are instead interrelated to all other beliefs. Such beliefs tend to be rooted in images based on early experiences as students or, as mentioned earlier, to evolve from what Lortie (1975) characterized as the apprenticeship of observation. Thus, when prospective teachers enter teacher education programs, they bring with them an accumulation of prior experiences that manifest themselves in the form of beliefs that tend to be quite stable and rather resistant to change.

Recent studies on the extent to which teacher education programs impact on learning to teach suggest that despite coursework and field experiences, preservice teachers' beliefs about teachers and teaching remain largely unchanged (M. W. McLaughlin 1991; Weinstein 1990). Some attribute this inflexibility, in part, to preservice teachers' lack of knowledge about how to adjust their beliefs to the realities of life in classrooms (Calderhead & Robson 1991). Yet, Pajares (1992) argues that teachers' beliefs are instrumental in shaping how teachers interpret what goes on in their classrooms and how they will react and respond to it.

Numerous studies in the fields of reading, writing, and second language education support the notion that teachers teach in accordance with their theoretical beliefs (Deford 1985; K. E. Johnson 1992a; Kinzer & Carrick 1986; Mangano & Allen 1986). For example, in a study I conducted on the relationship between ESL teachers' theoretical beliefs and their instructional practices (K. E. Johnson 1992a), Martha, an experienced secondary school ESL teacher, described her theoretical beliefs as being consistent with the communicative explanations of second language learning and teaching (Halliday 1973; Hymes 1972; Littlewood 1981; Widdowson 1978). She stated that she believes second language learning takes place in meaningful interactions in which students become participants in real-life activities. She also emphasized the importance of using authentic language within realistic contexts, with an emphasis on meaningful communication over grammatical accuracy. In one of our many interviews, Martha stated:

I believe students learn a second language by using it. But they have to use it in meaningful ways. I'd like my students to be comfortable with the language, not only reading, but expressing themselves and what they wanted to say, getting their meaning across effectively, being comfortable and being able to really use the language in real life. . . . I believe it is important to use realistic materials such as newspapers, magazines, pictures, and objects with second language students. These things engage them in meaningful communication and they simulate the types of experiences my students will encounter both inside and outside of school. (K. E. Johnson 1992a: 104)

After extensive observation of Martha's classroom teaching, I found that she provided instruction that was overwhelmingly consistent with her theoretical beliefs. For example, in all of her reading lessons, Martha used authentic texts and generally asked students to relate to the readings in some personal way. In Excerpt 2.3, Martha asks one of her students, Kim, to define the main idea of a reading passage by providing his own definition of the word "success."

Excerpt 2.3

1.	Kim: (S reads silently)
2. T: Do you understand anything there? What does it mean? Can you explain it to me?	
3.	Kim: Success . . . very difficult.
4. T: Do you know the word "success"?	
5.	Kim: Yes.
6. T: What is it? Can you explain it?	
7.	Kim: Good life . . . good life . . .
8. T: A good life? Yeah, OK, some people would say that is success. All right, people have different ideas about success . . . What do you think success means?	
9.	Kim: Good and happy life . . . no problems and family good and food, money, people feel good too . . .

Martha's theoretical beliefs about second language learning and teaching acted as a powerful filter through which she made certain instructional decisions and carried out certain instructional practices in the second language classroom.

Teachers' understandings of their teaching experiences

Although theoretical beliefs about learning and teaching may, in part, shape the nature of many teachers' instructional practices, this may not be the case for all teachers, in all instructional contexts. Some researchers, mostly in the field of reading, contend that at times the complexities of classroom life can constrain teachers' abilities to attend to their theoretical beliefs and provide instruction that is consistent with them (Duffy 1982; Duffy & Ball 1986; Lampert 1985). Instead, teachers' theoretical beliefs may be more situational and transferred into instructional practices only in relation to the complexities of the classroom.

Some teachers, especially inexperienced teachers, are frustrated by the realities of classroom life that they encounter as they try to provide second language instruction that is consistent with their theoretical beliefs. This was the case for Maja, a preservice ESL teacher who allowed me to observe her teaching during her 15-week TESOL practicum (K. E. Johnson, in press). During one of our post-observation interviews, Maja described a gap between what she believes is good second language teaching and what she saw herself doing during second language instruction. This gap caused Maja a great deal of tension – tension that Maja described as "the vision versus the reality."

Maja characterized her "vision" of second language teaching thus: "I have to know where I am going, and why I am going there, and I feel it is my responsibility as a teacher to let the students know where they are going too." Good teaching also seemed to include planning that leads to predictable, organized, and structured lessons: "The students need to be able to predict what is coming next, what is expected of them every day, and be ready for it." Maja's vision of herself as teacher was to organize the environment so that her "students are learning more than just the English language, but learning all sorts of new things through the English language." She added, "It's not that these kids can't learn, it's that they can't express what they learn, they can't raise their hands in class and answer the teacher's questions, they can't write up the lab reports, but they can learn, they really can learn."

The "reality," as Maja defined it, is what life is really like in an ESL classroom. There is the constant flow of interruptions, such as "knocks at the door, announcements over the loud speaker, the attendance sheet, students flying in, students flying out." Maja exclaimed, "This bothers me! There is so much crap going on that has nothing to do with education, the bell rings and I don't even realize it, and that bugs me. That drives me crazy! There is a real tension between do I cover all the things I had planned or do I say a quality discussion is more important." Maja found the reality of teaching ESL to be a process of "dummying down" the instructional material. Maja complained, "I had to act out, I'm brushing my teeth with toothpaste, as part of a grammar lesson! I felt like a fool, standing there saying this sentence and expecting the students to take me seriously."

There were many times when Maja felt caught between her vision of second language teaching and the realities of the ESL classroom. She said: "Sometimes I feel guilty because I feel like I am wasting their time. I am supposed to be teaching them English but unless the stuff they talk about is meaningful, the kids don't care about it, and it becomes a silly exercise to fill up time." Maja added: "Sometimes I know I am intentionally wasting time, just to get through the period, and I hate myself for doing that." This leads to feelings of guilt. "I know there is a gap between what I believe I should be doing and what ends up actually happening."

There were other times, however, when Maja seemed to reach a bit of the vision during her practicum experience. With the help of her university supervisor and her cooperating teacher, Maja developed a literature/social studies unit that centered on the play *The Diary of Anne Frank* within the historical period of World War II. Maja said she wanted the students not to just read the play, but to experience it from the point of view of the characters. Maja planned to accomplish this in several ways. The unit included a weekly schedule of class activities with daily homework assignments. The students would read a short segment of the play, answer a series of questions, discuss different aspects of the characters, write a series of journal entries through the eyes of their assigned characters, and design a collage depicting their characters. She hoped the students would be able to share in the experience of what it must have been like to live in hiding during World War II. She felt many of the students could relate to this sort of experience, because many had come to the U.S. under harrowing political and social conditions.

During the second half of the unit, Maja assigned groups of students to gather information about the personal and professional backgrounds of Churchill, de Gaulle, Hitler, Mussolini, Stalin, and Roosevelt, and to characterize their political perspectives. Maja collected biographical information on each leader and prepared reading guides and organizing questions to help the students understand the information. The groups would eventually write character sketches of their leader, illustrate three key political decisions that their leader had made, and present what they had learned about each leader in a formal class presentation. On the day of the formal presentations, Maja recalled:

In class [the university methods course] we talk about "the students" as these generic things, like faceless blobs, that are always out there waiting for us to teach them. But now when I think of students I see faces and names, and personalities, and real people who have real experiences, and I know these people. I know what they like and don't like. I know how they will act and what they will say if I call on them. Now that I know them, I can teach them. Before, it was just a shot in the dark, but now I know what I'm aiming at.

For Maja, her long-range planning and the strategies she had developed to cope with the realities of the classroom seemed to enable her teaching and her image of herself as a teacher to move a bit closer to her vision and lessened some of the tensions she had experienced earlier in the practicum:

I've learned a lot through all of this. Mostly what it's really like out there. I guess nothing prepares you for what it's really like, but I got through it, and so did the students. I think I learned more from them than they did from me.

Despite the complexities of the classrooms within which teachers teach, teachers like Maja make sense of their classroom teaching experiences through their own frames of reference and, of course, within the context of their own classrooms. The experiences of Kent, Martha, and Maja illustrate different aspects of teachers' frames of reference that shape how teachers conceive of themselves as teachers, make sense of their own teaching, and understand their own and their students' communicative behavior during second language instruction. Thus, teachers' frames of reference are central to understanding how teachers think, talk, act, and interact in second language classrooms.

Conclusion

This chapter describes (1) the ways in which teachers use language to control the patterns of classroom communication, and how that can shape the ways in which students participate in classroom activities, and (2) what teachers bring to the classroom that shapes, in part, what they do. If we combine these two dimensions, we can conclude that the ways in which teachers organize classroom communication tells us something about who these teachers are, what they know, what they believe, and how they think about teaching, teachers, students, and second language classrooms. In Excerpt 2.1, the teacher's use of a very structured learning task to present a particular grammatical rule reveals something about how he sees himself, his students, and what he considers to be the most effective way to teach this particular concept. In Excerpt 2.2, the teacher's willingness to allow for variability in the patterns of communication also suggests something about how she sees herself as a teacher, how she views her students, and what she considers to be appropriate language learning tasks.

Thus, the first component of the framework for understanding communication in second language classrooms enables us to recognize that the dynamics of classroom communication are shaped not only by what teachers say and do, but also by who they are and what they bring to the classroom. With this view of teachers in mind, the focus now shifts to how students perceive and contribute to the dynamics of communication in second language classrooms.

3 Students' perceptions of the patterns of classroom communication

When second language students enter classrooms, they enter into a communication context in which the norms of participation tend to be established by the teacher. Students' perceptions of these norms are generally based on a combination of how they perceive and respond to what their teachers say and do, and their expectations about what is and is not appropriate communicative behavior in classrooms. As with teachers (Chapter 2), the combination of these two dimensions – what students bring to classrooms and how they talk, act, and interact in classrooms – contributes to the dynamics of communication in second language classrooms.

This chapter focuses on students' perceptions of the patterns of classroom communication and the ways in which they perceive their role in classroom events. Once again, excerpts from actual second language classrooms are used to illustrate the ways in which second language students attempt to fit their communicative behavior into the structure of classroom events.

The examination of students' frames of reference extends over the next two chapters. In this chapter, the discussion is limited to aspects of students' frames of reference that are school-based: in other words, the norms and expectations that students hold about appropriate communicative behavior in classrooms based on prior school experiences. In Chapter 4, the discussion expands to aspects of students' frames of reference that are language-based: that is, students' culturally acquired knowledge and use of language, which determine, in part, the ways in which they participate in and learn from classroom events. Both aspects of students' frames of reference will enable us to appreciate how students perceive and contribute to the dynamics of communication in second language classrooms.

Students' perceptions of classroom events

Researchers interested in students' perceptions of classroom events agree that students actively engage, to a greater or lesser degree, in the creation of what occurs in classrooms and, thus, affect classroom events as much as they are affected by them (Pintrich et al. 1986; Schunk 1992; Wittrock

1986). Although this may seem to contradict the view that teachers retain control over the structure and content of classroom events, experienced teachers know that, in reality, teaching is much more of an adaptive than a rigid process. Most teachers admit that the success of any classroom event depends on how students perceive and respond to it.

Interestingly, researchers who have examined students' perceptions of classroom events claim that while students actively struggle to make sense of both social and cognitive aspects of classroom events, they often misinterpret teachers' expectations and intentions (Beam & Horvat 1975; Campbell 1978; Clark & Creswell 1979; Cooper & Good 1982). More importantly, such misinterpretations can interfere with student learning (Anderson 1981; Winne 1980; Winne & Marx 1980). In fact, it is believed that students' perceptions of classroom events mediate the effects of teaching (Wittrock 1986). That is, students' perceptions of themselves, their teachers, and classroom events and their role in those events, act as a filter between what is taught and what is learned. For example, the extent to which students believe that success in school is possible is a critical factor in the achievement of academic success (deCharms 1972; Wittrock 1986). Moreover, motivation to achieve in school is directly related to whether or not students attribute their school success to their own efforts, rather than to those of others or to factors beyond their control (Coleman et al. 1966; Nowicki & Strickland 1973; Reid & Croucher 1980). Clearly, academic success and motivation are closely linked to students' perceptions of themselves, as well as what they believe is and is not possible in classrooms.

While teachers' and students' perceptions of classroom events may not always be congruent, students are highly sensitive to teachers' differential treatment of students. Students perceive teachers as having high expectations for high-achieving students, granting them more freedom of choice and greater opportunities, while having low expectations for low-achieving students, to whom they give more direction, rules, work, and negative feedback (R. S. Weinstein & Middlestadt 1979; R. S. Weinstein et al. 1982). More importantly, it is through these perceptions of teachers' differential treatment that students tend to infer their own abilities and attributions toward academic success (Wittrock 1986). Thus, high or low teacher expectations regarding student achievement can actually create positive or negative student perceptions of individual academic abilities and achievements.

The structure of classroom events

While teachers and students may have differing perceptions of their roles in classroom events, student learning is enhanced when students accurately perceive teachers' expectations and intentions (C. S. Weinstein 1983). However, for students to do this, they must be able to recognize the structure of classroom events. One way in which the structure of classroom events has been examined is through a construct defined by Philips (1972: 377) as "participant structure," which refers to the rights and obligations of participation with respect to who can talk and when in any social event. Philips (1972, 1983) used this construct to characterize the ways in which teachers arrange verbal interactions with their students. For example, teachers may interact with only one, some, or all students in a particular manner and in doing so set certain controls over the rights and obligations of participation in that interaction.

Erickson (1982: 153), renaming this concept "participation structures," claimed that successful participation in classroom events requires that students accurately perceive both subject matter information and the social organization of participation. He described verbal interaction in classrooms as containing two interrelated structures: academic task structures and social participation structures. *Academic task structures* represent how the subject matter is sequenced in a lesson, or the logical operations involved in the task and its sequential steps. *Social participation structures* represent the allocation of interactional rights and obligations of participants that shape the discourse. These can include turns at speaking, pairs of turns, such as the question-answer or IRE pattern, as well as listening behavior in relation to speaking behavior. These structures are interrelated in the sense that mistakes made by students within the academic task structure may make it difficult for teachers to maintain the social participation structure. For example, if a student makes a content mistake, the teacher may have to interrupt the sequence of the lesson to offer a repair, thus not only breaking the logical operations necessary to complete the task, but also the instructional rhythm of the lesson. Likewise, if a student fails to conform to the social participation structure, teachers may have difficulty maintaining the academic task structure. For instance, right answers interjected into a lesson at the wrong time may require adjustments to the order of participation and the logical sequence of the lesson.

Of course, Erickson admits this is an ideal model of classroom communication. In reality, teachers and students make a variety of adjustments in these structures during classroom events. When students give unexpected or incorrect responses, teachers must make adjustments to either the academic task structures or the social participation structures, or both. These adjustments, Erickson claims, can actually enable teachers to not only simplify learning tasks for students, but also assess students' knowledge of the subject matter. Thus, Erickson characterizes classroom communication "as the collective improvisation of meaning and social organization from moment to moment" (1982: 153). Classroom communication may range from highly ritualized, formulaic speech events, in which who talks, when, and about what are predetermined, to highly spontaneous and adaptive speech events, in which neither the order nor content of talk are predetermined.

Besides accurately perceiving the academic and social structures embedded in classroom events, students must also be able to interpret what Gumperz (1977) calls *contextualization cues,* or the explicit and implicit means by which communicative intent and interpretative form are signaled. Furthermore, Gumperz claims that the ability to interpret these cues is critical to communicative competence. In classrooms, contextualization cues consist of what teachers do as much as what they say. Nonverbal features, such as voice pitch, facial expressions, and body posture, are critical cues for accurately interpreting the teachers' intentions and/or the structure of classroom events. In fact, a teacher's body posture alone has been found to have symbolic meaning to students and signals what is and is not acceptable social and verbal behavior during classroom interaction (Florio & Schultz 1979).

Finally, in order for students to understand the structure of classroom events, they must be able to accurately interpret the feedback teachers give them. Teachers generally view praise as having both a motivational function and an instructional function (Wittrock 1986), whereas students perceive it more as a means of obtaining information about correct answers, desirable behaviors, or teachers' expectations about appropriate social and verbal interactions (Brophy 1981). Teacher praise may actually inform students about the appropriateness of their participation rather than encourage and/or reinforce it. Yet, students' perceptions of the intent of teacher praise also depend on both their intellectual and personal characteristics. Students of high ability tend to regard teacher praise as a reward, and therefore they participate more as a result. Students of low ability, on the other hand, tend to perceive teacher praise as having an instructional function, providing social reinforcement (Morine-Dershimer 1982). Thus, what students infer from teacher praise may differ from their teachers' intentions and vary according to individual students.

In sum, students' perceptions of the patterns of classroom communication represent a critical component for understanding how students understand, participate in, and learn from classroom events. For students to participate in classroom events, they must accurately infer their teachers' expectations and intentions, the contextualization cues within the classroom, and the academic and social structures of classroom events at any given moment. Two excerpts taken from different second language classrooms illustrate how second language students do this.

Excerpt 3.1: Fitting into the structure of classroom events

The context for the transcript excerpted here was a class of beginning ESL students in secondary school. The teacher was leading a substitution drill that focused on constructing negative statements using "not" and the appropriate use of personal pronouns. The teacher's stated purpose in this lesson was for the students to use the substitution drill as a way to practice using these two grammatical structures. To complete the drill, students were expected to construct a negative statement with "not" and then a positive statement, based on the illustrations given in the textbook. For example, if the illustration in the textbook depicted a student, the correct exchange would begin with a teacher prompt, "Are you a teacher?", followed by a student reply, "I am not a teacher. I am a student."

As you read this transcript, take note of how the teacher sets up the academic task structure, that is, how the negative constructions and personal pronoun usage are sequenced in the lesson. Note also the social participation structure that the teacher sets up to regulate student participation. Pay particular attention to how the students, Kim and Petr, respond to the teacher's elicitations and attempts at repair. See if you can identify instances that illustrate how these students attempted to fit their communicative behavior into the structure of this classroom event.

Excerpt 3.1

1. T: So yesterday, what we were doing here on page forty-four and forty-five was following the examples here . . . We were saying a sentence with "no," or "not," and a sentence with "yes." So first of all you make a "not" sentence . . . "I'm not a student. I am a teacher." Yes? Let's begin. Kim? Are you a teacher? Now, you're pretending that you are the person and so if somebody asks you with "you," you answer with what? Are you from Vietnam? What would you answer?

2.   Kim: Yes, I am.

3. T: Yes. Yes, I am, right . . . So you're going to answer with "I am." Good . . . Are you a teacher? First you are going to make a sentence with "not," then you are going to tell me what you are. . . . Are you a teacher?

4.   Kim: No, I am not.

5. T: No, I'm not a teacher. . . .
What are you?

6.   Kim: I am a student.

7. T: No, not you, what is she?
(pointing to the textbook)

8.   Kim: Student.

9. T: Well, it looks like a
school but if she's not a teacher
she's not going to work in a
school. . . . She's a lawyer . . . so
what you say is, . . . "I am not a
teacher, I am a . . . ?"

10.   Kim: Student.

11. Well, if I asked you, you
would say you were a student,
but we're talking about this
picture and the lady in front of
a courthouse, although it is
hard to tell, so what she would
say is, "I am not a teacher. I am
a lawyer." Talking about her
work in the court . . . Are you a
teacher? Try that. Are you a
teacher?

12.   Kim: No, I am a student.

13. T: Well, yes, I know you are,
but look at the picture, she's not
a teacher, is she? Because this
isn't a school, it's a courthouse,
and lawyers work in a courthouse. So, she's a lawyer, not a
teacher. So, you put the "not"
sentence first, you would say, "I
am not a teacher, I am a lawyer."
Try that. Are you a teacher?

14.   Kim: I am not a teacher.

15. T: The woman in the picture,
right? "I am not a teacher, I am
a . . . ?"

16.   Kim: Lawyer.

17. T: Good, remember, you are
pretending you are the person in
the picture, so "I am not a

teacher, I am a lawyer." Try that
one again, "I'm not . . ."

18.   Kim: I am not a teacher.

19. T: Right, "I'm not a teacher.
I'm a . . . ?"

20.   Kim: Lawyer.

21. T: Very good. "I'm not a
teacher, I'm a lawyer." OK
Good. . . . Number two, "Are
you very bad students?" You're
talking about yourself and another person, what do you say?
Petr? Are you very bad students?

22.   Petr: Bad students.

23. T: "We," you say "we" are
not bad students. We are what?
What kind of students are we?

24.   Petr: Bad students.

25. T: We say "we" because you
and another person are in that
group. "We are not bad students." What kind of students are
we?

26.   Petr: We are bad students.

27. T: "We" are? No, we are not.
You aren't bad students, are you?
No, I think you are good students. What kind of students are
you?

28.   Petr: We are good students.

29. T: OK, but first with "no"
and then with "yes," "We are not
bad students. We are good students." I know you are all very
good students, right? OK. Good.
Number three.

In this excerpt, both Kim and Petr have difficulty understanding the academic task structures of the activity. The teacher cues the start of this
sequence by stating "Let's begin. Kim? Are you a teacher?" However,
before she gives Kim an opportunity to respond, the teacher reemphasizes
one part of the academic task structure, namely, correct pronoun usage, by
stating, "Now, you're pretending that you are the person and so if some-

body asks you with 'you', you answer with what?" The teacher then appears to test Kim's knowledge of pronoun usage by asking a question not related to the textbook or the task, but about Kim herself: "Are you from Vietnam? What would you answer?" To this, Kim answers in turn 2, "Yes, I am."

Kim's response could indicate two things: (1) that her response is a literal answer to the question, since Kim is, in fact, from Vietnam, and/or (2) that she understands the academic task structure of the activity, namely correct personal pronoun usage. The teacher appears to interpret Kim's response as the latter, since she praises Kim, in turn 3, by repeating, "Yes, Yes, I am, right . . . So you're going to answer with "I am. Good." and emphasizing the correct personal pronoun in the answer. The teacher then reinforces the academic task structure again by stating in turn 3, "First you are going to make a sentence with 'not', then you are going to tell me what you are. . . . Are you a teacher?" To this, Kim responds in turn 4, "No, I am not." Once again, Kim's response could be interpreted as a literal answer to the teacher's question and/or that she understands the academic task structure. However, when the teacher asks in turn 5, "What are you?", referring to the illustration in the textbook, Kim replies, "I am a student." The teacher suddenly realizes that Kim was referring to herself and not the illustration in the textbook, so she states in turn 7, "No, not you, what is she?" and points to the illustration in the textbook.

Until this point, Kim appeared to have been operating on a literal level, answering the teacher's questions without reference to the textbook. Sensing that Kim may have been confused by the illustration in the textbook, the teacher explains in turn 9 that the illustration is of a courthouse and that the person depicted in the illustration is a lawyer. However, when the teacher prompts Kim to complete the sentence, Kim continues to respond to the literal meaning of the teacher's question. The teacher makes two more attempts at repair, in turns 11 and 13, as she tries to get Kim to respond using the illustration in the textbook. These attempts at repair not only interrupt the academic task structure of the activity but also the social participation structure. Kim's confusion continues until the teacher explicitly states in turn 15, "The woman in the picture, right? I am not a teacher, I am a . . . ?" Finally, Kim answers in turn 16, "Lawyer," and the teacher then walks Kim through the academic task structure.

Throughout this entire sequence, Kim's confusion appears to stem from her misinterpretation of the academic task structure. If the teacher had intended her questions to be taken literally, Kim's responses would have been correct. However, the teacher's questions were directed at the illustration in the textbook, and as part of the academic task structure, Kim was expected to take on the role of the person depicted in that illustration. Kim's misinterpretation of the academic task structure created difficulty as she attempted to participate in the activity.

It is important to consider why Kim was unable to recognize the structure of this activity. Prior to turn 7, when the teacher physically pointed to the illustrations in the textbook, the teacher failed to make explicit when her questions were to be taken literally, as in line 1, "Are you from Vietnam?", and when they referred to the textbook, as in turn 11, "Are you a teacher?" Without explicit cues, Kim may have been at a loss as to how she should respond. In fact, the teacher made only one explicit reference (in turn 1) to the fact that Kim was supposed to pretend that she was the person in the illustration. Kim may have missed this, especially since this reference was followed by a literal question, "Are you from Vietnam?" If the teacher had given explicit directions for Kim to focus her attention on the illustration in the textbook, Kim might have been able to fit her verbal behavior into the academic task structure of the activity.

This same sort of confusion seemed to inhibit Petr's participation. In turn 21, the teacher cues Petr to use the correct pronoun by explaining, "You're talking about yourself and another person, what do you say? Petr? Are you very bad students?" Petr simply responds in turn 22, "Bad students." The teacher, intent on getting Petr to use the correct pronoun, repeats her explanation of "we" and once again prompts Petr in turn 25, "What kind of students are we?" Petr's response, in turn 26, "We are bad students," indicates that he knows the correct pronoun to use. Instead of acknowledging this, however, the teacher challenges the meaning of Petr's response in turn 27: "'We' are? No, we are not. You aren't bad students, are you? No, I think you are good students." This correction of Petr's response is given without explicit cues to indicate that the teacher has shifted her attention from pronoun usage to the literal meaning of Petr's response. Petr finally responds in turn 28: "We are good students," only to be corrected again because this time his response did not fit into the academic task structure that the teacher had set up earlier in the lesson.

It is not surprising that Kim and Petr had difficulty understanding the structure of this classroom event. At times the teacher enforced the academic task structure, but at others, she shifted out of that structure without explicit cues. This made it extremely difficult for Kim and Petr to recognize the academic structure of this activity, or to know how to fit their communicative behavior into that structure. Overall, Excerpt 3.1 illustrates difficulties second language students can have as they attempt to fit into the structure of classroom events and how the lack of explicit cues can inhibit successful participation in those events.

Excerpt 3.2: Variability in the structure of classroom events

The next classroom excerpt illustrates how variability in the structure of classroom events can influence the ways in which second language students participate in those events. Excerpt 3.2 is taken from an ESL classroom in an elementary school where members of the local community have been invited to speak to the fourth, fifth, and sixth grade classes as part of a schoolwide social studies unit on occupations. To support the unit, the school's ESL teacher is preparing her students for an upcoming visit by a police officer. In Excerpt 3.2, small groups of students have been assigned the task of creating a list of questions they would like to ask the police officer. Several small groups are working on this task at the same time; this excerpt focuses on one group of three students as they select a question and then, with the teacher's assistance, create the correct question formation. As you read this transcript, note the variability in the academic task structure and social participation structure of the classroom event. Pay particular attention to the nature of student talk in relation to teacher talk, and the ways in which these students participate in this classroom event.

Excerpt 3.2

1. 　　　　　　　　　　　　　Jay: I know, I know . . . gun . .
　　　　　　　　　　　　　　　　　[
2. 　　　　　　　　　　　　　Alex: on TV, police, um, gun . . .
　　　　　　　　　　　　　　I saw this show and this guy, and
　　　　　　　　　　　　　　they chasing him and they shot
　　　　　　　　　　　　　　him, and the car flip over, man!
　　　　　　　　　　　　　　Wow!
　　　　　　　　　　　　　　　　　[
3. 　　　　　　　　　　　　　Jay: They shoot him? His gun?
　　　　　　　　　　　　　　Yeah?
　　　　　　　　　　　　　　　　　　　[
4. 　　　　　　　　　　　　　Sung-su:　He shoot, bang!
　　　　　　　　　　　　　　shoot!

5. T: His gun? Do you think
you might want to ask him about
his gun? What about his gun?
6. 　　　　　　　　　　　　　Sung-su: Yeah, shoot his gun,
　　　　　　　　　　　　　　Yeah, bang! Ha, bang!

7. T: You want him to shoot his
gun? Do you think he will? In
here? I don't know if he'll do
that.
8. 　　　　　　　　　　　　　Jay: No, no, ha, ha, . .
　　　　　　　　　　　　　　　　　[
9. 　　　　　　　　　　　　　Sung-su:　　Yeah, shoot his gun
10. T: I don't think so, he better
not shoot it in here.
11. 　　　　　　　　　　　　　Sung-su: I say, you got gun, ha,
　　　　　　　　　　　　　　yeah, shoot!

12. T: Do you want to ask him
to shoot his gun? How would
you ask him that?
13.   Sung-su: Shoot! Shoot!
14.   Jay: No shoot, no, just looking,
                                                    just . .

15. T: Oh, so you just want to
look? That sounds good, maybe
he will let you look at it . .
16.   Jay: Just looking, hum, just look-
                                                    ing
                                                            [
17.   Sung-su: I have you gun...
                                                            [
18.   Alex: No, he's not giving you.
19.   Jay: No, hum . . . just looking,
                                                    just looking.

20. T: Yeah, I don't think he will
give it to you. Yeah, he can't
give his gun to anyone, right?
21.   Alex: Yeah, I know.
22. T: OK, so you just want to
look at it? Yeah, so what will
you say? How will you ask him
that?
23.   Jay: Can I, I, looking you gun?
                                                            [
24.   Sung-su: Hey, you got gun, I
                                                            have you gun?
                                                            [
25.   Alex: No, no way, he's not
                                                            . . .
26.   Jay: OK, I know, I know, I look-
                                                    ing you gun?

27. T: OK, yeah, let's try something. . . . Is that your watch?
28.   Jay: Yeah.
29. T: Wow, I've never seen a
watch like that before, look at
those colors, wow! It looks really
interesting, hum, I think I'd like
to look at it. Can I look at your
watch?
30.   Jay: Um?

31. T: Can I look at your watch?
Can I? OK?
32.   Jay: Yeah, sure . . . (holds out
                                                     arm)

33. T: (examines watch} Thanks,
that's a neat watch. . . . So if you
want to ask the police officer if
you can look at his gun, you
might say, "Can I look at your
gun?"
34.   Jay: Yeah, I just looking . . .

35. T: Yeah, he might not let you
hold it, in your hands, but if you
ask, he might let you look at it,
so, what if I were the police officer, what would you ask me?
36.   Jay: Can I, I look?
37.   Sung-su: Can I look at you gun?
                                                     OK?

38. T: Yeah. "Can I look at your
gun?" Yeah, or "Can we look at
your gun?" That would be nice,
wouldn't it?
39.   Alex: OK, so, yeah. Can we look
                                                     at your gun? OK?

The most noticeable feature of this excerpt is the variability in the social participation structures. There are several instances of overlapping student talk, as in turns 1–4, 16–18, and 23–25. The overlapping student talk creates opportunities for students to respond directly to one another instead of to the teacher. This is particularly evident when Alex corrects Sung-su by claiming he cannot "have" the gun, but can only look at it (turns 17–18, 24–25). This pattern of interaction contrasts sharply with the IRE sequence found in the typical classroom. In much of this excerpt, the teacher does not participate in the interactional sequences; rather, students exchange information among themselves.

Another feature of this excerpt is that the topic of discussion is student generated rather than teacher generated. When Jay mentions in turn 1, "I know, I know . . . gun . . . ," Alex, in turn 2, launches into a description of a recent television police show. Jay responds to Alex's description, in turn 3, with the question, "They shoot him? His gun? Yeah?" which prompts Sung-su to shout excitedly, "He shoot, bang! shoot!" Only after this exchange does the teacher suggest that the students use this topic to create a question to ask the police officer. In fact, throughout the excerpt, the teacher continues to allow the students to control the direction of the discussion. For example, their discussion moves from the idea of asking the police officer to shoot his gun to requesting that they be allowed to look at it. It is Jay who corrects Sung-su, in turn 14, by stating, "No shoot, no, just looking, just . . ." Picking up on the direction of the student talk, the teacher asks in turn 15, "Oh, so you just want to look? That sounds good, maybe he will let you look at it." As with overlap, instances of student-generated topics tend to occur less often in an IRE sequence.

Excerpt 3.2 also illustrates some variability in the academic task structures of this classroom event. Once the students have settled among themselves that they are interested in looking at the gun (turns 16–19) the teacher then directs their attention to how they might construct their request in a formal question (turn 22): "OK, so you just want to look at it? Yeah, so what will you say? How will you ask him that?" Clearly, the teacher has a specific academic task in mind: creating a formal question. However, she chooses to model question formation by asking to look at Jay's watch (turns 27–33), which is a meaningful context for the students. She then places herself in the role of the police officer and asks the students to construct a formal question. Without imposing a rigid academic task structure, or expecting the students to limit their language use to a "correct" answer, as we saw in Excerpt 3.1, this teacher provides a model of a formal question within the context in which it could be used. This seems to enable the students to participate successfully in this classroom event.

Clearly, the pedagogical purpose and participation structures of Excerpts 3.1 and 3.2 differ dramatically. Such differences are common in small group versus teacher-directed instruction. However, the most striking feature of Excerpt 3.2 is the way in which individual students chose to participate in this event. Specifically, the teacher did not enforce a rigid social participation structure, and therefore the students were free to self-select how and when they would participate in this event. The extent to which such variability in the structure of classroom communication impacts upon students' use of language for classroom learning and second language acquisition is discussed in Chapter 5.

Students' frames of reference

Think for a moment about your own experiences as a student. How were you expected to talk and act in classrooms? How did you talk and act? Did the norms of participation in those classrooms vary depending on the teacher? the grade level? the subject area? the school? If you have studied a second or foreign language in another country, do you recall if the norms of participation in those language classrooms were different from what you had expected? What did you have to do to adjust to those norms? Did your teachers help you adjust? If you were to walk into a classroom today, how would you know how to talk and act?

In Chapter 2, teachers' frames of reference were characterized in terms of what teachers bring to classrooms that shape, in part, what they do there. Students' frames of reference can be characterized similarly. This section limits the discussion to students' frames of reference that reflect the norms and expectations of appropriate classroom behavior that students hold based on their prior schooling experiences. The specific focus is cultural differences in classroom norms in both ESL and EFL instructional contexts. Chapter 4 expands the discussion of students' frames of reference to include students' knowledge and use of language.

Cultural differences in classroom norms

Many second language students come from countries where the patterns of classroom communication are quite different. Thus, the ways in which these students talk and act in second language classrooms may seem strange or inappropriate. More importantly, since the patterns of communication in most classrooms are not explicitly taught, but instead are implicitly enforced through teachers' use of language, second language students may find it difficult to infer the norms for participation in classroom events.

Thus, second language students are faced not only with learning a new language, but also with a new social code of conduct, according to which teachers' and students' intentions, behaviors, and emotions are expressed in different ways (Trueba 1987). Second language students must use social, cognitive, cultural, linguistic, and paralinguistic knowledge of the new language in order to successfully participate in classroom events. Paradoxically, to acquire this knowledge they must participate in interpersonal interactions in the language, but without this knowledge, their chances for such interactions remain limited. Adamson (1993) writes of the experiences of a 46-year-old Vietnamese man, Duc, who had extreme difficulty adjusting to the norms of participation in a graduate-level linguistics program at an American university. Adamson concludes:

The case study of Duc shows the enormous difficulty ESL students can have adjusting to the new school culture. Duc's comments indicate that for him learning new scripts for school was not just an intellectual exercise but a deeply personal matter that went to the heart of his culturally based beliefs about how human beings ought to relate to one another. Duc characterized his feelings toward his professors as one of respect, but apparently he felt a good deal of fear as well. This fear made it impossible for him to interact effectively with his teachers. Duc's comments show that he did not respect students who participated orally in class, even though he understood that this participation was expected and required. He says that students who speak in class, "ask questions they fully know, just to show off . . ." It appears that for Duc to adopt the kind of behavior he knew was expected of him would have required him to change his basic system of values to some extent. Duc was unwilling or unable to do this, and as a result finally dropped out of the program. (1993: 82)

Students' prior schooling experiences can also include their expectations about the roles that teachers and students should assume during classroom instruction. In some cultures, teachers and students uphold very strict roles that are rarely, if ever, violated. For example, an adult Taiwanese student in one of my research seminars, Sun-yu, described her prior experiences as a student in Taiwan and the difficulty she experienced adjusting to her graduate-level studies at an American university.

When I first came here, I couldn't believe how much Americans talked in class. In Taiwan, students never speak in class unless the teacher calls on them. At first, I was afraid to talk in class because I thought I might ask a question that I should know the answer, or I might say something that was already said. I was afraid that what was interesting to me might not be interesting to the rest of the students. I kept waiting for my teachers to call on me, but they never did. Then I realized that this way of talking was what teachers expected, and so I would have to get used to it. I think I have talked more in my classes here than all my years of schooling in Taiwan.

Sun-yu and Duc's frames of reference about appropriate norms of classroom communication and the roles of teachers and students are based on their prior experiences as students in non-Western style classrooms in Taiwan and Vietnam. Both characterize their teachers as having had a lecture style of teaching and report that students were expected to be silent. Few, if any, class discussions occurred and it was considered rude for a student to interrupt the teacher to ask a question. Moreover, their perceptions of appropriate norms of classroom communication are based on their culturally acquired ways of interacting, which include upholding the needs of the group over those of the individual and a reluctance to draw attention to oneself. For Sun-yu and Duc, differences in their frames of reference influenced their perceptions of the nature of classroom events and their role in those events.

Students' frames of reference in English as a foreign language classrooms

In EFL classrooms where the teacher and students share the same native language and educational enculturation, the norms of participation may be obvious to both teachers and students. However, this does not obtain in all EFL (English as a foreign language) settings. For example, in Japan, the

Ministry of Education currently subsidizes the hiring of native speakers of English as a way to enhance English skills beyond the grammar translation skills necessary for high school and university entrance exams, and in an effort to promote the more communicative skills of speaking and listening (Koike 1990). However, native-speaking English teachers in Japan often encounter difficulty adjusting to their Japanese students' norms of participation (Wordell 1985). These difficulties stem from a range of social and cultural norms that are specific to Japanese schooling. First, according to Confucian thought, appropriate student behavior includes a grateful acceptance of what is taught and keeping silent except when explicitly asked to speak (Scollon & Scollon 1990). In addition, Japanese attitudes about speech and silence come from the "Zen Buddhist idea that man is capable of arriving at the highest level of contemplative being only when he makes no attempt at verbalization and discounts oral expression as the height of superficiality" (LaForge 1983: 120). Moreover, since harmony is the object of communication in Japanese culture (Barnlund 1973), Japanese students tend to dislike a person who stands out and violates the unity of a class. Finally, nonverbal aspects of Japanese communication, such as avoiding eye contact when speaking to someone of a higher status and constantly nodding one's head as confirmation in conversation, are often misinterpreted as extreme shyness, uncooperativeness, or lack of comprehension (Kitade 1990). Given the culturally acquired norms for appropriate behavior in Japanese schools, native-speaking English teachers often encounter tremendous resistance from Japanese students as they attempt to implement more interactive styles of communication in EFL classrooms (Wordell 1985).

As mentioned earlier, when teachers and students share the same native language and educational experiences, EFL students are usually able to accurately perceive and participate in classroom events. However, in these EFL contexts, the English language itself sometimes becomes more of a subject matter than system of communication. This focus is often the result of externally imposed mandates, such as national curriculum standards or university entrance examinations. Thus, although such EFL students may develop a wealth of grammatical knowledge about the language, they are unable to use the language for communicative purposes. In such instructional contexts, students' frames of reference may not inhibit participation in classroom events, but the classroom events themselves may limit students' opportunities to acquire the English language for communicative purposes.

An example of this sort of EFL instructional context was identified in an exploratory study of the implementation of the national English language curriculum in Malaysia. Kaur (1993) found that while this curriculum was based on the theoretical premise of student-centered instruction – that is, teachers were to utilize and integrate student participation in order to tailor instructional materials and activities to meet predetermined student-oriented goals – the Malaysian EFL teachers struggled in their attempts to implement the curriculum accordingly. Instead, most continued to follow the traditional teacher-centered approach of second language instruction, used the curricular materials to teach grammar skills, and rarely created opportunities for their students to participate in communicative interactions in English. Thus, while the Malaysian EFL students were able to participate in these classroom events, they had limited success acquiring the English language for communicative purposes. As a result, the outcome of this sort of EFL instruction may be that EFL students are more likely to learn about the structure of the language but less likely to acquire nativelike interactional styles and use of the language for communicative purposes.

Conclusion

Second language students' perceptions of the patterns of classroom communication and their role in classroom events tend to be based on how they perceive and respond to what their teachers say and do, as well as the expectations they hold about what is and is not appropriate communicative behavior in classrooms. For second language students to participate in classroom events, they must accurately infer their teachers' expectations and intentions, the contextualized cues embedded within classroom events, and the academic task and social participation structures of those events. In Excerpt 3.1, Kim and Petr had difficulty recognizing and fitting into the structure of the lesson, mostly because they misinterpreted the academic task structure embedded in the lesson and misunderstood their teacher's verbal cues outlining that structure. On the other hand, in Excerpt 3.2, the teacher allowed for more variability in both the academic task and social participation structures. As a result, Jay, Sung-su, and Alex were able to use more exploratory language as opposed to correct answers, to self-select when and how they would participate, and to actively contribute to both the content and the structure of the lesson. The ways in which these students participated in these lessons represent a combination of how they understood their teachers' expectations and intentions, what they perceived the structure of the lesson to be, and what they deemed to be appropriate communicative behavior in their classrooms.

The next chapter expands the examination of students' frames of reference to include students' culturally-acquired knowledge and use of language, since this too determines, in part, the ways in which second language students perceive and participate in classroom events.

4 Students' knowledge and use of language

Second language students possess an accumulation of culturally acquired knowledge through which they interpret and respond to the world around them. Embedded in this knowledge is their use of language, the medium through which they understand and represent their experiences to themselves and to others. When students begin to operate in a second language, they must acquire a new means of understanding and representing their experiences. However, as they acquire a second language, most continue to rely on first language linguistic and cultural knowledge to interpret and participate in social interactions.

This chapter focuses on students' linguistic background knowledge, or learned ways of talking, and how such knowledge enables them to acquire both their native language and the social rules for how to use that language. In addition, students' cultural background knowledge, or learned ways of communicating, are explored as a factor enabling students to acquire patterns of social interaction that are deemed appropriate within their own specific culture. While this area of research has generated a large body of ethnographic field studies across a range of cultural and sociolinguistic contexts, only a few representative studies are reviewed in some detail here to get a better understanding of differences in students' linguistic and interactional competencies and the consequences such differences may have on their academic achievement. These examinations lead to a discussion of the discontinuities that sometimes exist between the language of the home and the language of the classroom, and how such discontinuities can create social and educational obstacles for second language students. The chapter concludes with examples of educational programs that have attempted to maximize second language students' knowledge and use of language to enable them to participate in and learn from classroom events.

Students' linguistic background knowledge: learned ways of talking

Even before children enter school, they have very sophisticated knowledge of the ways of talking in different social groups. In their early life experiences, much of this interactional competence is attributed to mother–child interaction, which enables children to behave in socially acceptable ways within their primary social group. As children become older, their social contacts often extend beyond this primary group to a wide range of second-ary social groups, such as religious institutions, the neighborhood, the community, or local daycare facilities. To successfully participate in these secondary social groups, children must learn ways of talking that match the social and interactional norms of these groups. Ways of talking in second-ary social groups are often fundamentally different from those of the pri-mary group, since secondary social groups rely on more decontextualized language and less shared background knowledge. Studies of Anglo-American children suggest that as early as age four, children acquire the social registers and functional uses of language and are able to mimic them in appropriate social contexts (Andersen 1986). Moreover, they are able to adjust their language to conform to the linguistic and interactional rules that are perceived as appropriate for a wide range of secondary social groups.

However, this is not always the case for second language students living within a dominant culture. In the United States, members of second lan-guage groups, such as Puerto Ricans, Mexican-Americans, Koreans, or Chinese, may not seek out and/or participate in social institutions within the middle-class Anglo-American culture. Less exposure to secondary social groups within the dominant culture means fewer opportunities for second language students to acquire the range of interactional competencies neces-sary to participate successfully in that culture. Thus, when these students enter school, they may not have acquired the norms of language use that are expected by Anglo-American teachers.

Probably the most well-known study of cultural differences between the language of the home and the language of the school was carried out by Susan Philips (1972, 1983) on the Warm Springs Indian Reservation. Phi-lips compared differences between the social conditions governing verbal participation in middle-class Anglo-American classrooms and in the Warm Springs community. She found that the Warm Springs students' willingness to participate in Anglo-American classrooms was related to the ways in which verbal interaction was organized and controlled. She characterized verbal interaction in Anglo-American classrooms as being organized by one of four participant structures. The first, and most common, was the teacher interacting with all students, controlling who will talk and when, with either voluntary student participation, through self-nomination, or compulsory participation, through teacher nomination. The second, also very common, was the teacher interacting with small groups of students, as in reading groups, where student participation was generally the result of teacher nomination and required individual performance. The third was students working individually at their desks, with the teacher available for student-initiated interaction. Finally, the fourth, more common in the higher than lower grades, was small group activities in which students were responsible for completing specific tasks with indirect supervision by the teacher.

Philips's observations of Warm Springs students in Anglo-American classrooms with regard to each of these participant structures revealed that Warm Springs students were less willing to participate verbally when speaking alone or in front of other students, if called upon by the teacher or asked to take on a leadership role. On the other hand, they were more willing to participate verbally in group activities when no distinction was made between the speaker and the audience, and when they could self-select when to speak. When comparing the conditions for verbal participation in the classroom with those in the Warm Springs community, these differences became clearer. Within the Warm Springs community, learning tasks generally follow a sequence of extensive listening and watching; then supervised participation, in which an older relative assists in segmenting the task so that the child can successfully complete it with assistance; and, finally, private self-initiated self-testing of what is learned. The use of speech in such activities is minimal, instructions are few, and competence is demonstrated without testing but through the completion of the task itself.

Thus, as Philips found, since the verbal competencies of Warm Springs children were incongruent with those expected in Anglo-American classrooms, Warm Springs children were less willing to talk during classroom events. Philips argues that when children of different cultural backgrounds come together in the classroom, "efforts [should] be made to allow for a complementary diversity in the modes of communication through which learning and measurement of 'success' takes place" (1983: 393).

Subtle differences in learned ways of talking have also been found between Chicano and Anglo-American mothers' use of teaching strategies when interacting with their very young children. Laosa (1981) found that Chicano mothers tended to teach their children by demonstrating or modeling an action or activity while the children observed. They also relied heavily on visual cues to attract their children's attention to a particular aspect of the action being modeled. Less often, these mothers used directives, praise, questions, and negative feedback. In contrast, Anglo-American mothers tended to teach their children through the use of praise and asking questions, relying less on visual cues, directives, modeling, or negative feedback. While Laosa makes no claim as to the value of these different styles of maternal behavior, it is implied that congruency between the teaching strategies of the home and school might enable Chicano children to make a smoother transition between the two. This is especially important since LeVine (1978) points out that praise and questioning are the predominant teaching strategies found in Anglo-American classrooms.

Common to these studies is the notion that children acquire learned ways of talking by interacting in predictable ways with caregivers or members of their primary social group. Thus, learned ways of talking enable children to acquire both their native language and the social rules for how to use that language. Peters and Boggs (1986: 81) define "modes of speaking" as a process reflecting key cultural values that guide a child's linguistic and socialization process. In short, language acquisition and socialization occur simultaneously. Learned ways of talking reflect the sociocultural values of a linguistic group and enable children to use language to successfully participate in that group.

With regard to the classroom setting, we can assume that all students enter classrooms with linguistic background knowledge, or learned ways of talking, that reflect the sociocultural values of their primary social group that have thus far enabled them to use their language to learn and to communicate within that group. Difficulties arise, of course, when students' learned ways of talking do not conform to the patterns of communication that are expected in classrooms. As the framework presented in Chapter 1 suggests, if the patterns of classroom communication do not allow second language students to utilize their learned ways of talking, then they may be less able to participate in and learn from classroom events.

Students' cultural background knowledge: learned ways of communicating

To understand differences in students' cultural background knowledge, or learned ways of communicating, we must look at the development of communicative style, or as Clancy (1986: 213) states, "the way language is used and understood in a particular culture, [which] both reflects and reinforces fundamental cultural beliefs about the way people are and the nature of interpersonal communication." Communicative style is thus equated with one's world-view (Whorf 1956), or the acquisition of culture-specific patterns of social interaction that represent learned ways of communicating within a specific culture.

Nowhere has the acquisition of communicative style been more closely scrutinized than in Japan. Clancy (1986) describes the communicative style of the Japanese as indirect, context dependent, rich in connotation, and consistent with the ideal of holding the interests of the group above those of the individual. Japanese place high value on silence as opposed to explicit verbal expression, on what is perceived as socially acceptable as opposed to individual feelings, and on an overwhelming need to not offend. Such features of the Japanese communicative style are continually reinforced in the relatively homogeneous Japanese society.

Clancy found that this sort of communicative style was acquired and reinforced through mother–child interactions in which Japanese mothers tended to tell their children what others were thinking, thereby encouraging a deep sense of empathy for others, and reinforced behavioral patterns that reflect conformity as opposed to individualistic expression. This combination of training in empathy and conformity is critical in the acquisition of an indirect, intuitive mode of communicating in Japanese culture. In addition, since Japanese people rely heavily on fixed verbal formulas in daily social interactions, Japanese children learn to use these formulas, and are not encouraged to express their feelings in more personal or individual ways. Japanese children learn at an early age that communication can often take place without actual talk, that by selecting the appropriate formula within the right social context, their meanings will be understood by listeners. The Japanese communicative style characterized by Clancy is in sharp contrast to that transmitted within Anglo-American culture, where emphasis is placed on extensive verbal interaction, where variability in the way in which meanings are expressed is not only accepted but valued, and where the speaker, not the listener, retains the responsibility for being understood.

Differences in culturally learned ways of communicating can also be found in the ethnographic descriptions of the communicative styles of various Aboriginal communities in Australia. S. Harris (1980) describes the communicative styles of the Yolngu of Milingimbi in the Northern Territory as based on two basic communicative rights: the right to speak and the right not to speak. Thus, the Yolngu reserve the right to pause at length before answering a question, or not to answer at all. Samson (1980) describes the communicative style of a fringe-dwelling Aboriginal group in Darwin as favoring and fostering reticence in most social interaction and the rules of speech as dominated by a sense of responsibility to the group as opposed to an individual speaker.

Malcolm's (1979, 1982) ethnographic descriptions of Aboriginal children in Western-style classrooms suggest that these children fail to participate in and learn from classroom events because of contrasting communicative styles. In an extensive examination of over 150 classrooms in 24 Western Australian schools, Malcolm identified a variety of classroom speech events in which Aboriginal students were unwilling to participate according to the rules that governed language use. When teachers tried to impart content through the typical IRE interactional sequence, Aboriginal students were unwilling to take up and respond to a teacher's initiations. Moreover, no amount of coaxing on the part of the teacher could get them to do so. Even in activities that allowed for more variability in student talk, such as discussions or talking about pictures, Aboriginal students failed to respond to open-ended bidding offers for voluntary student initiations or, if they did respond, their contributions were typically unelaborated. Instead, Aboriginal students were found to talk to one another in an overlapping style of interaction. They tended to call out when the teacher was not directly eliciting information from them. Much to their teachers' frustration, Aboriginal students were found to be talkative when they were part of the audience but silent when asked a direct question. Since this sort of communicative style violated the rules for participation in most Western-style classrooms, Aboriginal students were often left out of the teacher–student interactional patterns during classroom instruction. According to Malcolm, Aboriginal communicative style is governed by participant rights in a speech situation, reflected by such questions as "Who is this person who wants me to talk to him? Who is listening in? Do I want to say anything? Are my rights to noninvolvement being recognized? Have I the right to say something I want to?" (1982: 131). Malcolm argues that if teachers fail to recognize the significance of these rights, the communication problems of Aboriginal students in Western-style classrooms will continue to inhibit their participation in classroom events.

Thus, culturally learned ways of communicating that differ from those expected in school can create discontinuity between the home and the school, and ultimately inhibit students' abilities to fully participate in and learn from classroom events. Delgado-Gaitan (1987a) observed Mexican students at home and in their Anglo-American elementary schools and found that the communicative styles learned at home were not recognized at school. At home, Mexican students were expected to work collectively and cooperatively with others. There was an expected amount of turn taking, negotiation of shared responsibility, and collaboration in the completion of any task. While Mexican students were sometimes expected to demonstrate their ability to lead by assuming a more competitive role, more often than not they were encouraged to cooperate in collaborative ways with others. At school, Mexican students were found to resist working individually and instead seemed to want to share their answers with others. This, of course, violated their Anglo-American teachers' belief in the importance of individual work and was interpreted as "cheating," which was unacceptable.

Other sources of discontinuity were found in the differing authoritarian roles of Mexican parents and Anglo-American teachers. Mexican parents expected their children to obey and to respect their authority, but at the same time they afforded their children the freedom to select how parental requests would be accomplished, either with adult assistance, through peer collaboration, or individually. In contrast, Anglo-American teachers tended to control all aspects of an assigned task, allowing the students little, if any, opportunity to negotiate their role in how the task would be completed. Thus, while these Mexican students were found to possess competencies in collaboration, cooperation, and independent decision making, their communicative styles were not recognized, and in some cases were even discouraged, at school. Delgado-Gaitan (1987a) describes the need for Anglo-American teachers to recognize Mexican students' culturally learned communicative styles and create a wider range of learning structures through which Mexican students can utilize their communicative styles and thereby fully participate in and learn from classroom events.

Finally, culturally acquired patterns of communicating may affect not only how second language students participate in classrooms, but also their second language development. Willett (1987) compared the sociocultural environment and second language development of two non–English-speaking children in an American preschool. Through extensive observations of both children and interviews with their parents and teachers, Willett found that while both children were successful second language learners, they exhibited contrasting interactional and acculturation patterns in the classroom. Alisia, a Brazilian girl, had a strong desire to fit in with her peers. After a three-month silent period, in which she merely observed the interactional patterns of her peers, she began to speak using appropriate phrases and had nativelike pronunciation, which enabled her to successfully interact with her peers. Jeni, a Korean girl, began speaking English immediately but tended to ignore her peers and instead preferred to interact with adults. While her pronunciation remained non-nativelike, she exhibited superior syntactic development despite the fact that she relied on using one-word utterances in her initial interactions with adults.

In-depth interviews with the parents and teachers of both children revealed that their interactional competencies reflected their respective sociocultural environments at home. Alisia's sociocultural environment at home appeared to be congruent with that of the American preschool. Alisia's mother and her teachers shared the same views about peer socialization, adult roles, and discipline. They each maintained an informal, friendly, noncoercive relationship with Alisia. Both agreed on the importance of creating a stimulating environment in which the child retained the responsibility for social interaction. On the other hand, Jeni's sociocultural environment at home appeared to be in sharp contrast to that of the American preschool. Jeni had experienced more focused interaction with her parents and, thus, did not appear to have a strong need to be socially accepted by her peers. Willett concluded that the emphasis on adult guidance and supervision at home, in accordance with Confucian values, may in part explain why Jeni tended to play independently from her peers, selected structured activities, and sought out verbal interaction only with her teachers.

In her interpretation of the acculturation patterns of these two children, Willett contrasted the importance of peer acceptance and sociability in Alisia's home environment to the Confucian value of one-on-one learning interactions in Jeni's. Thus, social adjustment to the American preschool environment was easier for Alisia, who was not expected to act differently from the way she had been socialized at home. For Jeni, this adjustment was more difficult since she expected, but often did not receive, focused supervision from her teachers. When examining their second language acquisition patterns, Willett interpreted that Alisia's appropriate use of formulaic expressions and nativelike pronunciation as the result of more peer contact while Jeni's syntactic development may have been the result of more adult contact. Willett concluded that culturally learned language socialization patterns from home can affect children's learning styles, the developmental process of second language acquisition, and what is actually learned in the classroom.

At this point it should be evident that all students acquire learned ways of talking and communicating that reflect the sociocultural values of their social and/or cultural group. However, as the framework presented in Chapter 1 suggests, students' knowledge and use of language must conform to the patterns of communication that exist within the classroom; if it does not, they may be less willing or able to participate in classroom events, with the consequence that their academic abilities may be underestimated.

Thus far the discussion has focused on children and the ways in which they are socialized to use language to talk and to communicate. However, similar claims can be made about adults. In Chapter 3, both Duc and Sun-yu described the discontinuity between their culturally learned ways of talking and communicating and those expected in their second language classrooms. ESL and EFL teachers with whom I work are quick to offer anecdotal examples of adults who experience discontinuity between their culturally acquired knowledge and use of language and that which is expected in second language classrooms. Probably the most common discontinuity concerns differences in communicative styles among speakers from different linguistic and cultural backgrounds. An American ESL teacher, Kris, characterized this discontinuity in the following scenario:

In my beginning level ESL class at the Community Adult Education program, I have eleven adults. Five speak Spanish, four speak Japanese, and the remaining two speak Russian and are husband and wife. In large group activities the Spanish speakers tend to ask and answer most of the questions and dominate most of the student talk. Last week I tried an activity in which I paired up different native language speakers, but again the Spanish speakers tended to dominate while the Japanese speakers sat quietly and when it was their turn to speak they appeared to be very uncomfortable. While I am pleased with the Spanish speakers' eagerness to participate and do not want to squelch their opportunities to speak, I am very concerned about providing opportunities for the Japanese and Russian speakers to participate in class. I am also keenly aware of how uncomfortable the Japanese speakers appear to be when they are forced to speak in class. At this point, I'm not sure what to do!

Clearly, Kris recognized that the patterns of communication that she expected in her classroom have created discontinuities for some of her adult students. Since they have acquired different ways of talking and communicating, some were more likely to participate in classroom events than others.

A linguistic and/or ethnic community can have a powerful influence on the extent to which some second language adult students are able to adjust to the norms of communication in second language classrooms. An American colleague of mine who worked as an ESL tutor was asked by her adult Korean student, Kim, not to tell other Koreans of their tutoring arrangement. Kim spoke of the ridicule he would face within his own community if it was known that he was trying to improve his English. He described a shared sense in the importance of accommodating to the American university community in which the Koreans lived while at the same time maintaining an unwillingness to assimilate into that community.

Gibson (1987) found a similar phenomenon in her study of the social and cultural adjustment and academic performance of Punjabi immigrants in an American high school. Despite cultural and language differences, the Punjabi students did well in school; however, she characterized their adjustment to the American school system as accommodation without assimilation. That is, Punjabi high school students were encouraged by their parents and social community to fit in to school life in order to receive an education that would lead to future employment opportunities, but not to become like Americans. Gibson writes, "To understand language minority students' school performance we must look at the social structure of the host society and the cultural background of the minority group – and the minority group's position in the host society – its perception of opportunities and its historical relationship with that group" (1987: 272).

Finnan (1987) supports Gibson's findings. In a study of the role of one Vietnamese community in helping newly arrived refugees develop a new occupational identity, Finnan found that the Vietnamese community had more influence on the process of matching one's self-image to an image of a professional occupation than did educational training and/or individual interest. She concluded that education can only provide access to the professional training for a new occupation, and that one's own community has the strongest influence on the development of occupational identity.

It appears that second language students, whether they are adults or children, can experience discontinuity between their learned ways of talking and communicating and that which is expected in second language classrooms. How do such discontinuities create social and educational obstacles for second language students?

Discontinuities between the language of the home and the school

Thus far, much of the discussion has drawn on anthropological research that highlights the differences between how the native language is used in the home and how the second language is expected to be used in school.

DIS

Route Item   11/18/2013 5:52:58 PM

ROUTE ITEM Item Barcode: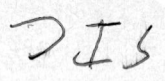

all Number: 418.007 J677
TO Library:
Morris Library - SIUC

Location: SIUC CIRCULATION
Address: ILDS: SIC
Morris Library, SIUC
605 Agriculture Drive
Carbondale, IL 62901
USA
Patron Category:UBReg
Patron Barcode:

S I U 8 5 1 2 5 7 6 6 7

Callslip Request   11/18/2013 4:03:51 PM

Request date: 11/17/2013 06:17 AM
Request ID: 42883
Call Number: 418.007 J677
Item Barcode:

Author: Johnson, Karen E.
Title: Understanding communication in second
Enumeration: c.1 Year:
Patron Name: Abdulsamad Yahya Abdulrahma
Patron Barcode:

Patron comment:

Request number:

Route to:
I-Share Library:

Library Pick Up Location:

The recognition of this sort of discontinuity between the home and school has contributed to what is known as the *cultural discontinuity hypothesis* (Spindler 1974). This hypothesis suggests that second language students acquire different learned ways of talking and communicating, and when they enter school, their linguistic behavior and communicative styles are unappreciated and misunderstood. The cultural discontinuity hypothesis can function in more pronounced ways, as when teachers know the target language but not the native language and/or culture of their students, or in less pronounced ways, as when teachers fail to recognize subtle differences in aspects of communicative styles, such as touching, distance between speakers, gesturing, and speaking rights.

Ogbu (1982, 1987) claims that some discontinuities are inherent in all formal schooling and are universally experienced by all children, while others are experienced only by certain linguistic and ethnic minorities. He suggests that universal discontinuities exist in school because initially all children must learn new ways of talking, communicating, and learning. Cole and Scribner (1974) have characterized schools as places where children learn how to learn. In school, learning takes place in mostly decontextualized environments, it is based more on written than on oral language, and children begin to process new information by learning to read, write, and speak in new ways. Thus, all children experience universal discontinuity between the home and school.

However, Ogbu (1982) questions why some students are more successful at overcoming these discontinuities than others. He recognizes the cultural discontinuity hypothesis as accounting for the fact that students who come from different linguistic and cultural backgrounds will have more difficulty overcoming universal discontinuities. However, he goes on to suggest that it is not just cultural differences that cause language minority students to fail in mainstream schools, but the types of differences that exist. Ogbu identifies these differences as primary and secondary discontinuities. Primary discontinuities consist of cultural differences that existed in a given population before contact with the new culture. Most often associated with non-Western immigrants entering Western-type schools, primary discontinuities represent differences in the curricular content, learning and teaching styles, and language use. Primary discontinuities are generally overcome by non-Western immigrants because of the perceived value of the Western-type schooling as a means of obtaining social and economic status. In addition, non-Western immigrants are often willing to overcome primary discontinuities because these do not threaten their individual or ethnic identity.

In contrast, secondary discontinuities are defined as differences that develop after two populations have been in contact for an extended period of time, or after one population has begun to participate in the educational or social institutions that are controlled by another. Secondary discontinuities are most often associated with nonimmigrant minorities, or what Ogbu describes as "castelike minorities" (1982: 299). In his view, castelike minorities in the United States, such as African-Americans, Native Americans, Chicanos, and Puerto Ricans, have historically been incorporated into the dominant Anglo-American society involuntarily and permanently, and tend to possess communicative styles and attitudes that set them apart from the dominant culture.

Ogbu's distinctions between the types of cultural discontinuity explain to some extent the importance of recognizing the sociocultural context from which second language students come when they enter school. It is not just differences in students' knowledge and use of language that create discontinuity between the home and school, but the broader aspects of the sociocultural context that will determine the extent to which they are willing to overcome the discontinuities they experience at school. This issue is discussed in further detail in Chapter 8, which addresses both community and school-based issues that impact upon second language classrooms.

We turn now to some well-known examples of educational settings in which deliberate attempts have been made to maximize second language students' knowledge and use of language at school so as to enable them to overcome the discontinuities between the language of the home and school.

Maximizing students' knowledge and uses of language in the classroom

There are several well-known examples of educational programs that have attempted to mitigate discontinuities between students' learned ways of talking and communicating at home and school. Designed for different populations of second language and ethnic minority students, each creates instructional situations that attempt to maximize students' culturally acquired knowledge and use of language while at the same time developing their repertoire of interactional competencies so that they can successfully participate in and learn from a wider range of classroom events.

The Papago Early Childhood Head Start program

The Papago Early Childhood Head Start (PECHS) program was designed specifically for preschool-age children of the Papago Native American Reservation in Arizona. As Macias (1987) reports, caregivers in Papago culture generally teach children through nonverbal behaviors and rely on minimal speech. The Papago culture emphasizes individual rights and autonomy, and children are allowed to interact freely without having to conform to the wishes of others. Papago culture devalues drawing attention to oneself or separating from the social group. Papago caregivers rarely scold or coerce children into doing something they choose not to do. In mainstream classrooms, the communicative style of Papago children is often mistakenly perceived as reticent, unwilling, and socially deferential.

To reduce the negative impact of the discontinuity between the home and school, Papago teachers in the PECHS program have developed what Macias describes as a "hidden curriculum" (1987: 377). That is, PECHS teachers use a variety of strategies to enable the Papago children to acquire the prerequisite knowledge and skills for successful participation in the mainstream classroom, while maintaining an appreciation of their own culturally acquired communicative style. To encourage Papago children to be more verbal, PECHS teachers create instructional activities that combine both doing and talking. For example, Macias describes an arts and crafts activity in which the teacher verbally explains how the activity should be carried out and then models the activity for the children. In addition, PECHS teachers encourage Papago children to talk in group activities, but do not require them to do so. To enable Papago children to feel more comfortable when singled out for individual interaction, PECHS teachers are careful to work with groups of students, and turn their attention to an individual child only when members of the group are busy working on their own. During large group instruction, PECHS teachers address their questions to the entire class and rarely single out individual students to speak unless they have volunteered to do so. The PECHS curriculum integrates experiences that are both familiar and new to Papago children. Macias describes field trips to both unknown and familiar places, lunches served that are common to Papago and the mainstream communities, and social activities that are common to both students from the Papago reservation and those living in nearby towns and cities. PECHS teachers maintain a high tolerance for nonparticipation. Papago children are not punished for nonparticipation, but at the same time they are expected not to violate the rules for acceptable behavior in the classroom. In the PECHS program, Macias states, "the teaching style of the Papago staff is characterized first by attention to the immediate needs of the child, her emotional welfare and understanding of her own place in the new school environment and, second, by attention to the task of instructing the child in how to fit into the overall organization of the classroom" (1987: 377).

Macias recognizes that the discontinuities between home and school for Papago children reflect the cultural differences between Papago culture and mainstream American society. However, he claims that the PECHS program creates an opportunity for Papago children to develop a new way of learning that will eventually enable them to participate more successfully in mainstream classrooms without denying them the right to maintain their own cultural values and communicative style. Ultimately, the PECHS program acts as an intervention, in which the range of experiences and the communicative competencies of Papago children are widened.

The Kamehameha Early Education program

The Kamehameha Early Education program (KEEP) was designed for children of Polynesian descent in Hawaii. After almost eight years of investigation into both the home community and the school environment of Hawaiian children, it became apparent that during mainstream American classroom reading instruction, these children found themselves in instructional situations that were not congruent with the interactional competencies familiar to them at home (Boggs 1972; Jordan 1981; Watson 1972). In fact, they did not recognize reading lessons as situations in which they needed to apply their full range of cognitive and linguistic abilities (Au 1980; Au & Jordan 1981). Thus, steps were taken to create a reading program that included instructional practices that were more congruent with the interactional competencies these children had acquired in their own culture.

The KEEP reading program has several unique features that distinguish it from typical reading instruction. First, direct instruction focuses on understanding what is read, as opposed to learning how to read, or decoding skills. Second, the classroom is organized into smaller learning centers where students self-select to work with other students on language-arts tasks. Third, direct reading instruction lasts only about twenty minutes, centers on a story from the basal reader, and is followed by a storytelling or "talk story" mode of teacher–student interaction. The "talk story," a common linguistic event for children in Hawaiian culture, represents the co-narration of a story by two or more people. KEEP reading lessons and "talk story" share many of the same interactional features. Teachers in KEEP classrooms, like adults in the Hawaiian community, must establish themselves as socially relevant figures whose approval is highly valued. This social relationship is critical to these children, since without proper interpersonal relationships, Hawaiian children will not respond to the storyteller (Boggs 1972). Both KEEP reading lessons and "talk story" are characterized by mutual participation. That is, both teacher and students participate in the telling of the story and, more importantly, the teacher's contributions to the story are no more important than the students'. This process of co-narration represents a style of interaction more common to informal learning than school learning (Au & Jordan 1981; Scribner & Cole 1981).

However, KEEP proponents are quick to point out that a KEEP reading lesson is not identical to "talk story" in the Hawaiian culture. Rather, they claim it contains some of the key features of this unique linguistic event and, thus, enables Hawaiian children to maximize their interactional competencies so that they can successfully participate in and learn from their reading lessons. They recommend that schools develop learning situations that are more congruent with those that second language students have experienced in their own culture. However, they are evasive on how to translate culturally sensitive instructional practices into the educational experiences for all second language students.

A related project, carried out by some of the same KEEP researchers, attempted to transplant the KEEP reading lessons into classrooms with Navajo students on the Rough Rock Indian reservation (Tharp 1982). It was found that what was culturally compatible and educationally effective for Hawaiian children was not relevant for Navajo students. Thus, while maintaining cultural compatibility may help explain school success, it is not the sole reason for school failure. Tharp (1982) concluded that the KEEP program may be culture specific, but its underlying instructional principles can be adjusted to fit other cultural communities. Tharp recommends examining classrooms in which second language students are succeeding to determine the essential characteristics of the instructional practices that lead to this success.

Questioning in rural Appalachia

Heath's (1982) ethnographic research in three English-speaking communities in a rural Appalachian area of the American Southeast identified subtle differences in language socialization patterns. Over a five-year period, Heath examined the literacy event of "book-reading" and its relationship to the development of children's narrative skills in Maintown (representing mainstream, middle-class, school-oriented culture), Roadville (a white mill community of Appalachian origin), and Trackton (a black mill community of recent rural origin). She found that each community used different ways of talking and interacting in this particular literacy event. The most striking differences were found with the working-class blacks in Trackton, where parents rarely used questions as a mode of interaction with their children. Trackton children were not expected to be information givers or conversational partners, and although their linguistic environments were rich, language was not directed at them. When asked questions, these children were expected to relate an entire incident, but rarely to identify or name its individual parts. Consequently, when Trackton children entered classrooms with Anglo-American teachers, where the asking of "known-answer" and identification questions dominated classroom talk, they were suddenly expected to respond to questions in ways that were unlike what they had experienced at home. This incongruence caused a great deal of frustration for their teachers, who perceived the Trackton students' lack of appropriate responses as an unwillingness and/or inability to participate in classroom activities.

Heath (1982, 1983) also participated in collaborative work with Anglo-American teachers of the Trackton children by first helping these teachers become aware of the questioning patterns that were familiar to Trackton children, and then by creating an intervention program in which they adapted curricular techniques and materials to include more open-ended, or probing type, questions. For example, instead of asking children to identify specific objects from a photograph for a social studies unit on "our community," the teachers asked more open-ended questions, such as "What's happening here? Have you ever been here? Tell me what you did when you were there? What's this like?" (Heath 1982: 124). Such slight adaptations in their questioning patterns resulted in increased participation and involvement on the part of the Trackton children.

The next step was to enable the Trackton children to acquire the questioning patterns that were used most often by their Anglo-American teachers. To do this, teachers tape recorded the Trackton children's responses to specific lessons, and then added sample "known-answer" and identification questions and answers to the tapes. During informal learning-center activities, the children had access to these tapes and, thus, were able to hear the kinds of question-answer patterns that their teachers tended to use during classroom instruction. In addition, the teachers made a point of openly discussing the different types of questions used in class and eventually helped the Trackton children create and use their more favored type of questioning pattern.

Heath concludes that the success of this sort of program was the result of the two-way nature of the teacher-designed intervention. That is, the language of the community and the language of the school were not placed at odds, but instead each was used to learn about the other. Heath claims it is critical for educators to "tap the uses of language and ways of 'talking about things' of the culturally different and to bring these skills into the classroom" (1982: 126). Heath also stresses the importance of encouraging teachers to become investigators into how they and their students act and talk, and to use resulting insights to adapt and adjust their own classroom talk to match that of their students.

Conclusion

Several conclusions can be drawn about students' knowledge and use of language. First, differences in students' linguistic and interactional competencies may be the result of culturally acquired socialization patterns learned at home and/or in a student's social community. Moreover, such competencies may influence how students participate in and learn from classroom events. While all students must learn to recognize the patterns of classroom communication and adjust their linguistic and interactional competencies accordingly, when discontinuities exist between the competencies of the home and those expected at school, students may be less willing or able to participate in classroom events. Ultimately, for second language students to participate successfully in classroom events, they must be aware of the implicit rules for participation that are expected by teachers and are thereby embedded in classroom events.

Teachers must recognize that differences in second language students' linguistic and interactional competencies exist and, more importantly, that these competencies are the result of a process of socialization and do not represent cognitive or social deficiencies. Second, teachers must create classroom events that allow for greater variability in both the academic task structures and the social participation structures, so as to maximize second language students' competencies. Teachers must also make their expectations and intentions clear, and in doing so, make explicit the implicit rules for participation in classroom events.

The orientations of the educational programs reviewed here are based on the premise that second language students come to classrooms competent in learned ways of talking and communicating. If recognized by teachers, students' knowledge and uses of language can be maximized through the creation of instructional activities that allow students to utilize their competencies in such a way that they are able to participate in and learn from classroom events. The discussion now moves to the final component of the framework: that is, students' use of language for learning and second language acquisition.

5 Students' use of language for learning and second language acquisition

As has been shown thus far, the patterns of communication that are established and maintained in second language classrooms are jointly constructed by teachers, as they control the content and structure of classroom communication, and by students, as they interpret and respond to what teachers say and do. Moreover, both teachers and students perceive and respond to what happens in second language classrooms through their own frames of reference. This chapter examines the final component of the framework for understanding communication in second language classrooms by exploring the ways in which the patterns of classroom communication can both foster and constrain students' use of language for classroom learning and students' opportunities for second language acquisition.

It is important to remember that Cazden (1988) warns against assuming a direct relationship between how language is used and what is actually learned. For example, in Excerpt 2.1, even though Bin eventually produced the superlative adjective in the sentence, "It's the warmest it has ever been," his utterance did little to indicate whether or not he understood this grammatical structure or if he would be able to use that structure in another context. Thus, the relationship between language use and learning is a complex one, as is the relationship between language use and second language acquisition.

In this chapter, language use in second language classrooms is seen as having primarily two functions (Fillmore 1982). The first is to convey the content of what is to be learned, such as concepts or factual information related to a specific content area, or as in most second language classrooms, information about the language itself and/or functional aspects of how to use the language in a variety of contexts. The second is to provide opportunities for second language students to receive linguistic input and to generate linguistic output in order to acquire a second language.

It is important to evaluate what role teacher–student interaction actually plays in students' use of language for classroom learning and second language acquisition. To explore this issue, I focus primarily on the work of cognitive psychologist L. S. Vygotsky (1978), particularly his theory on the role of social interaction in learning and cognitive development, and examine the applications of Vygotsky's theory for classroom instruction and student learning. These applications are illustrated through classroom transcripts that demonstrate how the patterns of classroom communication can either foster or inhibit the ways in which students use language for classroom learning. Moreover, I review several prominent theories of second language acquisition that have attempted to describe the relationship between classroom interaction and second language acquisition. This review highlights the optimal conditions for classroom second language acquisition and illustrates how the patterns of communication can foster students' opportunities to use language for second language acquisition.

Finally, the optimal conditions for both classroom learning and second language acquisition are presented. These will illustrate the applications of cognitive learning theory to understanding the processes of second language acquisition. The chapter concludes with a review of the framework for understanding communication in second language classrooms.

Students' use of language for classroom learning

In order to understand how students use language for classroom learning, it is necessary to first examine the role that language plays in learning. A comprehensive review of the theories on the relationships between language, learning, and cognitive development is beyond the scope of this chapter. Rather, attention is focused on theories that have examined the role of interaction in the teaching–learning process.

Traditionally, cognitive psychologists have viewed the role of interaction in learning as one in which adults act as providers of new information, as models of how to use that information, and as selective reinforcers of children's attempts at correct performance (L. B. Resnick 1985). Thus, most research on the teaching–learning process has focused on how learners can improve their performance of specific skills. An alternative position, based on the writings of Vygotsky (1978), views the teaching–learning process as taking place in social interactions in which the child shares responsibility for producing a complete performance with an adult (Wertsch 1979, 1984).

The social-cognitive view put forth by Vygotsky (1978) focuses on the social processes that contribute to cognitive development. He argues that learning and cognitive development are interrelated, in that cognition develops as a result of social interactions in which the child learns how to complete a task by sharing responsibility for that task with a more competent adult or peer. Thus, cognitive development lags behind learning and, ultimately, creates a gap between what can be done on one's own and what can be done with assistance. To explain this gap, Vygotsky posits two developmental levels, the first of which he refers to as the *actual developmental level,* defined as "the level of development of a child's mental functions that has been established as a result of certain already *completed* developmental cycles" (1978: 85). The second developmental level, the *zone of proximal development,* is *"the distance between the actual developmental level as determined by independent problem solving and the level of potential development as determined through problem solving under adult guidance, or in collaboration with more capable peers"* (p. 86; emphasis in original). For Vygotsky, learning is a dynamic social process in which the dialogue between adult and child fosters the development of higher cognitive processes. In addition, given the emphasis on the social processes involved in cognitive development, Vygotsky recognizes that each child possesses a wealth of prior experiences – what I have been referring to as the accumulation of culturally acquired knowledge about language use and learning.

For Vygotsky, the child's language use represents the actual level of cognitive development. However, since he proposes that cognitive development lags behind learning, the language of instruction should be geared beyond the actual level of development, to the zone of proximal development. Instructional efforts should focus on the child's potential abilities, creating opportunities for the child to assume joint responsibility for learning tasks that could not be completed on one's own, but with the assistance of the teacher.

Although the writings of Vygotsky were not directed at teachers, his theory on the relationship between learning and cognitive development offers tremendous insight into the role of social interaction and language use in learning. As illustrated in Chapter 4, early socialization patterns between caregivers and children foster learned ways of talking and communicating within specific social and cultural contexts. Caregivers provide opportunities for their very young children to participate in social interaction long before their cognitive or linguistic abilities would enable them to do so on their own. The structure of these social interactions has been referred to by Bruner (1978) as "verbal scaffolds." Some classic examples of verbal scaffolds are found in caregiver-infant language games, such as peekaboo (Ratner & Bruner 1978) and picture-book reading (Ninio & Bruner 1978). In such language games, the caregiver initially enacts the entire activity, performing both parts of the script. The caregiver provides temporary support that is adjusted to the individual needs of the child; as the child begins to take on more responsibility for the game, the scaffold is slowly removed. Later the caregiver either varies the structure of the game or initiates a new game for the child to learn. Throughout this process, the dialogue between the caregiver and the child is what provides the support and adjustment for scaffolded instruction. Thus, verbal scaffolds make it possible for learners to participate in social interaction that is beyond their actual developmental level, but is instead in Vygotsky's zone of proximal development.

In applying Vygotsky's theory and Bruner's notion of scaffolds to classrooms, Applebee and Langer (1983) describe scaffolded instruction as including the following components. First, the teacher selects a learning task that has a clear goal or purpose, one that is focused more on an intended outcome as opposed to the individual parts that may lead to that outcome. The learning task must be based on the teacher's knowledge of the skills that are emerging from the students' repertoire but are not yet mature, or in Vygotsky's terms, abilities that are "ripening" as opposed to "ripe" (1978: 86). Once the task is selected, it is evaluated to determine what aspects may create problems for the students. Based on this evaluation, the teacher then sets up the task in such a way that best enables students to successfully complete the task with an appropriate amount of assistance. To do this, the teacher must sequence the steps from simple to more complex, highlight aspects of the task that may create stumbling blocks, and adjust the level of instructional support to the specific abilities of the students. During instruction, the teacher emphasizes student participation and makes every effort to ensure high levels of interest and attention by modeling, questioning, and explaining, and making the critical features of the task explicit. Evaluation is carried out only as a means of assessing appropriate levels of difficulty so that the teacher's scaffolds can be adjusted if necessary. Finally, as students begin to assume more responsibility for the task, the scaffold is gradually withdrawn. Eventually, the students internalize the necessary skills to demonstrate their competence in the task, and are ready to move on to the next task.

Scaffolded instruction includes not only the instructional design of what occurs in classrooms, but the teacher–student dialogue embedded in that instruction. Palincsar (1986) describes the effective use of teacher–student dialogue in scaffolded instruction as being contingent on how well the teacher supports students' contributions to the dialogue and uses those ideas as links to new knowledge. If, in an IRE sequence, the teacher's E acts more like an expansion than an evaluation, students' contributions can actually become part of that dialogue. Once this occurs, the teacher can create a scaffold upon which students can link what they already know to new knowledge that they need to learn to complete the task. Palincsar also stipulates that effective teacher–student dialogue be focused on a specific and manageable task, that the purpose of the task be made explicit to students, and that teachers' evaluation statements be more positive than negative. In essence, "the teacher receives what the students offer, recasts their offerings, and evaluates their understandings" (1986: 89). Palincsar goes on to say that "teacher attention is directed to the profile of the learner, to the profile of the skill being learned, and to matching the skills of learners to the way new skills are presented to them. Dialogue has a critical role to play in scaffolding instruction, facilitating the collaboration necessary between the novice and expert for the novice to acquire the cognitive strategy or strategies" (p. 95).

Teachers who create verbal and instructional scaffolds that enable students to practice the individual parts of a task within the context of full performance are, in essence, operating within the students' zone of proximal development. In doing so, teachers are encouraging students to formulate new understandings of what they are learning as well as creating opportunities for them to acquire the requisite skills needed to carry out that learning on their own.

However, just as children are socialized to use language appropriately within the home community, in classrooms, students are also socialized to use language in socially and academically acceptable ways. In fact, teacher–student interaction in classrooms enables students to adopt the language use and conceptual understandings of the teacher. Edwards and Mercer (1986) describe this process as the development of educational knowledge, or the shared meanings and ways of talking that are mutually constructed between teachers and students in classrooms. They claim that "educational development is not simply a matter of individual cognitive growth, but rather a joint enterprise in which shared understandings, terms of reference, and forms of discourse are established in the process" (1986: 200).

Thus, classrooms act as communication contexts within which students are socialized to use language in specific ways. Lemke (1989) claims that teachers' use of language socializes students into specific ways of talking and thinking. In reference to a high school chemistry lesson on electrons and orbitals, Lemke claims, "a way of talking chemistry is being developed here, a shared way of making sense between a teacher and the wider academic-scientific community and the little community of teacher and students in this class, a way shared also by the writers of science textbooks, and even by working scientists" (1989: 12). Thus, by enacting verbal scaffolds, teachers are in essence doing what caregivers do, that is, socializing students into using language in specific ways and initiating them into the broader "world-views" held by a specific academic community. The following excerpt helps illustrate how teachers use language to do this, as well as how the patterns of classroom communication can create opportunities for students to use language for classroom learning.

Excerpt 5.1: Students' use of language for classroom learning

Excerpt 5.1 is taken from an advanced ESL literature/social studies lesson in a secondary school. The students are reading the play *The Diary of Anne Frank*. In this excerpt, a student, Tanzi, and the teacher are discussing the symbolic meaning of the Star of David during the Nazi occupation of Europe. Notice how the teacher reformulates her questions to help Tanzi understand the concept "symbolize." Pay particular attention to the teacher's use of verbal scaffolds, which help Tanzi as she struggles to understand this concept. In addition, notice how the teacher encourages both Tanzi and another student, Yuko, to express their personal understandings of the play, and then relate those personal understandings to the main characters in the play.

Excerpt 5.1

1. T: . . . and not only did he make them live in one part of the city but then he started making them wear these yellow stars, I'll show you what that star looked like, it's called the Star of David, and it looks like this. (draws on board)

2.   Tanzi: What does star mean?

3. T: What does this star mean?

4.   Yuko: It's in the sky.

5.   Tanzi: I know, but what does that mean?

6. T: Oh, what did it mean . . . what did it symbolize?

7.   Tanzi: Yeah, symboli . . . ?

8. T: What did it symbolize? . . . What did it stand for? . . . when you saw that star what did you think of?

9.   Tanzi: Yeah, what, symboli . . . what did . . . ?

10. T: What did it symbolize?

11.   Tanzi: What did it . . . ?

12. T: Symbolize, what did it symbolize? OK, for the Jews, it symbolizes David – one of their religious leaders – and for the Jews, this star is a symbol of their belief in their religion.

13.   Tanzi: It symboli . . .

14. T: Symbolizes

15.   Tanzi: It symbolizes Jew religion?

16. T: Yes, it symbolizes the Jewish religion. And Hitler made all of the Jewish people wear a yellow star on their clothing, so everywhere they went, people knew they were Jewish . . . and Hitler wanted his people to blame the Jews for all the problems they were having at the time.

17.   Tanzi: Anne, Anne Frank was . . . ?

18. T: Anne Frank was a Jew.

19.   Tanzi: Anne Frank was a Jew?

20. T: Yes, Anne Frank was a Jew.

21.   Tanzi: She had a yellow star?

22. T: Yes, she had to wear a yellow star.

23.   Tanzi: Oh, she had to wear a yellow star? Oh, no, I, I wouldn't wear a star. . . . I just wouldn't tell anyone.

24. T: So, you wouldn't wear a star? If you were Anne Frank you wouldn't wear a yellow star?

25.   Tanzi: No. If I were her, I wouldn't . . . I would run away.

26. T: If you were Anne Frank, you would run away?

27.   Tanzi: If I were her, I would run away and they wouldn't find me. . . . I don't know, it makes me scared a little bit . . .

28. T: Do you think Anne Frank was scared?

29.   Tanzi: Yeah, if I were her, I think I would be scared, I think she was a little bit scared.

30.   Yuko: But she had to wear it.

31.   Tanzi: No, I wouldn't . . . I would hide like Anne Frank, I would run away . . .

32. T: What would you do,
Yuko? If you were Anne Frank?

33.   Yuko: I don't know, maybe if I
                                       were her, I would have to wear
                                       it. My parents would say I have
                                       to.

34.   Tanzi: No, my parents wouldn't,
                                       they wouldn't wear it, we
                                       wouldn't wear it.

35. T: How do you think Anne
Frank's parents felt about it?

36.   Yuko: Maybe they get in trouble
                                       if they don't, so they have to
                                       wear it.

37.   Tanzi: Maybe they have to, but I
                                       wouldn't, I wouldn't care, I just
                                       wouldn't wear it.

At the beginning of this excerpt, Tanzi initiates a question about the symbolic meaning of the yellow star that Anne Frank wore in the play. In turn 6, the teacher responds to Tanzi's question by introducing the word "symbolize." In turn 8, the teacher reformulates her question several times: "What did it symbolize? . . . What did it stand for? . . . When you saw that star what did you think of?" Such reformulations are characteristic of how teachers can simplify a concept so that it becomes comprehensible to the student. In addition, the teacher–student dialogue in turns 2 through 15 acts as a verbal scaffold, since the teacher begins the exchange by assuming full responsibility for the script by using, pronouncing, and defining the word "symbolize." However, in turn 9, Tanzi begins to take over some of that script, when she asks, "Yeah, what, symboli . . . what did . . . ?" She continues in turns 11, "What did it . . . ?", 13, "It symboli . . . ," and 15, "It symbolizes Jew religion?" The more Tanzi attempts to use this new word, the less verbal support is given by the teacher, until Tanzi is able to reformulate her original question without the teacher's assistance.

Midway through this exchange, the teacher appears to shift the focus of her instruction from the meaning of Tanzi's question to the form of the language she is using. The teacher could have easily explained what the Star of David meant without introducing the word "symbolize," but instead she chose to use this opportunity to embed form-focused instruction (teaching a new vocabulary word) in meaning-focused interaction (teacher–student dialogue). The teacher may have had two reasons for doing this. First, when second language teachers shift between meaning- and form-focused instruction, they often are trying to manage the dual functions that language plays in second language classrooms: namely, conveying the content of what is to be learned and creating enough linguistic input and output for second language acquisition. Second, this may have been an opportunity to indirectly socialize Tanzi into using language in a particular way. Semantically, there was little difference between Tanzi's question in turn 2, "What does star mean?", and her question in turn 15, "It symbolizes Jew religion?" However, the second question reflects what Lemke (1989) would describe as more academically oriented language use. Thus, we might characterize this teacher use of both meaning- and form-focused instruction as an attempt to not only teach the language, but also to socialize Tanzi into using the language in academically appropriate ways.

As the exchange continues, the teacher helps Tanzi understand the significance of the Star of David by confirming her contributions. In turn 17, Tanzi asks, "Anne, Anne Frank was . . . ?", to which the teacher responds, "Yes, Anne Frank was a Jew." Tanzi continues, in turn 21, "She had a yellow star?", which the teacher confirms: "Yes, she had to wear a yellow star." This sort of confirmation of student's contributions allows Tanzi to assume more responsibility for the teacher–student dialogue, initiating the question sequence of the script, a role that is generally reserved for the teacher.

Tanzi next begins to relate her personal reactions to the wearing of a yellow star in the play. In turn 23 she claims, "I wouldn't wear a star. . . . I just wouldn't tell anyone." The teacher accepts Tanzi's statement and asks, "So, you wouldn't wear a star?", and then asks Tanzi to relate her statement to the play: "If you were Anne Frank you wouldn't wear a star?" Tanzi responds in turn 25, "No. If I were her, I wouldn't . . . I would run away." The teacher once again accepts Tanzi's statement and asks her to relate it to the main character in the play. A similar pattern emerges when Tanzi expresses her fears (turn 27) and the teacher asks if Tanzi thinks Anne Frank might have experienced those same fears (turn 28). In the midst of this pattern, Yuko challenges Tanzi's statements, in turn 30: "But she had to wear it." The teacher first allows Tanzi to respond to Yuko's challenge, and then asks Yuko to relate her statement to the main character in the play (turn 32). This interaction illustrates what Palincsar (1986) describes as the effective role of teacher–student dialogue in scaffolded instruction. That is, the teacher receives what the students offer in a positive manner, and then recasts those offers in terms of the content of the lesson. This teacher's consistent pattern of acceptance and then request for expansions creates opportunities for Tanzi and Yuko to use language to express their personal understandings and then relate those understandings to what they have read.

Finally, at several points in the exchange, the teacher gradually removes parts of her verbal scaffolds so that the students can begin to assume more responsibility for the interaction. For example, in turn 26, the teacher asks Tanzi to relate her personal reactions to Anne Frank. However, after Tanzi incorporates part of the teacher's script into her response, in 27, "If I were her, I would run away . . .", the teacher, in turn 28, drops the explicit request from her follow-up question: "Do you think Anne Frank was scared?" Tanzi continues to assume this part of the script when she responds in turn 29, "Yeah, if I were her, I think I would be scared . . ." When Yuko enters the discussion, the teacher reenacts her explicit request by asking, "What would you do, Yuko? If you were Anne Frank?" After Yuko successfully assumes one part of the script, the teacher once again removes it, as in turn 35, "How do you think Anne Frank's parents felt about it?"

Overall, this excerpt illustrates some of the ways in which teacher–student interaction can create opportunities for students to use language for classroom learning. Teachers can lower the complexity of classroom language by reformulating their own language in such a way as to make it comprehensible to students. Teachers can create verbal scaffolds that enable students to participate in an activity without assuming full responsibility for that activity. Verbal scaffolds encourage students to express their emerging understandings of a concept as well as reconceptualize those understandings in terms of the content of a lesson. Verbal scaffolds also socialize students into using language in academically appropriate ways. Finally, teachers can gradually remove verbal scaffolds as students begin to assume more responsibility for the interaction.

At this point it seems clear that the patterns of communication that are established and maintained by teachers can create opportunities for students to use language for classroom learning. Again, we must be careful not to assume that language use equals student learning. However, we can assume that the teacher–student interactions that take place in classrooms can, and probably do, have an important impact on how students use language and what they ultimately learn.

Students' use of language for second language acquisition

While most researchers in the field of second language acquisition recognize classroom interaction as having the potential to create opportunities for second language acquisition, there continues to be a general lack of agreement, and more critically, a lack of empirical evidence, on how classroom interaction actually contributes to second language acquisition (Ellis 1990). Given this current state of affairs, the discussion begins with a brief overview of the most prominent theories that have attempted to describe how classroom interaction might contribute to second language acquisition. The overview also highlights some of the optimal instructional characteristics that might create opportunities for students to use language for second language acquisition.

Theories that help us understand the complex relationship between class-room interaction and second language acquisition are based on two as-sumptions. First, the classroom represents an environment that is conducive to second language acquisition. The second is that what goes on in class-rooms, for better or worse, involves communication, and thus can be viewed as some form of interaction. Ellis (1990) describes both reception- and production-based theories of classroom interaction and second lan-guage acquisition. Reception-based theories contend that interaction con-tributes to second language acquisition via learners' reception and com-prehension of the second language, whereas production-based theories credit this process to learners' attempts at actually producing the language. While Ellis claims that neither theory adequately describes how much or what kind of classroom interaction is best for second language acquisition, he concludes that both must be considered when determining how class-room interaction can best be organized in order to create opportunities for second language acquisition.

Probably the most well known, although not necessarily the most widely accepted, reception-based theory has been put forth by Krashen (1981, 1982, 1985). The Input Hypothesis, a fundamental principle of Krashen's Monitor Model, holds that if input is made comprehensible to the learner, either through the context within which it is used, or as a result of simplified input (foreigner talk), acquisition will follow. Hence, acquisition occurs when learners understand input that contains structures that are beyond their current level of competence. Known as the $i + 1$ *hypothesis,* the i represents students' current level of language proficiency, and the $+1$ repre-sents linguistic forms or functions that are beyond this level. Krashen's $i + 1$ hypothesis has striking parallels to Vygotsky's zone of proximal develop-ment presented earlier in this chapter. That is, to provide comprehensible input, teachers (more mature adults) must be attuned to students' $+1$ ("ripening" skills) and adjust the complexity of their language accordingly. By doing so, teachers can create opportunities for students to participate in meaningful interaction (full performance) before they have acquired the necessary skills to do so on their own (zone of proximal development). Thus, in second language classrooms teachers adjust the complexity of their language and/or the cognitive tasks they expect students to participate in, and in doing so create opportunities for students to use language for both learning (Vygotsky) and second language acquisition (Krashen). While these parallels can be carried only so far, both Vygotsky and Krashen focus on the importance of social interaction for both learning and language acquisition.

Krashen credits second language classrooms as having the potential to provide a rich source of comprehensible input. He describes optimal input as being first and foremost comprehensible, that is, focused on meaning, not form. It must also be interesting to students or at least relevant to their own lives. Optimal input should not be grammatically sequenced; it need merely be comprehensible, in which case it will provide plenty of $i + 1$ input. Finally, optimal input must be sufficient in quantity. Despite Krashen's overemphasis on the role of input, he does credit output as indirectly contributing to second language acquisition. He claims output can become comprehensible input to the speaker, since language production usually occurs during interaction and, thus, generates comprehensible input directed at the speaker. Output can also build conversational skills by allowing speakers to control the topic of conversation and participate in meaningful interaction – all necessary, Krashen claims, to generate the kind and amount of input that is required for successful second language acquisition.

There are many published critiques of Krashen's Input Hypothesis (Faerch & Kasper 1986; Gregg 1984; McLaughlin 1987; White 1987). Most complain that his theory is more interpretative than empirically grounded, and represents only a partial description of the processes involved in second language acquisition. In fact, Ellis (1990) claims that Krashen offers no direct evidence in support of the Input Hypothesis. However, Ellis describes its value to language teachers as "a statement of important principle, namely that for successful classroom acquisition learners require access to message-oriented communication that they can understand . . . [however] there is more to teaching than comprehensible input" (1990: 106–7). Thus, while Krashen's Input Hypothesis may have little empirical basis, it has powerful descriptive powers and captures features of the second language acquisition process that teachers intuitively recognize as important.

Another prominent reception-based theory, the Interaction Hypothesis proposed by Long (1981, 1983, 1985), emphasizes the importance of comprehensible input in the form of conversational adjustments. That is, the more adjustments speakers make in their attempts to communicate, the greater the opportunities for second language acquisition. Such adjustments, like those found in foreigner talk, indicate a speaker's attempts at trying to be understood, or the negotiation of meaning; thus, they create comprehensible input. Long suggests that when speakers have the opportunity to receive and participate in conversational adjustments, it maximizes their opportunities for second language acquisition. Like Krashen, Long stresses the importance of comprehensible input but places more emphasis on the interaction that takes place in two-way communication and the adjustments that are made as a result of the negotiation of meaning. Like Krashen, Long's hypothesis is more interpretative than empirically grounded; such interactional adjustments may only partially explain the role of interaction in second language acquisition.

In his critique of these reception-based theories, Ellis (1990) concludes that comprehensible input may facilitate more than determine second language acquisition. Thus, he assumes that if the patterns of communication that exist in second language classrooms foster meaning-oriented interaction between teachers and students, then the nature of that interaction, at the very least, is providing a source of comprehensible input that can, in turn, facilitate second language acquisition.

Production-based theories of the relationship between classroom interaction and second language acquisition place a heavier emphasis on learners' attempts at producing the language. The Output Hypothesis (Swain 1985) states that besides the necessary comprehensible input, learners must have opportunities to produce the language if they are to become fluent, nativelike speakers. Swain describes learners as being "pushed" into developing their linguistic abilities when they participate in meaningful interaction. Moreover, for learners to actually produce the language, they must attend to both the meaning of what they say and the form of how to say it. This, Swain claims, forces learners to move from semantic to syntactic processing in ways simple access to comprehensible input does not. However, language production must occur within the context of social interaction, since this, unlike language production in isolation (for example, repetition of language patterns in a language lab), gives learners opportunities to try out their knowledge of the language.

Other production-based theories emphasize different factors as contributors to second language acquisition. These include the social situations within which the language is used, the ways in which learners jointly construct discourse, and the extent to which learners are allowed to control the topic of conversation. The Discourse Hypothesis (Givon 1979) assumes that learners will acquire only the type of language that is found in the communicative contexts in which they tend to participate. Thus, if learners participate only in informal/unplanned contexts, for example, they will acquire only the type of language used in such contexts. To acquire the full range of linguistic competencies, learners must participate in a variety of communicative contexts.

Based on examinations of how speakers jointly construct discourse within naturalistic contexts (Hatch 1978; Long & Sato 1984; Wagner-Gough 1975), the Collaborative Discourse Hypothesis (Ellis 1990) assumes that more proficient speakers create syntactic structures, or scaffolds, that enable less proficient speakers to produce language that is beyond their current proficiency level. Thus, speakers who actively participate in the joint construction of discourse may have more opportunities for second language acquisition.

Finally, the Topicalization Hypothesis stresses the importance of providing opportunities for learners to select and control the topic of conversation as a means of facilitating second language acquisition (Ellis 1984; Long 1983). As with the reception-based theories, Ellis (1990) warns that no empirical evidence exists that adequately describes how language output, collaborative discourse, or topic control actually contribute to second language acquisition.

Optimal conditions for second language acquisition

Based on a review of both reception- and production-based theories, Ellis (1990) characterizes what he considers to be the optimal conditions for second language acquisition. Essential to these conditions is that students have the need and desire to communicate. In part, this comes from their involvement and interest in what is being talked about, and abundant opportunities to control the topic of conversation and self-initiate in class. Teachers and students must make every effort to be understood by negotiating meaning using language patterns, routines, and strategies. Second language students must be challenged to operate slightly beyond their current level of language proficiency and, in doing so, have opportunities to perform a range of language functions. They must also have opportunities to participate in both planned and unplanned discourse that is similar to what they will encounter outside the classroom. To do this, teachers must provide scaffolds for students to try out new linguistic structures and language functions that are beyond their current level of language proficiency. They must also provide sufficient planned discourse with many examples of the linguistic features that students are trying to learn. Finally, students' output should not be forced; they must be free to self-select when they will participate.

Van Lier (1991) proposes similar optimal conditions for second language acquisition; however, he emphasizes the importance of moving students from noticing the language, to understanding it, and then to using it appropriately. To notice the language, van Lier suggests, takes more than mere language exposure. For language exposure to be "usable," students must be receptive to it, which in turn focuses their attention on the language. Such attention allows the language itself to become comprehensible input. However, input is not enough. Van Lier claims that students then need to make some sort of investment in learning the language if the input is to be processed. This investment requires that students understand the language by making sense of it in terms of what they already know. This prior knowledge may be linguistic (knowledge of linguistic structures) as well as cognitive (knowledge of cognitive operations). Once this occurs, the language then becomes intake. Intake must then be practiced until it is under conscious control of the students and successfully retained. Van Lier describes intake as becoming uptake when students are able to use the language under authentic conditions and as part of the entire language system. This process, which is characterized as both cyclical and spiral, leads to second language proficiency.

The commonalities among these descriptions of optimal conditions for second language acquisition are clear. They stress the importance of creating opportunities for students to have reason to attend to the language, of giving them ample opportunity to use the language for both meaning-focused communication and form-focused instruction, of their receiving enough instructional support from teachers to be able to participate successfully in language-related activities that are beyond their current proficiency levels, and of creating a range of authentic contexts that allow full performance of the language.

To illustrate how the patterns of communication can create opportunities for students to use language for second language acquisition, let us reexamine segments of Excerpt 5.1. In this excerpt, Tanzi initiated the topic of conversation by asking, "What does star mean?" This sort of self-initiated question on Tanzi's part suggests that she had both reason and desire to attend to the language. Thus, her receptivity was demonstrated by her self-selected attention to the language.

Tanzi's attention to the language, in turn, led the teacher to adjust the complexity of her language in order to create input that was comprehensible. The teacher did this by reformulating her questions in turn 8: "What did it symbolize? . . . What did it stand for? . . . When you saw that star what did you think of?" The teacher also chose to introduce a new linguistic form, the word "symbolize," not yet in Tanzi's vocabulary, and thus beyond her proficiency level. Tanzi's attempt to use the new word, as in turn 13, "It symboli . . . ," suggested that the teacher's input had begun to move from input to intake; later, in turn 15, Tanzi was actually able to reformulate her original question using this new word. Thus, we are able to follow Tanzi as she notices the language, understands it, and then uses it appropriately in this context.

This teacher also shifted between form- and meaning-focused instruction as she moved from Tanzi's original question about the meaning of the Star of David, to the linguistic form and correct pronunciation of the word "symbolize," and then back to the meaning of Tanzi's reformulated question. Swain (1985) might characterize this as creating opportunities for both semantic and syntactic processes, two essential aspects of second language acquisition. Both Ellis (1990) and van Lier (1991) support the importance of form- and meaning-focused instruction for classroom second language acquisition.

Later in Excerpt 5.1 we see other opportunities for students to use language for second language acquisition. The teacher consistently created comprehensible input by confirming Tanzi's contributions, as in turn 22, "Yes, she had to wear a yellow star," and created opportunities for Tanzi to produce the language by requesting that she relate her contributions to the characters in the play, as in turn 28: "Do you think Anne Frank was scared?" Tanzi's investment was reflected in her continued attempts at moving from input to intake, that is, from understanding the language to using it. The patterns of communication set up by this teacher created opportunities for both Tanzi and Yuko to express their personal understandings and then relate those understandings to the content of the play.

These examples from Excerpt 5.1 exemplify how this teacher created opportunities for her students to use language for second language acquisition by establishing patterns of communication that allowed students to initiate topics and/or questions of interest. This teacher also created verbal scaffolds that enabled her students to actively participate in the classroom discussion and to engage in the negotiation of meaning, and provided form-focused instruction so that they could attend to specific linguistic features of the language. Finally, this teacher created an authentic context within which her students could use the language appropriately.

The opposite might be said for segments of Excerpt 3.1. In this excerpt, Kim and Petr were not encouraged to initiate the topic of conversation. Few of the teacher–student interactions were meaning focused. In fact, the teacher's attention tended to center on getting the students to produce utterances that contained appropriate negative constructions and correct personal pronoun usage. Moreover, there was little, if any, negotiation of meaning, in that the teacher focused more on the grammatical accuracy of student responses than on the meaning of what they said. Finally, Kim and Petr's attempts at creating any sort of authentic context, namely, by responding to the literal meaning of the teacher's questions as opposed to those given in the textbook, were met with error corrections and reprimands. Excerpt 3.1 exemplifies the ways in which the patterns of communication can constrain more than enhance opportunities for students to use language for second language acquisition.

Optimal conditions for classroom learning and second language acquisition

It should be evident by now that what have been described as the optimal conditions for students' use of language for classroom learning are quite similar to those described as optimal for second language acquisition. These similarities stem from the commonly held belief that learning a second language is like learning any other cognitive skill. This belief has prompted some to claim that "language-related codes and structures are stored and retrieved from memory much like other information, and that language acquisition follows the same principles of learning as do other complex cognitive skills" (O'Malley, Chamot, & Walker 1987: 288). Such claims have led many to assume that the basic principles of cognitive learning theory (Anderson 1980, 1983, 1985) provide powerful explanatory powers for understanding the processes of second language acquisition.

Bialystok (1988) posits a cognitive theory of second language learning in which second language proficiency is characterized as having both an analyzed and an automatic dimension. The analyzed dimension represents the extent to which learners are aware of the structure and organization of their linguistic knowledge, and the automatic dimension represents their ready access to that knowledge. Thus, in the early stages of second language acquisition, the learner has limited knowledge of the linguistic system and minimal control over that knowledge. However, as language acquisition occurs, the learner becomes more aware of the formal structure and organization of the linguistic system and, if opportunities for practice are provided, develops greater access to that information and thus more fluent performance. Bialystok's model also predicts that the context within which language learning occurs will influence the kind of acquisition that takes place. For example, informal language acquisition will result in greater nonanalyzed and automatic knowledge, whereas formal language learning will result in greater analyzed and nonautomatic knowledge.

While Bialystok uses cognitive learning theory to explain how learners develop their knowledge of and control over a second language, Ellis (1990) points out that cognitive learning theory fails to explain aspects of second language acquisition that are governed by linguistic rather than cognitive factors. Specifically, Ellis claims cognitive learning theory cannot account for the natural-order hypothesis: namely, that there is a particular developmental sequence, regardless of direct instruction, in which linguistic structures are acquired. If cognitive learning theory could fully explain second language acquisition, then learners would be able to acquire any linguistic features, in any order, after adequate attention to and practice with them. On the contrary, much research has shown that second language learners acquire certain linguistic structures in a particular acquisitional order, regardless of direct instruction (Gass 1979; B. McLaughlin 1987; Pienemann, 1988).

Second, Ellis claims cognitive learning theory fails to explain the role that explicit knowledge (formal instruction) plays in second language acquisition. Cognitive learning theory assumes that explicit knowledge is in some way a prerequisite for the development of implicit knowledge. It is assumed that the learning process moves from the cognitive stage, in which learners pay attention to new information and relate it to what they already know, to the associative stage, in which learners apply what they know about this new information and use it in some way, finally, to the autonomous stage, in which learners are able to use this new knowledge without conscious attention to it (Anderson 1980, 1983, 1985). Ellis counters that second language learners can, and do, acquire certain linguistic features without explicit attention to them or the ability to articulate what they have acquired. Thus, Ellis's position is more in line with Krashen's emphasis on the importance of comprehensible input for second language acquisition.

However, Ellis does believe that explicit knowledge can facilitate the development of implicit knowledge by making the learner conscious of specific features of the language, but that explicit knowledge is not a prerequisite for implicit knowledge. Ellis claims that "different kinds of input result in different kinds of knowledge and, more significantly, different kinds of input are needed to achieve acquisition of different kinds of knowledge" (1990: 187). Thus, in second language classrooms, meaning-focused instruction will create more opportunities for students to use language for learning and to perform a range of language functions, while form-focused instruction will create more opportunities for students to reflect on the structure and organization of the language. Ideally, he believes, second language classrooms should create opportunities for students to participate in both meaning- and form-focused instruction, since both are believed to contribute to second language acquisition.

At this point, we can assume that students' use of language for classroom learning and second language acquisition operate under some, but not all, of the same theoretical principles. Thus, the patterns of communication that are established between teachers and students in classrooms will determine the extent to which students are given opportunities to use language for classroom learning and for second language acquisition.

Conclusion

To conclude Part I, it is important to review the theoretical assumptions and basic components of the framework for understanding communication in second language classrooms presented thus far. First, and probably most important, is the assumption that classroom communication is a process of negotiation between teachers' meanings and students' understandings that are constructed through face-to-face communication in the classroom. Moreover, the patterns of classroom communication represent a crucial aspect in the learning process, in that they can constrain, to a greater or lesser degree, students' opportunities to participate in and learn from classroom events.

The framework for understanding classroom communication begins with the recognition that second language students possess an accumulation of culturally acquired linguistic and interactional knowledge through which they interpret and respond to the world around them. The extent to which second language students are given opportunities to demonstrate that knowledge will depend on the patterns of communication that are established and maintained in second language classrooms. Within second language classrooms, the patterns of communication are jointly constructed by teachers as they control the content and structure of classroom communication, and by students as they interpret and respond to what teachers say and do. The ways in which teachers choose to organize classroom communication may be the result of the pedagogical purpose of their lessons and the frames of reference through which they make sense of their own and their students' communicative behavior. Students' perceptions of the patterns of classroom communication are based on how they perceive and respond to what their teachers say and do, their culturally acquired linguistic and interactional competencies, and their prior experiences as students in classrooms. Thus, the patterns of classroom communication are jointly constructed as what teachers and students bring to the classroom merges with and shapes what occurs during face-to-face classroom communication. Finally, the patterns of classroom communication that are established and maintained between teachers and students will influence students' opportunities to use language for classroom learning and for second language acquisition.

It is important to remember that the teacher plays a critical role in understanding, establishing, and maintaining patterns of communication that will foster, to the greatest extent, both classroom learning and second language acquisition. As mentioned previously, teachers must recognize that differences in second language students' linguistic and interactional competencies exist and, more importantly, that these competencies are the result of a process of socialization and not cognitive or social deficiencies. Once teachers recognize students' competencies, they can begin to create instructional activities that allow students to utilize those competencies, allow for greater variability in both the academic task and social participation structures of their lessons, and make explicit the implicit rules for participation in classroom events.

PART II
EXAMINING PATTERNS OF
COMMUNICATION IN SECOND
LANGUAGE CLASSROOMS

6 Teacher–student interaction

In this chapter the framework for understanding communication in second language classrooms presented in Part I is used to examine the patterns of communication that exist between teachers and students in two very different second language classrooms. I examine how these teachers use language to control the structure and content of classroom communication. I also explore the ways in which the students respond to their teachers' use of language, their own language use, and the extent to which they are able to fit their language into the patterns of communication that exist in each classroom. Finally, I assess the ways in which the patterns of communication found in each classroom create opportunities for students to use language for classroom learning and for second language acquisition.

The goal in this chapter is to examine teacher–student interaction and to understand the ways in which this interaction shapes the patterns of classroom communication. Therefore, the examination is limited to transcribed excerpts of actual second language lessons. Given this limited data source, both teachers' and students' perceptions of the patterns of communication can only be inferred from what they say and do. Nonetheless, examination of these excerpts will help illustrate how the framework can create a lens through which teachers can begin to construct an integrated view of communication in second language classrooms.

Excerpt 6.1: Teacher-directed patterns of communication in teacher–student interaction

Excerpt 6.1 is taken from a secondary school (form four level, or American grade 10) intermediate EFL class in Malaysia. The teacher and students speak the same native language; however, the entire lesson is conducted in English. The lesson is based on the prescribed national curriculum in Malaysian schools known as the *Kurikulum Bersepadu Sekolah Menengah,* or the New Integrated Secondary School Curriculum. The lesson covers a vocabulary exercise based on an advertisement for a clearance sale printed in the English textbook. The vocabulary lesson is actually a prelude to an assignment in which the students will write a letter to a friend or relative requesting that a particular item from the clearance sale be purchased.

As you read this excerpt, see if you can determine the ways in which the teacher uses language to control the structure and content of classroom communication. Try to identify the academic task structures and the social participation structures embedded in this lesson. Note how the teacher reinforces these structures. In addition, pay attention to how students use language during the lesson. Try to characterize the type of language they use. See if you can identify how they fit their language into the patterns of communication established by this teacher. Finally, try to assess the ways in which the patterns of communication create opportunities for these EFL students to use language for classroom learning and second language acquisition.

Excerpt 6.1

1. T: What is this advertisement about?

2.   Peersak: Radio . . . sale.

3.   Milo: Cheap sale . . .

4. T: What is the word that is used there?

5.   Suchada: Clearance sale.

6. T: Clearance sale. OK, in the first place, do you know the meaning of "clearance sale"?

7.   Suchada: Clearance sale.

8. T: Clearance sale. Let's look at the word "clearance." What word does it come from?

9.   Peersak: Clear.

10. T: Therefore, "clearance" sale will mean what?

11.   Suchada: To clear up.

12. T: To clear up, that's right. To clear up all the goods in the store. OK, let's look at the items which are for sale. Where is the photographic department? Peersak, look at the advertisement and tell me, where is the photographic department?

13.   Peersak: Ground floor.

14. T: Yes, on the ground floor. Now, if you go to the photo-

graphic department, what can
you get there?
15.   Peersak: Camera.

16. T: A camera. Can you be
more specific? What kind of
camera?
17.   Peersak: A Kodak . . . Instamatic
                                            76X camera.

18. T: OK, a Kodak instamatic
camera. What is the usual price
of the camera?
19.   Peersak: Twenty-seven and forty
                                            cents.

20. T: Twenty-seven dollars,
forty cents. And what is its price
after the sale?
21.   Peersak: Twenty-three dollars,
                                            seventy-five cents.

22. T: Twenty-three dollars,
seventy-five cents. Now, if you
buy that camera what free gift
will you get?
23.   Peersak: . . . Ball.
24. T: A ball. Now, let's move
on to some other department in
the store. Milo, where is the
housewares department?
25.   Milo: First floor.
26. T: What can you buy there?
27.   Milo: Stainless steel kettles.
28. T: How many sizes of ket-
tles?
29.   Milo: Five.
30. T: OK, these stainless steel
kettles come in five sizes. And
what is the special feature of this
kettle?
31.   Milo: Imported.
32. T: What other special fea-
tures?
33.   Milo: Movable handle.
34. T: Yes, they have movable
handles in addition to being
stainless steel. OK, now,

Suchada, if you want to buy a
rattan picnic basket, which
department will you go to?

35.   Suchada: First floor.

36. T: Which department?

37.   Suchada: Flower department.

38. T: Yes, flower department.
Where does this picnic basket
come from?

39.   Suchada: China.

40. T: What is its special feature?

41.   Suchada: Complete with tray and
                                           two flask holders.

42. T: Yes, and what is a flask
holder? You know what a flask
is, right? What about holder? It
comes from the word "hold." It
holds the flask. OK, all right . . .

Teachers' control of the patterns of communication

Most of the teacher–student interaction in this lesson follows the IRE
interactional sequence (Mehan 1979). The IRE sequence begins with a
teacher initiation, followed by a student response, and then the teacher's
evaluation of that response. In this excerpt, the structures of this teacher's
evaluations differ depending on whether the students' responses are correct
or incorrect. If a response is incorrect, the teacher ignores the incorrect
response, and simply gives a second initiation. This occurs in turn 1 when
the teacher initiates, "What is this advertisement about?", and Peersak and
Milo respond, "Radio . . . sale" and "Cheap sale." Neither of these responses appears to be correct, because in turn 4 the teacher ignores both
responses and asks, "What is the word that is used there?" This second
initiation acts as an evaluation because it indicates to the students that their
responses were incorrect; at the same time, it represents an open bid for
other responses. Alternatively, when a student's response is correct, the
teacher repeats that response as an affirmation before giving the next initiation. This occurs in turn 5 when Suchada responds, "Clearance sale," to
which the teacher replies, "Clearance sale. OK, in the first place, do you
know the meaning of 'clearance sale'?" Thus, in the first six turns of this
excerpt we see a pattern of teacher–student interaction emerging. That is,
the IRE sequence dominates the patterns of communication, and the teacher
evaluates incorrect responses by reformulating her initiations to elicit the
correct response, then moves to the next initiation.

As the excerpt continues, we can also see the development of both the academic task structures and the social participation structures (Erickson 1982). In turns 12 through 24, the academic task structure follows a consistent pattern of first establishing location in the store, next identifying an item at that location, and, finally, reviewing specifics about that item. The teacher begins this structure by identifying a particular department and asking the students to identify the location of that department in the store. In turn 12 she asks, "Where is the photographic department? Peersak, look at the advertisement and tell me, where is the photographic department?" In turn 13, Peersak responds correctly, "Ground floor," to which the teacher provides a positive evaluation in turn 13, "Yes, on the ground floor." She then moves on to request the identification of an item at that location: "Now, if you go to the photographic department, what can you get there?" In turn 15, Peersak correctly responds, "Camera," to which the teacher provides another positive evaluation and then requests specifics about that item: "A camera. Can you be more specific? What kind of camera?" This continues as Peersak generates several specifics about the item, namely, the type of camera, the original price, and the sale price.

The social participation structures follow the IRE interactional sequence. Students wait for a direct nomination from the teacher before speaking. Once students are nominated, they become responsible for completing the entire cycle of naming the location, item, and specifics about the item. The content of the students' responses is limited to information given in the clearance sale advertisement. In summary, the social participation structures require that students wait for a nomination before speaking, confine the content of their responses to a specific set of information, and limit their responses to one or two words that directly answer the teacher's initiation. The teacher maintains control over all initiations and evaluations of students' responses.

Throughout the remainder of the excerpt, the academic task structure and social participation structure are maintained. In turns 24 through 32 the teacher selects a different department, asks for its location, identifies an item at that location, and then requests specifics about that item. The students identify the location ("First floor"), the item ("Stainless steel kettles"), and specifics about the item ("Five," "Imported," "Movable handle"). The only variation in the teacher's use of language is that she begins to withdraw her positive evaluations of repeating correct responses and, instead, moves directly to the next initiation in the sequence. For example, when Milo responds correctly in turn 25, "First floor," the teacher does not repeat this response but moves directly to the next question, "What can you buy there?" This occurs again in turn 27, when Milo correctly responds, "Stainless steel kettles," after which the teacher moves directly to, "How many sizes of kettles?" Only in turns 30 and 34 does the teacher repeat Milo's responses, but in both cases these utterances act as summations more than direct repetitions of Milo's responses. Thus, it appears that as these students begin to recognize and respond correctly to the academic task structure (location, item, and specifics about that item), the teacher begins to withdraw her positive evaluations.

In turns 34 through 42, the academic task structure is repeated again, but this time with a slight variation. Instead of identifying a specific department and asking for its location, the teacher identifies the item first and then asks for the name of the department where it is sold. Thus, in turn 34 the teacher asks, "OK, now Suchada, if you want to buy a rattan picnic basket, which department will you go to?" This slight variation seems to confuse Suchada, who responds in turn 35, "First floor." Apparently fooled by the previously established academic task structure, Suchada provides the location even though the teacher had actually requested the name of the department. When this occurs, the teacher returns to her pattern of negative evaluation, in which she ignores the incorrect response and provides another initiation. Suchada's corrected response in turn 37, "Flower department," is positively evaluated, "Yes, flower department," followed by an initiation for specifics about the item: "Where does this picnic basket come from?" In this exchange, Suchada seems to attend to the academic task structure more than the meaning of the information embedded in that structure. In addition, when Suchada violates the academic task structure, the teacher returns to her earlier established pattern of evaluating students' responses to repair the error, and then reestablishes the academic task structure.

Besides controlling the patterns of communication, this teacher is also controlling the content of the lesson. She does this by using the interactive questioning strategies of preformulation and reformulation (MacLure & French 1980). In turn 1, the teacher's preformulated question, "What is this advertisement about?", acts to orient the students to the context of the question and provides some indication of how it should be answered. Since neither student provides the correct response, the teacher reformulates the question in turn 4, "What is the word that is used there?", to make her question less complex and more specific. This strategy seems to work, because in turn 5, Suchada is able to provide the correct answer.

Finally, this teacher has a particular way of generating the meaning of unfamiliar vocabulary. This occurs twice in this excerpt, first in turns 8 through 12, and later in turn 42. In turn 8, the teacher identifies the unfamiliar word "clearance sale" and asks, "What word does it come from?" In turn 9, Peersak responds, "Clear," and in turn 11 Suchada responds, "To clear up." The teacher evaluates in turn 12, "To clear up all the goods in the store." This pattern is found again in turn 42. The teacher asks, "Yes, and what is a flask holder? You know what a flask is, right? What about holder? It comes from the word 'hold'. It holds the flask. OK, all right." This pattern carries the implication that the meaning of unfamiliar vocabulary can be found within the word itself, as opposed to within the context in which the word is used. Thus, we can speculate that this approach for examining unfamiliar vocabulary may possibly be based on this teacher's frames of reference about how meaning is derived from language. On the other hand, this teacher may find this approach to be the most effective for these particular words, but in another lesson she might use other strategies for other vocabulary words.

Overall, we can characterize the teacher–student interaction in this excerpt as being tightly controlled and teacher-directed. It is important to remember that the ways in which teachers organize the patterns of communication often depend on the pedagogical purpose of the lesson. This vocabulary lesson was to be followed by a writing activity in which the students use the information in the advertised clearance sale to compose a letter to a relative. Thus, the teacher may have decided to exert greater control over the patterns of communication during this portion of the lesson in order to ensure that the students understood what she perceived as necessary vocabulary to carry out the follow-up writing activity.

Students' perceptions of the patterns of communication

As discussed in Chapter 3, students' perceptions of the patterns of classroom communication are shaped by a variety of factors. Probably the most important is the ability to accurately infer teachers' expectations and intentions. To do this, students must be able to infer both the academic task structure and the social participation structure, and to fit their language into those structures. The ability to make such inferences and adjustments can be enhanced or inhibited by students' culturally acquired linguistic and interactional competencies, which shape how they interpret and respond to the world about them.

Since we are limited to the information given in Excerpt 6.1, we can only infer students' perceptions of the patterns of communication from what they said and did during this lesson. However, in this excerpt, the students seemed to be able to fit their language into the established academic task structures and the social participation structures, since their responses, except for one instance, were given in the appropriate form and at the appropriate time. That exception, as mentioned earlier, was when Suchada anticipated the sequence of the academic task structure and, therefore, did not attend to the teacher's variation in that structure (turn 35).

While the students seemed to recognize the patterns of communication established by their teacher and were able to adjust their language so as to successfully participate in this activity, the content of their language was limited to one- or two-word responses generated directly from the advertisement given in the textbook. In fact, the longest student response, "Complete with tray and two flask holders" (turn 41), was a direct quote from the advertisement. Moreover, students seemed to know to wait for a direct nomination from the teacher before offering a response, and maintained that responsibility until one complete cycle of the academic task structure was carried out. From our limited data source, we are unable to determine whether or not such patterns of communication maximized these students' linguistic and interactional competencies. However, given their apparent ability to infer the academic task structures and social participation structures so quickly and without error, we can speculate that this sort of teacher–student interaction is a common pattern of communication in this EFL classroom.

Students' use of language for classroom learning and second language acquisition

If we compare the students' use of language in this excerpt to the optimal conditions for classroom learning and second language acquisition presented in Chapter 5, we find few similarities. The optimal conditions for classroom learning and second language acquisition stress the importance of students having the need and desire to communicate. Such investment comes from opportunities to initiate, to control the topic of discussion, and to self-select when to participate. These conditions also stress the importance of creating opportunities for students to use language for both meaning-focused communication and form-focused instruction. Moreover, students need enough instructional support from their teachers to be able to participate successfully in language-related activities that are beyond their current proficiency level. Finally, students must have opportunities to use language for both planned and unplanned discourse, within a range of authentic contexts, and within the context of full performance.

Few, if any, of these conditions are evident in Excerpt 6.1. However, we must remember that teachers' control of the patterns of communication often depends on the pedagogical purpose of the lesson, and the frames of reference through which they judge the appropriateness of their own and their students' classroom communicative behavior. With these considerations in mind, we must be cautious in our assessment of the extent to which the patterns of communication found in this excerpt appear to create opportunities for students' use of language for classroom learning and second language acquisition.

Yet, we can assert that there is little evidence of opportunities for students to initiate, control the topic of discussion, or engage in meaning-focused interaction. They did not seem to be challenged to operate beyond their current level of language proficiency, to participate in the negotiation of meaning, or to perform a range of language functions. On the other hand, the students did appear to be participating in the lesson, and given that we found no violation of the social participation structures and only a slight violation of the academic task structures, we can assume that they were aware of and able to fit their language into the patterns of communication established by this teacher. The follow-up writing activity may create opportunities for these students to use language for more meaning-focused communication within a more authentic context.

To conclude, the framework for understanding communication in second language classrooms has enabled us to examine the ways in which this teacher used language to organize the patterns of communication, as well as how she used language to control both the structure and content of the lesson. We were able to infer students' perceptions of the patterns of communication from the extent to which they were able to participate in this classroom event. Finally, we were able to make some assumptions about the extent to which the patterns of communication found in this excerpt created opportunities for students to use language for classroom learning and second language acquisition.

Excerpt 6.2: Variability in the patterns of communication in teacher–student interaction

The next excerpt is taken from an intermediate-level ESL conversational English course at an American university. Much of the content in the course focuses on current social and cultural issues facing university students. In this particular lesson, the students have just finished reading an article from the university newspaper about the upcoming celebration of Gay Pride Week on campus. Excerpt 6.2 is a vocabulary lesson of sorts, in that the focus of the discussion is on understanding the meaning of the slogan "Straight, Secure, and Supportive," referred to in the newspaper article and seen on pins worn by students on campus.

Once again, as you read this excerpt, pay particular attention to how this teacher controls the patterns of communication. See if you can characterize the ways in which this teacher uses language to control the structure and content of classroom communication. Try to identify the academic task structures and the social participation structures embedded in this lesson. How does she reinforce these structures? Notice the ways in which students use language during this lesson. How do they fit their language use into the patterns of communication in this lesson? Finally, try to characterize the ways in which the patterns of communication that exist in this excerpt create opportunities for these ESL students to use language for classroom learning and second language acquisition.

Excerpt 6.2

1. T: So, what other questions
do you have about this (the arti-

cle), or Gay Pride Week in general?

2.

   Stan: What is this pin?

3.

   Rosa: Oh, I saw that too . . .

4.

   Stan: I saw this on some people, but I didn't know. I thought it some politics or something . . .

5. T: OK, It says, "Straight, Secure, Supportive." Do you know what that means?

6.

   Stan: Maybe some politics.

7. T: You thought it had to do with politics? Well, you are sort of right, because Gay Rights has become a political issue, but let's think about the words on the pin, it says, "Straight, Secure, Supportive." Do you have any ideas about what "straight" means in reference to what we have been talking about, in terms of Gay Rights Week?

8.

   Rosa: Opposite, not gay.

9. T: The opposite of gay, or the opposite of homosexual.

10.

   Rosa: Not gay.

11. T: Right, the opposite of gay, or heterosexual.

12.

   Stan: Straight is not gay, oh, OK.

13. T: Exactly, OK, so "straight" means not gay, or heterosexual. OK, do you know what "secure" means?

14.

   Stan: Safe, secure.

15. T: Safe, secure, what do you think that might mean in terms of gay rights?

16.

   Stan: No shame?

17.

   Zhang: That you think it's OK, they are normal too, like everyone.

18. T: Exactly, that you think they are just like everyone else,

that there is no reason to be
ashamed . . .

19.

20.

Stan: So, it's OK to be that way.
Rosa: You're not like them but
that's OK.

21. T: Right, and that helps us
understand what "supportive"
means, right?

22.

Zhang: That we can support them
too.
Rosa: To support but not to be
like them.

23.

24. T: Yes, that we can support
them as people who have social
and legal rights, but we don't
have to be like them.

25.

Stan: But maybe they think you
are gay too, maybe they think
you are because they see your
pin and that's what they think.

26.

Rosa: No, you're not like them
but it's OK.

27.

Stan: What if they see this pin on
you, they might just think you
are too.

28. T: Well, what would you
think if you saw someone wearing this pin?

29.

Stan: I don't know, I think maybe
they are too because why would
they wear it?

30.

Rosa: No, because "straight"
means not gay, and secure means
it's OK, like I'm not gay, but I
think it's OK.
Stan: Oh, "straight" is not gay?

31.

32. T: Right, in this context,
"straight" means not gay, or heterosexual.

33.

Stan: "Straight" means heterosexual. Oh, OK . . . and "secure" is
it's OK.

34. T: Right, "secure" means I'm
comfortable enough with myself

that I think it's OK that others
are gay.

35.   Stan: So if you wear this pin it
                                                 means you are heterosexual, but
                                                 if they are, it is OK, it doesn't
                                                 bother me, so I support them . . .

36. T: Exactly. "Straight, Secure,
Supportive," those three words
make a statement, a statement
about how you feel about gay
rights . . .

37.   Stan: Yeah, but anyway, I don't
                                                 think I would wear it.

38.   Zhang: Me too, I wouldn't wear
                                                 it.

39. T: Sure, a lot of people feel
that way, that's OK, but if you
see someone wearing this pin on
campus at least you will know
what it means . . .

Teachers' control of the patterns of communication

The substantial amount of student talk versus teacher talk in this excerpt suggests that this teacher is exerting less control over the patterns of communication. There was obvious variation in the IRE interactional sequence; in fact, there were many instances where the students took on both the initiation and the evaluation part of the sequence, or the sequence was abandoned altogether as students interacted with one another.

The social participation structure that emerges from this excerpt encourages students to initiate questions, to control the topic of discussion, and to self-select when to participate. For example, Stan initiates a new topic by asking in turn 2, "What is this pin?" Before the teacher has a chance to respond, Stan qualifies his initial question in turn 4, "I saw this on some people, but I didn't know. I thought it some politics or something." The teacher takes up Stan's initiation and asks an open-ended question in turn 5, "OK, It says 'Straight, Secure, Supportive.' Do you know what that means?" Thus, the teacher allows Stan to initiate the topic of conversation and encourages him to offer his own interpretation of the slogan as a starting point for the discussion. Later in the lesson, Stan once again controls the topic of discussion by voicing his personal concern about how a person wearing this pin might be perceived. The teacher appears to be comfortable with this topic shift since she allows Stan and Rosa to direct comments to one another before asking another open-ended question in turn 28, "Well, what would you think if you saw someone wearing this pin?"

The social participation structures also encourage students to self-select when to participate. Throughout the excerpt, Rosa and Zhang self-select when to participate in response to open bids from the teacher. However, at times Rosa responds directly to Stan's comments without a direct bid from the teacher. Thus, the social participation structures of this lesson indicate that a certain amount of variability was allowed in the rights and obligations that determined who talked and when.

The teacher uses language to maintain the social participation structures in several ways. First, she asks open-ended questions, as in turn 15, "Safe, secure, what do you think that might mean in terms of gay rights?", and in turn 28, "Well, what would you think if you saw someone wearing this pin?" Both questions require that students generate their own opinions and/ or understandings of the question, as opposed to some sort of "right" answer. Second, she receives students' contributions and then recasts those contributions in terms of the content of the discussion. For example, in turn 18, she takes up both Stan's and Zhang's contributions of "No shame" and "That you think it's OK, they are normal too, like everyone," and recasts those contributions into a summation: "Exactly, that you think they are just like everyone else, that there is no reason to be ashamed." Finally, she allows students to respond directly to one another. In fact, in turns 23 through 30, Rosa takes on a teacherlike role, responding directly to Stan's comments and attempting to correct what she sees as his misunderstanding of the slogan.

Besides allowing for greater variability in the social participation structures, this teacher also allows for greater student contributions to the content of the academic task structures. The teacher sets up the sequential steps for understanding the slogan by first requesting student-generated interpretations of each word in the slogan, and then by constructing a shared (teacher–student) meaning of each word. For example, in turn 7 the teacher asks, "Do you have any ideas about what 'straight' means in reference to what we have been talking about, in terms of Gay Rights Week?" This question requires a student-generated interpretation of the word "straight," which is offered by Rosa in turn 8, "Opposite, not gay." The teacher then takes up Rosa's contribution and introduces the vocabulary words "homo-sexual" and "heterosexual." The teacher uses Rosa's and Stan's contributions of "Not gay" and "Straight is not gay, oh, OK" to construct the shared meaning given in turn 13, "Exactly, OK, so 'straight' means not gay, or heterosexual." Once this meaning is established, she repeats the same academic task structure for the words "secure" and "supportive." The academic task structure is also evident later in this excerpt when the teacher initiates in turn 28, "Well, what would you think if you saw someone wearing this pin?", which acts as a request for a student-generated interpretation of the entire slogan. The teacher then allows Stan to offer his opinion in turn 29, "I don't know, I think maybe they are too because why would they wear it?", and Rosa's negative evaluation of Stan's comment in turn 30, "No, because 'straight' means not gay, and secure means it's OK, like I'm not gay, but I think it's OK." The teacher then waits until Stan asks for clarification before she confirms, "Right, in this context, 'straight' means not gay, or heterosexual." Thus, the academic task structures that emerge from this excerpt begin with student-generated interpretations and move to the joint construction of shared meanings between the teacher and students.

Despite considerable student contributions to the content of the discussion, this teacher does, at times, control the content of this lesson. There are two ways in which she does this. First, she uses students' contributions as an opportunity to introduce unfamiliar vocabulary. For example, in turn 8, she takes up Rosa's response, "Opposite, not gay," to introduce the words "homosexual" and "heterosexual." She then combines Rosa's contribution with these new vocabulary words to offer the new definition, "so 'straight' means not gay, or heterosexual." Thus, she accepts Rosa's more simplified language and at the same time introduces more academic or conventionalized language. Second, she recasts students' contributions in her own words, based on her own interpretations. For example, in turns 22 through 23, neither Zhang's contribution, "That we can support them too," or Rosa's contribution, "To support but not to be like them," mentions anything about the social or legal rights of homosexuals; however, when the teacher recasts these contributions in her own words (turn 24), she includes the idea of such rights: "Yes, that we can support them as people who have social and legal rights, but we don't have to be like them." Thus, we find this teacher interjecting her own interpretations into students' contributions. As Cazden (1988) warns, she may believe she is helping her students develop their own understandings, when in fact, she is actually imposing her own belief on her students so that they understand the issue as she does. Lemke (1985) and Edwards and Mercer (1986) characterize this as the socialization that all students go through as they develop educational knowledge, or the shared meanings and ways of talking that are mutually constructed by students and teachers in classrooms. However, we must recognize that such shared meanings sometimes reflect teachers' understanding more than students'.

Overall, we can characterize this teacher's control over the patterns of communication in this excerpt as allowing for greater variability and for mutually constructed meaning by the teacher and students. Students were given opportunities to control when and how they would participate in the lesson. Their interpretations of the issues being discussed were not only accepted by the teacher but they also contributed to the content of the lesson. The teacher–student interaction was spontaneous, adaptive, and meaning-focused. Students carried out a range of language functions, from requesting information to voicing an opinion, within the context of meaningful interaction.

Students' perceptions of the patterns of communication

Once again, since we are limited to the information given in Excerpt 6.2, we can only infer students' perceptions of the patterns of communication from what they said and did during this excerpt. However, the students' use of language in this excerpt suggests that they were able to fit their language into the social participation structures established by this teacher. As already mentioned, they took full advantage of opportunities to initiate, to control the topic, and to self-select when to participate. Variability in the social participation structures was also evident when Stan initiated a series of requests for clarification, and the teacher confirmed and then expanded upon his responses. For example, in line 31 Stan asks, "Oh, 'straight' is not gay?" and the teacher repeats the previously established definition in turn 32, "Right, in this context, 'straight' means not gay, or heterosexual." Once again Stan initiates in turn 33, "'Straight' means heterosexual. Oh, OK . . . and 'secure' is it's OK," to which the teacher responds in turn 34, "Right, 'secure' means I'm comfortable enough with myself that I think it's OK that others are gay." The teacher's confirmation and expansion upon Stan's comments seemed to foster his continued willingness to participate. It is also clear that student–student interaction was encouraged. In several instances, Rosa and Stan responded directly to each other's comments without a bid from the teacher.

The content of the students' language in this excerpt is generally meaning-focused. That is, they used language to express their personal interpretations, to understand the teacher and each other, and to make themselves understood. This was especially true for Stan, who throughout the exchange requested information, offered his opinions, asked for clarification, and confirmed his understandings. This was also true for Rosa, who remained intent on making sure Stan correctly interpreted the meaning of the slogan. Moreover, since the content of their language was meaning-focused, these students also produced more extended pieces of discourse.

Requesting student-generated interpretations, taking up student contributions, and constructing shared meanings also encouraged meaning-focused language use by encouraging students to express their own opinions. The opinions were both acknowledged and accepted by the teacher. At the end of the excerpt, both Stan and Zhang maintained their position that despite understanding the meaning of the slogan, they would feel uncomfortable wearing this pin. Stan states in turn 37, "Yeah, but anyway, I don't think I would wear it," and Zhang concurs: "Me too, I wouldn't wear it." We can infer that the teacher's acceptance of their sentiments fostered their willingness to express such personal opinions. Overall, from our examination of students' language use in Excerpt 6.2, we can assume that these students accurately inferred this teacher's expectations and intentions as well as the academic task and social participation structures; therefore, they were able to participate successfully in this classroom event.

Student's use of language for classroom learning and second language acquisition

If we compare the students' use of language in Excerpt 6.2 to the optimal conditions for classroom learning and second language acquisition, we find a good deal of overlap. As already indicated, the students were given ample opportunity to initiate, to control the topic of discussion, and to self-select when to participate. They also had extensive opportunities to use language for meaning-focused communication, in that much, if not all, of the excerpt focused on understanding the meaning and implications of the slogan "Straight, Secure, Supportive." The students enjoyed greater opportunities to participate in the discussion and contributed knowledge to the content of that discussion. They had opportunities to participate in a range of language functions, for example, requesting information, stating an opinion, clarifying a statement, agreeing and disagreeing, and asking for confirmation. Finally, they had many opportunities to use language in unplanned discourse. Overall, the patterns of communication that emerge from Excerpt 6.2 appear to create ample opportunities for students to use language for classroom learning and second language acquisition. Once again, the extent to which this teacher chose to control the patterns of communication may have been the result of the pedagogical purpose of this lesson. That is, understanding the meaning of an unfamiliar slogan may lend itself to more meaning-focused teacher–student interaction.

To conclude, the framework for understanding communication in second language classrooms has enabled us to see how this teacher used language to allow for greater student participation in and contributions to the structure and content of this lesson. It also illustrated the extent to which students were able to use language to participate in this classroom event. Finally, we were able to make some assumptions about the extent to which the patterns of communication found in this excerpt created opportunities for students to use language for classroom learning and second language acquisition.

Conclusion

In comparing these two excerpts, we find contrasting patterns of classroom communication. Excerpt 6.1 illustrates tightly controlled, formulaic patterns of teacher–student interaction in which who talks, when, and about what are controlled by the teacher. Excerpt 6.2 illustrates highly spontaneous, adaptive patterns of teacher–student interaction in which the structure and content of the interaction are mutually constructed by both the students and the teacher. Moreover, the language use of the students in these two excerpts is vastly different. In Excerpt 6.1, students' language use is limited to individual words, generated directly from the textbook, and given in direct response to a teacher nomination. In Excerpt 6.2, students' language use reflects more extended discourse, is meaning-focused, and is self-initiated. Finally, we find differences in the ways in which the patterns of communication in each excerpt create opportunities for students to use language for classroom learning and second language acquisition. In Excerpt 6.1, the patterns seem to limit such opportunities whereas in Excerpt 6.2 they seem to foster them.

Given this comparison, should we conclude that Excerpt 6.2 represents effective teacher–student interaction and, thus, that all teachers should emulate these patterns of communication during second language instruction? My response to this commonly asked question is no, probably not. First of all, these two excerpts represent very different patterns of classroom communication that could be placed on a continuum. On one end we might have tightly controlled patterns of communication and on the other greater variability in the patterns of communication. The appropriateness of either depends on the pedagogical purpose of the lesson, the language proficiency of the students, and the frames of reference through which both teachers and students judge the appropriateness of their classroom communicative behavior. More appropriate questions for teachers to consider might be:

1. When is more or less teacher-directed control over the patterns of communication appropriate for the goals of a particular lesson?
2. What variations along this continuum are most appropriate for a particular group of students?
3. To what extent do variations in the patterns of communication inhibit or enhance student's opportunities to use language for classroom learning and second language acquisition?

Other questions that were not addressed because of our limited data source might be why these teachers chose to establish and maintain the patterns of communication that were found in each excerpt. What was the pedagogical purpose of the lessons? How did the teachers attempt to carry out that purpose? What conceptions of second language teaching do these teachers hold? Why do the teachers seem to be so different? What prior experiences may have influenced how they understand their roles as teachers? In other words, what constitutes these teachers' frames of reference, and how do these frames of reference shape the ways in which they chose to organize the patterns of communication in their second language classrooms? Similar questions might be asked about the students. What sorts of linguistic and interactional competencies do these students possess? How do these competencies shape the ways in which they interpret and respond to what their teachers say and do? How closely do these competencies match those expected by their teachers? What sorts of prior experiences have these students had in classrooms? In short, what constitutes these students' frames of reference and how do these frames of reference shape the ways in which students participate in and learn from classroom activities?

Such questions represent important issues that teachers must address for themselves and their second language students if they are to fully understand the complex nature of communication in second language classrooms. As the framework for understanding communication in second language classrooms suggests, it is the interrelatedness of these two dimensions that contributes to the dynamics of communication in second language classrooms. At this point, let us examine student–student interaction as another type of communication that exists in second language classrooms.

7 Student–student interaction

Thus far, much of our attention has focused on understanding classroom communication by looking at the interaction that occurs between teachers and students. However, by doing so we have ignored another important dimension of classroom interaction, that is, the interaction that occurs between students themselves, and the impact that student–student interaction has on the patterns of communication, classroom learning, and opportunities for second language acquisition.

This chapter once again relies on the framework for understanding communication in second language classrooms presented in Part I to examine student–student interaction. Among the aspects examined are how teachers exert variable control over the structure and content of student–student interaction, how students perceive and participate in student–student interaction, the ways in which students use language during student–student interaction, and the opportunities that student–student interaction creates for students to use language for classroom learning and second language acquisition.

Several transcribed excerpts of student–student interaction taken from both ESL and EFL classrooms provide the basis for the analysis; as before, we can only infer teachers' and students' perceptions of student–student interaction from what they say and do. However, the variable nature and instructional impact of student–student interaction on the patterns of communication in second language classrooms will become evident. In addition, these excerpts will highlight the opportunities that student–student interaction can create for students to use language for classroom learning and second language acquisition.

Student–student interaction in the classroom

Attention to the nature and impact of student–student interaction on classroom learning has been virtually ignored in much of the classroom-based educational research. D. W. Johnson (1981: 5) faults much of this research as being "adult centrism," which implies that real learning occurs only

111

between teachers and students and that student–student interaction represents off-task behavior, discourages achievement, and leads to classroom
disruptions. On the contrary, Johnson argues, student–student interaction
may actually be more important for educational success than teacher–
student interaction. In fact, he claims, constructive student–student interactions influence students' educational aspirations and achievement, develop
social competencies, and encourage taking on the perspectives of others.
Johnson is not alone in his assessment of the value of classroom student–
student interaction. Slavin (1980), Sharan (1980), and Webb (1982) each
provide in-depth reviews of research that overwhelmingly conclude that
cooperative learning tasks in small groups enhance students' academic
achievement, self-esteem, relationships among students of different ethnic
backgrounds, and positive attitudes toward school.

Although they emphasize the educational and social value of student–
student interaction, many researchers warn that simply putting students in
groups is not enough. If student–student interaction is to be a successful
instructional strategy, teachers must control two important aspects: namely,
how learning goals are structured and how conflicts among students are
managed (D. W. Johnson & Johnson 1979). Such learning goals may be
cooperative, competitive, or individualistic; thus students may work collaboratively, compete for fun and enjoyment, or work on their own. However, each goal structure promotes a different pattern of interaction among
students. A cooperative goal structure promotes positive collaborative interaction among students; a competitive goal structure promotes cautious
and defensive student–student interaction; and, of course, an individual
goal structure allows for little or no student–student interaction. Therefore,
the selection of a particular type of structure depends on teachers' instructional goals as well as the type of student–student interaction they want to
promote.

Besides selecting an appropriate learning goal structure, teachers must
also effectively manage the conflicts that are inevitable in student groups.
Teachers often find this difficult to do, since most teachers tend to avoid or
suppress conflicts among students' ideas. However, D. W. Johnson and
R. T. Johnson (1979) propose that cognitive conflict among students, if
managed effectively, can be highly constructive, leading to increased student motivation and to higher levels of cognitive development and moral
reasoning. When students are exposed to alternative or contradictory view-
points from their peers, they are often encouraged to seek more information
or to take on alternative perspectives. When this occurs, new or reorganized
conclusions can be reached that often include the reasoning of others.
Cazden (1988: 126) calls this "discourse as catalyst," in which the cognitive
conflict generated from student–student interaction can challenge students
to reorganize, or rethink, their prior understandings. Thus, it is believed that
student–student interaction can induce cognitive conflict, which in turn can

result in cognitive restructuring and growth (Forman & Cazden 1985; D. W. Johnson & Johnson 1979; Perret-Clermont 1980). However, for cognitive conflict to be constructive, teachers must establish a supportive climate that is more cooperative than competitive, promote a general sense that conflict is constructive, recognize and respect the differing perspectives of individual students, and, finally, deal with students' feelings as well as the ideas and information being discussed (D. W. Johnson & Johnson 1979).

The nature of the language that is generated as a result of student–student interaction is also believed to have cognitive benefits for students. Barnes (1976) claims that most classroom language reflects what he characterizes as "final draft talk" (p. 113), in that what is said and how it is said represents a sort of final presentation given mostly for teacher approval. "Exploratory talk" (p. 113), on the other hand, represents the false starts, detours, and cognitive rearranging that occur as students come to understand a particular concept, or work through a particular instructional task. When students work collaboratively in groups they are more likely to engage in exploratory talk and, thus, use language to learn as opposed to merely demonstrate what has been learned. Therefore, exploratory talk fosters more informal language use and student-centered styles and strategies of learning that are generally inhibited during teacher-directed instruction.

In recent years, the field of composition has not only recognized the cognitive benefits of student–student interaction but has also incorporated student–student interaction, in the form of peer writing conferences, into classroom writing instruction (Carroll 1981; George 1984; Gere & Abbott 1985; Grimm 1986; M. Harris 1986). Peer conferences, in which students share their written texts with one another, encourage exploratory talk as writers come to terms with what they want to say. Moreover, peer writing conferences encourage students to elicit explanations from their peers, restate what their peers have written, offer suggestions, voice their opinions, and explain unclear content or ideas (Mendonca & Johnson, in press). Thus, peer writing conferences foster more exploratory talk, promote cognitive conflict, encourage students to take a more active role in their own learning processes, and enable students to recognize the impact of their own writing on others. While peer writing conferences are intended to enhance student's writing abilities, they are also believed to foster higher levels of cognitive development and overall student learning (Cazden 1988; Kamler 1980).

We can conclude that student–student interaction, if structured and managed appropriately, can play an important role in students' cognitive development, educational achievement, and emerging social competencies. Student–student interaction can induce cognitive conflict, and thus foster cognitive restructuring and development. It can foster the use of more exploratory language and encourage informal learning styles and strategies among students. It can enhance students' abilities to work collaboratively, encourage collaborative rather than competitive social relationships among students, and foster positive attitudes toward school. Clearly, student–student interaction is an important dimension of classroom communication that should not be underestimated or overlooked.

The structure of student–student interaction

Despite the fact that student–student interaction allows students to interact with one another, more often than not, teachers still maintain a certain amount of control over the structure and, sometimes, even the content of student–student interaction. However, the extent to which teachers exert this control depends on the instructional goals of the lesson, the classroom activities designed to reach those goals, and the type of student–student interaction teachers hope to promote. Students also exert a certain amount of control over the structure of student–student interaction through how they perceive and participate in small groups. To understand the structure of student–student interaction, we will examine a variety of cooperative learning techniques that promote different patterns of student–student interaction, and then consider the characteristics of students that shape their perceptions of and participation in student–student interaction.

Cooperative learning techniques based on peer-tutoring methods require the class to function as an aggregate of groups who rehearse teacher-taught materials, act as both teacher and learners, and focus on tasks that emphasize the acquisition of information and/or specific skills. One example of this is the Jigsaw Method (Aronson et al. 1978), in which teachers divide the academic content to be learned into parts and delegate individual parts to each group member. Thus, group members are responsible for learning only one part of the content and then teaching that part to the rest of the group. Another example is the Teams-Games-Tournament technique (De-Vries & Slavin 1978), which requires student groups to work cooperatively to rehearse information and/or skills before competing in a tournament against other groups. Teachers assign tasks to be completed collaboratively in groups, and eventually groups compete as teams against other teams. A third example is the Student Teams and Academic Divisions technique (Slavin 1978), in which teachers rank students by academic ability levels and then create groups of students with differing ability levels so they can tutor each other within each group. Teachers present the academic material, allow groups to work cooperatively to complete assigned tasks, and then follow up with individual assessment. In all three of these techniques, teachers maintain a considerable amount of control over the structure of student–student interaction, and to some extent, they even control the content of that interaction. Students, on the other hand, compete more with themselves than with their peers and share equal opportunities to contribute to their group's achievement.

Cooperative learning techniques based on group investigation methods focus on problem-solving tasks in which students gather necessary information, engage in the exchange and interpretation of ideas, and produce a final product that is generated collaboratively and may differ from those produced by other groups. An example of this is the Group Investigation technique (Sharan & Lazarowitz 1978), which involves organizing student groups by particular interests, allowing the groups to gather necessary information, analyze and evaluate that information and, finally, summarize the essential features of that information in a formal presentation made to the class. Teachers evaluate student performance based on both the individual's contribution to the group and the group's final presentation. Teachers exert control only over the procedures that the groups will follow, while students are free to establish the rules for group participation, as well as the content of what will be talked about.

Slavin (1980) claims that cooperative learning techniques involving peer tutoring may be better suited for low-level learning outcomes, such as the acquisition of a specific body of knowledge, calculations, and the application of principles, since they require the performance of all team members and are structured to reinforce previously specified content. On the other hand, group investigation cooperative learning techniques may be better suited for high-level cognitive concepts, such as problem solving, identifying concepts, and evaluating information, since they require students to maintain a high level of autonomy and involvement in the generation of knowledge, and active participation in the decision-making process. However, both types of cooperative learning techniques have been found to foster students' academic achievement, enhance self-esteem and positive student relationships, and improve students' attitudes toward school (D. W. Johnson & Johnson 1979; Sharan 1980; Slavin 1980; Webb 1982).

Besides varying amounts of control that teachers can exert over student–student interaction, the prior experiences and the competencies of students themselves can also shape the structure and content of student–student interaction. In Chapters 3 and 4, differential experiences among students – whether in the home, as with the children of Trackton; in an ethnic community, as with the children on the Warm Springs Reservation; or in a particular cultural group, as with the Aboriginal children in Australia – were found to shape students' perceptions of and participation in student–student interaction. Similar claims have been made for second language classrooms. For example, Sato (1982) found different turn-taking styles among Asian and non-Asian students. Asian students took fewer self-selected turns and tended to wait for a bid before initiating a turn during student–student interaction. Duff (1986) found different styles of participation in Japanese and Chinese dyads; Chinese students tended to dominate all aspects of language production during student–student interaction whereas the Japanese did not. Thus, students' differential experiences lead to different interactional competencies, competencies that determine how and when students will participate in student–student interaction.

Besides differential experiences, perceived status within a group can also determine how students will perceive and participate in student-student interaction. If one group member is perceived as having stronger academic and/or linguistic skills, or higher social status, this student is often allowed to control not only the structure of the student–student interaction but also the content of that interaction. Other characteristics, such as, age, gender, race, social class, and personality traits, also shape students' perceptions and involvement in student–student interaction. Therefore, we cannot assume that student–student interaction will automatically foster equal opportunities for students to participate. Differential experiences, interactional competencies, social and academic status, and individual personality traits also determine how students will act and interact in student–student interaction. We can conclude, however, that both teachers and students contribute to the structure and content of student–student interaction.

Student–student interaction in second language classrooms

The recent shift toward more communicative approaches of second language teaching has prompted a shift in instructional styles; as a result, more classroom time is allotted for students to actively communicate with one another. This shift reflects the premise that a communicative curriculum should include structural, functional, and communicative aspects of the language (Littlewood 1981). That is, second language learners must be aware of the structural or grammatical features of the language, be able to relate those features to their functional usage, and have the ability to use both forms and functions appropriately within the context of meaningful communication with others. While the structural and functional aspects of the language lend themselves to formal teacher-directed instruction, the communicative aspects of the language must be acquired through more informal and meaning-focused interactions with others (Littlewood 1981). Hence, student–student interaction in second language classrooms can create opportunities for students to participate in less structured and more spontaneous language use, negotiate meaning, self-select when to participate, control the topic of discussion, and, most important, draw on their own prior knowledge and interactional competencies to actively communicate with others. Moreover, since student–student interaction provides a more meaningful social environment for promoting language use than traditional teacher-directed instruction, student–student interaction in second language classrooms can increase students' opportunities to use language for second language acquisition.

Obviously, student–student interaction has the potential to play an important role not only in shaping the patterns of communication in second language classrooms but in creating opportunities for students to use language for classroom learning and second language acquisition. Thus, in each of the following transcribed excerpts, we will examine student–student interaction by exploring the extent to which teachers exert control over the structure of student–student interaction. In addition, we will explore students' perceptions of and participation in student–student interaction, and students' language use in these interactions. Finally, we will explore the ways in which student–student interaction creates opportunities for students to use language for classroom learning and second language acquisition.

Excerpt 7.1: Peer tutoring model of student–student interaction

One of the more common types of student–student interaction found in second language classrooms is small groups of students reviewing and/or practicing teacher-taught materials. Similar to the peer tutoring model of cooperative learning mentioned earlier, student groups are given a specific instructional task in which each group member has the opportunity to teach and/or share some information with other group members while at the same time practicing the structural, functional, and communicative aspects of the language previously taught by the teacher. Thus, the learning goal structure is cooperative, yet at the same time, students are expected to act as teachers, or at least as group leaders, as they share information and/or practice a particular aspect of the language. This type of student–student interaction is often intended to reinforce a particular language skill, and therefore the teacher generally exerts a good deal of control over the structure of the interaction and, to some extent, the content of that interaction.

Excerpt 7.1 is an example of this sort of student–student interaction. The excerpt is taken from an adult beginning-level EFL conversational class in the Federal Czech Republic. In this excerpt, the teacher has just completed a lesson on demonstrative pronouns, singular and plural forms of the verb "to be," and vocabulary on the family. The class has generated sentences on the board, such as "This is my mother. These are my brothers. This is my son," and so on. The teacher had requested that students bring in photographs of their families. At the beginning of Excerpt 7.1, the teacher places the students in groups, instructs each group member to take turns describing his or her family photographs, and reminds the students to use the sentences generated on the board in their descriptions.

As you read this excerpt, pay particular attention to how the teacher sets up the structure of the student–student interaction. Also note the roles that group members maintain during the interaction. See if you can describe the type of language that is generated as well as the type of language functions that are carried out by each group member. Finally, try to assess the extent to which this type of student–student interaction creates opportunities for these students to use language for classroom learning and second language acquisition.

Excerpt 7.1

1. T: Now, I want you to take turns in your group. Each person should have a chance to talk about the photograph of your family, and remember you can use these sentences to help you, like we practiced, right? (reads from the board) This is my mother. This is my father. These are my brothers. These are my children. This is my son. . . . and so on, OK?

(Student group of Lena, Joseph, Hanka)

2. Lena: You? yes?
3. Hanka: No, please, you, please . . .
               [
4. Joseph: OK please.
5. Lena: Yes? OK, I have book, here.
6. Hanka: Oh, you have lots of photos.
7. Lena: This is my family, not all, but here, at my home, this is my home . . .
8. Hanka: Your home is very big, hum, . . .
9. Lena: No, not so big, here I live, I, my family live here, this no, this here, (points to half of the house in the photo) this is for my family, only here, . . . (to Joseph) You see?
10. Joseph: Yeah, oh, yeah . . .
11. Lena: This is my husband, Fredrico, he is very young here, now he is not so young, his hair is old, he is old . . .
12. Hanka: Old? How old?
13. Lena: Fredrico?
14. Hanka: How old?
15. Lena: Fifty now, I think, yeah, his hair is old . . .
16. Joseph: Gray?
17. Lena: Gray?
18. Joseph: His hair is gray?
19. Lena: Yeah, gray, yeah, his hair is gray . . . but I like, so Fredrico, yeah, and my sons, these, these are my sons, Stephen and Karl . . . and the children . . . here
20. Hanka: Two sons?
21. Lena: Yeah, Stephen and Karl, yeah two, I have two sons, and the children, Gabriella and Frances and Theresa.
22. Hanka: Your children?

23. Lena: No, no, my grandchildren, Gabriella, Frances, Theresa, my grandchildren. (reads from the board) These are my grandchildren. These are my sons here, . . . these are my grandchildren here.
24. Hanka: I think, no, I think you're too young.
25. Lena: Oh, no. (laughs)
26. Hanka: You're too young, I think no, you don't have . . .
27. Lena: No, these are my grandchildren, I am old, yeah, too old . . . (laughs)

At the beginning of the excerpt, the teacher establishes the structure of the student–student interaction. She instructs the students to take turns describing their family photographs and reminds them to practice the sentences listed on the board. Thus, each group member is expected to have an opportunity to lead the group by describing his or her photographs to the other group members, and in doing so, use the sentences generated on the board.

As Lena describes her home, her husband, her sons, and her grandchildren, some interesting patterns emerge from the student–student interaction. First, the entire interaction is meaning-focused. Much of the language generated by the students consists of sentence fragments; however, throughout the entire exchange the language appears to be comprehensible. Hanka's fragmented questions in turn 14, "Old? How old?", in turn 20, "Two sons?", and in turn 22, "Your children?", are understood and answered appropriately by Lena. Moreover, while much of Lena's language also consists of sentence fragments, she does use the grammatical constructions on the board. This occurs in turns 11, "This is my husband"; 19, "these are my sons"; and 23, "These are my grandchildren." In turn 24, Hanka expresses her surprise that Lena has grandchildren in the form of a compliment, "I think, no, I think you're too young," and while her compliment may have been incomplete or non-nativelike, it is clearly comprehensible to Lena, who laughs in turn 27, "No, these are my grandchildren, I am old, yeah, too old." Thus, despite the fragmented nature of the language generated by these students, the entire interaction was meaning-focused and generated meaningful communication between group members.

Each group member takes on a specific role in this interaction. Hanka becomes an active participant, commenting on and/or requesting further details about the information Lena shared with the group. Hanka's comment on the size of Lena's home in turn 8, "Your home is very big," forces Lena to clarify that her family only lives in one half of the house, as she points out in turn 9, "No, not so big, here I live, I, my family live here, this no, this here, this is for my family, only here." Later on, Hanka initiates several requests for more information about Lena's family. For example, she inquires about the age of Lena's husband, she asks about Lena's sons, and she questions whether or not the younger children in the photograph are Lena's. In each instance, Lena is encouraged to provide additional information to answer Hanka's queries. Thus, Lena acts as the group leader, while Hanka assumes the role of active listener and participant.

Joseph, however, participates much less, and in turn 9 Lena actually attempts to draw Joseph into the conversation by offering him an open bid for a turn, to which he responds minimally. Later in the excerpt, Joseph offers assistance to Lena as she attempts to describe her husband. In turn 15, Lena describes her husband's hair as old, and Joseph offers the word "gray" and the sentence "His hair is gray?" in response. Lena takes up Joseph's offer and uses the sentence to describe her husband's hair in turn 19: "Yeah, gray, yeah, his hair is gray." Thus, while Hanka and Joseph clearly assume different roles in this student–student interaction, both seem to be participating to a greater or lesser degree in the interaction.

Finally, it seems clear that the student–student interaction that occurred in Excerpt 7.1 matches some, if not all, of the optimal conditions for students' use of language for classroom learning and second language acquisition. Each member of the group eventually has an opportunity to initiate and control the discussion, and throughout the entire exchange they are able to self-select when to participate. The interaction was meaning-focused and group members participated in a range of language functions, namely, describing a picture, asking for and/or providing clarification, requesting information, stating an opinion, and giving a compliment. There were opportunities for both planned and unplanned discourse. Group members were participating in the negotiation of meaning as they used confirmation and comprehension checks and made requests for clarification. The teacher's instructional goals appears to have been met, since students did use the appropriate expressions within the context of their group discussion.

Excerpt 7.2: Group investigation model of student–student interaction

In the group investigation method of cooperative learning mentioned earlier, group members are encouraged to contribute their personal opinions or knowledge of a particular issue, support those opinions, discuss differences of opinion within the group, and eventually, report back to the whole class. The learning goal structure is cooperative and students are expected to work collaboratively as they share information, discuss this information, and reach a group consensus. The group investigation type of student–student interaction is intended to foster the exchange of ideas, the generation of knowledge, and active participation in the decision-making process. Therefore, teachers allow group members greater autonomy and exert less control over the structure of the interaction and little, if any, control over the content of that interaction.

Excerpt 7.2 was taken from a high-intermediate ESL listening and speaking class for entering university level students in the United States. The teacher has just completed a lesson on the speech acts of agreeing and disagreeing. The class listened to a series of audiotaped dialogues that illustrated different ways of agreeing and disagreeing in different social contexts, followed by a review of several useful expressions for agreeing and disagreeing given in the textbook. The teacher then put the students in pairs and gave each pair a list of ten controversial statements. She then instructed the students to read each statement, state whether or not they agree or disagree with the statement, and give reasons to support their opinions. If differences of opinions arise, the pairs were encouraged to discuss those differences and eventually reach a consensus. The teacher has also reminded the students to use the expressions for agreeing and disagreeing given in the textbook.

As you read this excerpt, pay particular attention to the structure of the student–student interaction. Also note the type of language that is generated and the various language functions that are carried out. Notice the ways in which the students use language to resolve differences of opinion. Finally, try to assess the extent to which this type of interaction creates opportunities for students to use language for classroom learning and second language acquisition.

Excerpt 7.2
(Student pair of Kumiko and Eva)
1. Kumiko: (reads from handout) Too many women hold jobs today.
2. Eva: What's this?
3. Kumiko: What?
4. Eva: Hold jobs?
5. Kumiko: Woman that have the job, "holding a job" means keeping a job, I have a job . . .
6. Eva: Oh, OK, not hold like this? (signals with her hand)
7. Kumiko: No, "hold a job" means I have a job so I hold it, like I hold on to it because it is my job, so I hold a job.
8. Eva: I don't agree.
9. Kumiko: Yeah, I think only men agrees, they want women to get back in home, to clean and cook and be with children. In Japan, all men think this way, but women don't agree. They want to work and have a job and money and be independent from men, but it is very difficult there because everyone think it's better if women are home.
10. Eva: Yeah, but in my country there are too many jobs so the woman must work, and some don't want to but they must,

so they are not happy, some want to work but some don't
want to, so it is a problem, when I was in my country I
had a job, but I want the job, but my friend, she don't
want to work, but she must, and her daughter must go to
the mother, and she must go to work.

11. Kumiko: Yeah, I think this is in Japan too, maybe some want and
some don't . . .

12. Eva: I think the woman must decide and if she don't want to go
to work then she can be home, but she must decide what
she want to do, I think is OK. . . .

13. Kumiko: OK, I agree with you, women must decide what they
want.

14. Eva: Yeah, I think that is best, OK?

15. Kumiko: (reads from handout) The legal drinking age should be
eighteen years old.

16. Eva: I think it's not so important, twenty-one or eighteen because everyone drinks anyway so . . .

17. Kumiko: Yeah, but some kids get drunk and they go crazy, I can
hear them in my apartment, at night, they are crazy and
yelling and throwing bottles, and people get hurt.

18. Eva: But it doesn't matter if they are eighteen or twenty-one,
right?

19. Kumiko: No, if they are older maybe they will be more mature.

20. Eva: Yeah, I know, but now they must be twenty-one, but when
they are eighteen they still go to bars and they get drunk
and so it doesn't matter, right?

21. Kumiko: No, but they check everyone in the bars, me too, we went
with some friends and they check everyone.

22. Eva: Yeah, but they still get in or they get someone to buy for
them and they still get drunk, even when they are eighteen, so it doesn't matter what age it is, eighteen or
twenty-one, right?

23. Kumiko: Yeah, but I think it helps a little bit, because it is harder to
get and they have to be careful at parties . . .

24. Eva: I think the age should be nothing, that everyone can drink
when they are little with their parents and so when they
are eighteen or twenty-one it is the same, so they don't go
crazy, like here.

25. Kumiko: Yeah, OK, if the age is nothing then it is normal to drink,
I think this is good too, but I don't think this very real, I
mean, not very real.

26. Eva: Real?

27. Kumiko: I mean not real, it would be difficult to happen, not very
real . . .

28. Eva: Not very realistic?
29. Kumiko: Yeah, not realistic, that's what I mean, it would be difficult here because people already think that way and it would be difficult to change how people think.
30. Eva: Yeah, maybe, but I think it is best not to have it . . .
31. Kumiko: Yeah, I agree with you but I don't think it will change here.

Throughout this entire exchange, Eva and Kumiko maintain the structure set up by the teacher in her initial directions to the class. They begin by stating their personal opinions, then provide reasons to support those opinions, discuss their differences, and, finally, reach an agreement. However, neither student takes on a teacher or group leader role; instead they share responsibility for maintaining the structure of the interaction. They also work collaboratively to complete the task at hand. Both students offer assistance to one another, as in turns 2 through 7, where Eva asks Kumiko to explain the meaning of "hold jobs" and Kumiko provides a definition and several examples to illustrate the meaning. They switch roles in turns 26 through 29, when Eva offers Kumiko the phrase "not very realistic" to help Kumiko express the idea that having no set drinking age would be unrealistic.

The entire interaction is meaning-focused. Both students freely contribute their personal opinions, seem comfortable disagreeing with one another, and, eventually, are able to negotiate a consensus in spite of differing opinions generated in their discussion. For example, Kumiko describes the cultural pressures in her country for women to stay at home, but Eva counters that in her country some women want to stay home but are unable to do so. In turn 11, Kumiko acknowledges Eva's opinion and admits that women in her country may face the same dilemma. In turn 12, Eva proposes a possible solution, namely, that women should have a choice of whether or not they want to work, and Kumiko agrees. Thus, after stating their opinions and providing supporting evidence for those opinions, a possible solution was proposed, and a consensus was reached.

The same pattern of interaction was followed in the second half of the excerpt. Both students express their personal opinions; in turn 16, Eva argues that the legal drinking age is inconsequential since minors have access to alcohol through other means, and in turns 19 and 23, Kumiko argues that a higher legal drinking age acts as a deterrent. In turns 16 through 23, they engage in a lengthy discussion in which each student offers reasons to support her opinion and listens to counterarguments from her partner. For example, Eva claims in turn 18, "But it doesn't matter if they are eighteen or twenty-one, right?" and Kumiko counters with "No, if they are older maybe they will be more mature." Then in turn 20 Eva claims, ". . . when they are eighteen they still go to bars and they get drunk and so it doesn't matter, right?", and Kumiko counters, "No, but they check everyone in the bars . . ." Finally, in turn 24, Eva offers an alternative solution to the conflict, that there should be no drinking age. Kumiko agrees with this alternative; however, she attempts to describe it as unrealistic. Eventually, they reach an agreement about the statement, but both appear to feel comfortable maintaining their differences of opinion. For example, Eva agrees, in turn 30, but maintains her earlier position, "Yeah, maybe, but I think it is best not to have it, . . ." while in turn 31, Kumiko states, "Yeah, I agree with you but I don't think it will change here."

Thus, Eva and Kumiko are actively participating in the exchange of ideas, recognizing each others' perspectives, and reaching new or reorganized conclusions. These students use language to express and support their opinions, agree and disagree with one another, negotiate meaning, and, eventually, reach a consensus. Thus, we can conclude that the student–student interaction in Excerpt 7.2 provided a variety of opportunities for Eva and Kumiko to use language for classroom learning and second language acquisition. They had equal opportunities to initiate, state their opinion, and self-select when to participate. The interaction was entirely meaning-focused, and both students participated in a range of language functions, stating and supporting an opinion, agreeing and disagreeing, and asking for clarification. Moreover, the teacher's instructional goals appeared to be met as well, since Kumiko and Eva were actively agreeing and disagreeing with one another and using the expressions given in the textbook.

Excerpt 7.3: Peer writing conference in student–student interaction

A third type of student–student interaction, one commonly found in second language writing instruction, is the peer writing conference. As mentioned earlier, during peer writing conferences, students share their written texts with one another and are encouraged to use exploratory talk as they discuss the ideas expressed in their own and their peer's texts. Peer writing conferences are similar to the peer tutoring model of cooperative learning in that students exchange roles as reader and writer. As readers, they assume a tutor or teacher type of role and may elicit explanations, restate a writer's idea, offer suggestions, voice an opinion, or request clarification from the writer about an unclear point in the text. As writers, they respond to readers' queries, formulate or reformulate their ideas based on the reader's reactions to their texts, and ideally begin to recognize the impact of their own writing on others. Before peer writing conferences, teachers usually provide some guidelines that set up both the procedures to be followed and, to some extent, the structure of the student–student interaction. For example, a teacher may provide a list of questions that readers should ask, such as, "What is the thesis? Who is the intended audience?" Or the teacher may specify some specific features that readers should look for in the text, such as, "Is there an introduction, a body, and a conclusion? Has the writer provided enough supporting details to support the main points in the text?" Students, on the other hand, are free to express their own interpretations of each other's texts, formulate their own questions about unclear aspects of the text, and negotiate meaning as they respond to each other's texts.

Excerpt 7.3 is taken from a peer writing conference that took place in an advanced-level writing class for ESL university students in the United States. The students were first-year graduate students from a range of academic majors who had just completed the first draft of a research paper on a topic in their own fields of study. The teacher instructed the writers to begin their conferences by explaining what their texts were about and, as they read their peer's texts, to take note of any ideas or sections that were unclear. Readers were encouraged to focus their comments on ideas in the writer's drafts that they had difficulty understanding. In this particular excerpt, the writer, Miko, has written a research paper on the economic decline of the world's superpowers after the end of the Cold War. The reader, Asha, questions Miko about the meaning of the term "pluralism" mentioned throughout the text.

As you read this excerpt, pay particular attention to the roles that each student assumes and the structure of the student–student interaction. Try to describe the type of language that is generated and the type of language functions that are carried out. Also, assess the extent to which this type of student–student interaction creates opportunities for students to use language for classroom learning and second language acquisition.

Excerpt 7.3

1. Asha: Here the first one, pluralism, for me is not clear, what is "pluralism"?
2. Miko: Is not clear to you?
3. Asha: No, I think maybe you define . . .
4. Miko: Pluralism . . .
5. Asha: A little bit. OK, this word, I didn't understand.
6. Miko: OK. OK.
7. Asha: The thing is . . . no, let me see. I think that this word "pluralism." This is one of the reasons of the changing of the international. But I don't really understand what is pluralism.
8. Miko: Eh hum. Eh I . . .
9. Asha: I like . . . you say here that you wrote that the powers Europe and Japan could recover their economic vitality from the ruins of . . . like they get together? They work together?
10. Miko: Uh . . . In the Cold War, there is only one superpower and is

the United States. In the Cold War, the only superpower in
the international politics. But after that time, after 1970s,
only 1970s, Japan and Europe, eh . . . European community,
became another superpowers in the international politics.
And the power of the United States . . .

11. Asha: Began to decline . . .
12. Miko: Began to decline. So, this situation is pluralism.
13. Asha: Oh, this is pluralism.
14. Miko: Yes, I . . . I give three examples of pluralism here. Here is
one . . . They could recover their economic vitality, and another one is . . . here, the United States's trade deficit and
decline its power, and the third part, the third aspect of pluralism is the increasing importance of the Third World.
15. Asha: OK. OK, but I think that when you talk here about pluralism,
this example is good about pluralism, now I understand that
Europe and Japan. But here . . . I think you are stating reasons why pluralism started.
16. Miko: Hum, hum. Right, right.
17. Asha: There are reasons because the United States power started to
decline. And, and . . . the other thing is the countries of the
Third World, is getting more importance . . . OK. So, I guess
you have to define or explain better what is . . .
18. Miko: More, more, more clearly what is pluralism. OK.

Asha, as the reader, clearly assumes the role of tutor or teacher. She
begins by asking Miko to explain the meaning of "pluralism," and then
reformulates her question several times in order to help Miko understand
exactly what aspect of this concept was unclear. In fact, her questions move
from rather broad, as in turn 1, "what is 'pluralism'?", to more specific, as
in turn 7, "This is one of the reasons of the changing of the international.
But I don't really understand what is pluralism," to very specific and based
on what Miko had written in the paper, as in turn 9, "you say here . . . that
the powers Europe and Japan could recover their economic vitality from the
ruins of . . . like they get together? They work together?" Thus, Asha
reformulates her questions, much in the way that teachers do, in order to
make them more specific and easier to answer. However, the difference
between Asha's questions and typical teacherlike questions is that Miko,
not Asha, possesses the "right" answer. So while Asha may ask teacherlike
questions, only Miko can answer them; thus, they are genuine questions as
opposed to known-answer questions common in most teacher-directed instruction. Asha's language is also teacherlike in that throughout much of the
exchange, Asha generates most of the input and does most of the conversational work by maintaining control over the topic as well as using questions
to engage Miko in the interaction.

Miko, as the writer, assumes a studentlike role. She responds directly to Asha's questions and provides an explanation of the concept of "pluralism," in turn 10; later, in turn 14, she cites three examples of pluralism given in the text. Thus, the content of the text, or Miko's knowledge of that content, is not being questioned by Asha. Instead, Miko appears to be struggling to understand why the definition and examples of pluralism given in the paper were unclear to Asha. In turn 18, Miko admits that she should provide a better definition of pluralism; however, it remains unclear if Miko knows exactly why Asha was confused. Theoretically, this exchange might help Miko at least understand how a naive reader, such as Asha, had difficulty understanding this term, and perhaps Miko will attend to this problem when she revises the paper.

The language generated during this interaction was meaning-focused. In fact, both students participated in the negotiation of meaning in that they used confirmation checks, comprehension checks, and clarification requests. For example, in turn 12, Miko explains, "Began to decline. So, this situation is pluralism." Asha checks her comprehension of this in turn 13, "Oh, this is pluralism." In fact, much of Asha's language represents requests for clarification, as at the end of turn 7, "But I really don't understand what is pluralism," and at the end of turn 9, ". . . like they get together? They work together?"

The student–student interaction in Excerpt 7.3 clearly created opportunities for Asha and Miko to use language for classroom learning and second language acquisition. Since the structure of the peer writing conference was set up on the peer tutoring model of cooperative learning, Asha was able to assume a more active and, at times, more controlling role in the interaction. However, when this pair moves to Asha's paper they will exchange roles in the interaction.

Thus, peer writing conferences provide students with equal opportunities to initiate, state their opinion, and self-select when to participate. The interactions tend to be meaning-focused, and students are encouraged to participate in a range of language functions, namely, asking questions, checking comprehension, requesting clarification, explaining concepts, and giving suggestions. Moreover, students are encouraged to focus their attention on unclear aspects of their peer's texts and indicate to one another how they have understood the ideas expressed in their texts.

Conclusion

Using the framework for understanding communication in second language classrooms, we find that the patterns of communication that occur in student–student interaction may still be shared by teachers and students. Teachers can choose to control the structure and content of student–student interaction based on their instructional goals, the nature of their classroom events, and the type of student–student interaction they hope to promote. The extent to which teachers choose to control student–student interaction will shape the roles that students assume, as well as the type of language they generate. Students also exert a certain amount of control over the structure and content of student–student interaction based on their differential experiences, interactional competencies, and individual personality traits. Finally, student–student interaction generally creates opportunities for students to participate in meaning-focused communication, to perform a range of language functions, to participate in the negotiation of meaning, to engage in both planned and unplanned discourse, to attend to both language forms and functions, to assume differing roles in that interaction, and, finally, to initiate, control the topic of discussion, and self-select to participate. Thus, student–student interaction in second language classrooms will more than likely have a positive impact upon students' opportunities for both classroom learning and second language acquisition.

8 Community- and school-based issues and second language classrooms

Recently, a teacher in one of my graduate seminars fondly described what she enjoyed most about teaching:

> I close my door and it's just me and my students without any outside distractions or pressures. We create our own little world where no one bothers us and we can do whatever we want.

This idealized image of the autonomous classroom is probably shared by many teachers, but, of course, it is true only in the figurative sense. In fact, closing one's classroom door does little, if anything, to eliminate the broader social and contextual issues that impact upon what goes on inside classrooms. Classrooms do not operate in isolation from society. In fact, schools tend to not only reflect but also transmit the social and cultural values and beliefs of the dominant society in which they exist (Wilcox 1982). In most countries, the ultimate goal of formal schooling is to prepare students to assume adult roles within the dominant society.

The framework for understanding classroom communication is now placed within the broader social context of second language classrooms. This chapter begins with an examination of community-based issues that exist outside the immediate classroom, but that directly affect what goes on inside the classroom. First is an exploration of how a range of historical, social, and psychological factors shape the ways in which second language groups perceive and respond to formal schooling. This is followed by an examination of how the perceived status of the target language, particularly English within EFL instructional settings, can determine not only how the language will be taught, but how it will be learned. Another focus is the role that school-based issues, such as commercial materials, as well as the complex social nature of the classroom itself, play in determining what and how teachers teach. Ultimately, the goal of this chapter is to place our view of classroom communication within much broader social contexts and to examine how such contexts impact upon the nature of the communication that occurs there.

Community-based issues and second language classrooms

The cultural discontinuity hypothesis (Ogbu 1982, 1987; Spindler 1974) states that second language students acquire learned ways of talking and communicating at home, and when they enter school, their linguistic behavior and communicative styles are often unappreciated and misunderstood. For example, the curricular content and instructional styles of the school often differ from the cultural content and learning styles they have experienced at home. It follows, then, that mitigating such discontinuities is critical if second language students are to participate in and learn from their formal school experiences. However, one criticism of the cultural discontinuity hypothesis is that it fails to recognize that not all minority students do as poorly in school as others. In the United States, several published reports have found that Asian-American students perform better academically in schools than African-Americans, Mexican-Americans, Native Americans, and Puerto Ricans in all academic skill areas (Coleman et al. 1966; Ogbu 1982; Slade 1982; Wigdor & Garner 1982). Similar trends have been found in other countries as well. For example, in Britain, Asian students perform better academically than West Indian students (Ogbu 1987; Yates 1987), while in Ontario, Canada, French Canadian students perform worse academically than other Canadian-born children of immigrant minorities (Cummins 1982).

These studies suggest there is variability in the ways in which different second language groups respond to formal schooling. Ogbu (1987) attributes this variability to historical, social, and psychological factors that not only shape the ways in which they perceive of and respond to formal schooling, but also how different minority groups are perceived within the dominant society. To explain this variability, Ogbu (1987) distinguishes between nonimmigrant and immigrant minorities. Nonimmigrant, or castelike, minorities, have historically been incorporated into the dominant society through an act of imperialism, such as slavery, conquest, or colonization, and thus are generally perceived to be inferior by the dominant society. In response to what they perceive as institutionalized discrimination (Lewis 1981; Ogbu 1987) castelike minorities tend to assume a cultural frame of reference that is in direct opposition to the traits and values of the dominant society. Moreover, castelike minorities equate school with the dominant society and perceive schooling as one-way acculturation or assimilation into the dominant group, which they are trying to resist. Consequently, their school behavior does little to enable them to experience academic success, and, in fact, encourages an attitude of low effort and at best ambivalence toward school in general.

Immigrant minorities, on the other hand, have experienced voluntary immigration, generally for economic, social, or political reasons, and while they tend to experience the same sort of subordination and exploitation as castelike minorities, they respond to it in vastly different ways. Most immigrant minorities tend to see their economic problems as temporary, and because they often have opportunities for employment within their own ethnic community, they may be less dependent on the dominant society. Immigrant minorities also tend to measure success within their own minority community as opposed to the dominant society, and thus assume a cultural frame of reference that is, if not identical to that of the dominant society, at least not in direct opposition. Immigrant minorities see schooling as a means to economic success and tend to adopt "an alternation model of schooling" (Ogbu 1987: 275), which allows them to act one way in school and another at home in their own community. Thus, immigrant minorities are willing to cross cultural and linguistic boundaries to get jobs and economic benefits, yet at the same time they are able to maintain their own social and cultural identity. Gibson's (1987) study of the social and cultural adjustment of Punjabi immigrants in an American secondary school, mentioned in Chapter 4, is an example of the adaptation strategy of accommodation without assimilation. Punjabi students were encouraged by their parents and the Punjabi community to fit into school life in order to receive an education that would lead to future employment opportunities, but not to become like Americans. A similar pattern of accommodation without assimilation was found in a study of the cross-cultural adaptation and learning of Iranian students in U.S. high schools (Hoffman 1988). Once again, Iranian students' desire to retain their Iranian cultural identity kept them from adopting the cultural perspective of the school; although they were open to learning about and, to some extent, participating in school life, they did not accept as their own the cultural perspective of the school.

Variability in second language groups' responses to schooling has also been found within what may be perceived as a single minority group. For example, Suarez-Orozco (1987) found variability in Hispanic American students' academic performance in school. Mexican-American students, whose ancestors experienced long histories of depreciation by Anglo-American groups, tend to respond to schooling by rejecting the educational system as forced acculturation. They see schooling not as enhancement, but as enculturation by a dominant society with which they do not identify. On the other hand, more recent Central American immigrants, often fleeing political strife or economic hardship at home, see Anglo-American education as an important step in improving their economic status, and thus tend to hold greater expectations from the American educational system. Suarez-Orozco (1987) claims that educators must differentiate between Hispanic American groups and not view them as the same or as facing similar problems, but in fact as having different social histories, present realities, and adaptive strategies that enable them to succeed academically to a greater or lesser degree in the American educational system.

Variability in second language groups' responses to schooling is not unique to the United States. In Britain, Yates (1987) found that Asian students did better than West Indian students in school largely because formal education was not seen as forced acculturation into the dominant group, but instead as a means of maintaining and transmitting the cultural values of the minority group. For the Asian minority group (Patidar) that Yates (1987) studied, an individual's educational achievement was interpreted within the context of the minority group and seen as a resource for the entire minority group.

Other community-based issues, such as the relationship between parents and teachers, or a community's willingness to accept and support social change, can also affect a second language group's response to schooling. Warren (1988) examined parent–teacher relations in three different educational settings: a rural, southwest German village; an Anglo middle-class neighborhood in a northern California metropolis; and a lower middle-class Mexican-American neighborhood in a southern Californian metropolis. Working from the premise that parents and teachers are key agents of socialization in children's lives, Warren found that when teachers and parents shared the same core system of norms and values, they tended to have better relations and, thus, created a unifying factor in sustaining successful educational programs. However, continuity between parents' and teachers' cultural values and norms did not always resolve other differences, and while they tended to cooperate with one another, conflicts still arose.

How communities react to changes in schools with new refugee populations depends on the nature and degree of that change, the extent to which the community has been warned and prepared for this change, and whether the minority group is visibly different from the community. Finnan's (1988) examination of the effect of Southeast Asian refugees on schools and school districts suggests that the extent to which a community is willing to accept and support social change within the community itself will have an important effect on the success or failure of schoolwide refugee programs.

Thus, variability in second language groups' responses to schooling may be due not only to cultural discontinuities between the home and school, but also to wider social and historical issues surrounding the perceived status, identity, and cultural frames of reference held by different second language groups and those held by the dominant society. To understand differences in second language students' academic success or failure, teachers must recognize the broader social issues that are deeply ingrained within the historical and current relationships between different second language groups and the dominant society.

The issue facing second language teachers then becomes how to mitigate these societal and largely extralinguistic forces that shape how their second language students are likely to perceive and respond to what happens in second language classrooms. One way to address this issue is to presume that if second language students are to succeed in mainstream classrooms, teachers must maintain a balance between the second language students' own cultural frames of reference and those of the dominant society. In addition, teachers must create learning opportunities that utilize students' linguistic and interactional competencies and encourage the values and attitudes that students already have that will support their second language classroom experiences. Chapter 4 reviews several educational programs that have attempted to do this.

However, Gee (1986, 1988, 1990) believes maintaining a balance between students' own cultural frames of reference and the frames of reference of the dominant society – or specifically, those who speak the target language – may be difficult, if not impossible, to do. He claims that all language use, or "discourse practices" (1990: 270), are embedded in the cultural frames of reference, or world-view, of a particular social group. Hence, learning a second language becomes a form of enculturation: socializing second language students into particular ways of making sense and perceiving their experiences. It follows that acquiring a second language means, in all likelihood, acquiring new cultural frames of reference, ones that, for some second language students, may conflict with their own cultural frames of reference and cultural identity.

In fact, Gee speaks directly to English language teachers by suggesting that the teaching of English enculturates students into standard-English discourses – that is, specific ways of using language, creating meaning, and making sense of experiences – at the expense of students' own cultural identities. Moreover, Gee describes ESL teachers as "gatekeepers" (1986: 743), since second language students will be unable to gain access to educational or economic opportunities within the English-speaking society unless they acquire the oral, written, and communicative discourse practices of that society.

Thus, Gee believes students cannot truly acquire a second language unless they assume a new cultural perspective and take on, as their own, the literacy practices of the dominant society. If native and second language cultural perspectives conflict, or are diametrically opposed, second language students may be forced to give up their own cultural perspective in order to assume the cultural perspectives of the target language society. Like Ogbu, Gee agrees that second language students' willingness to assume a new cultural perspective will be closely tied to the historical and social relationships between the second language group and the dominant society.

Combining these perspectives, we can conclude that second language teachers must recognize the broader historical, social, and psychological issues that impact on students' linguistic and academic performance; at the same time, they must recognize that second language teaching in itself can act as a form of enculturation that socializes students into the cultural perspectives of the target language society. This may cause conflicting cultural perspectives for some second language students and, thus, will more than likely affect the extent to which they are willing and able to successfully participate in and learn from their classroom experiences.

Attempting to resolve these seemingly conflicting outcomes of second and, particularly, English language teaching, Peirce (1989) argues for an expanded definition of communicative competence by suggesting that the teaching of English can, and should, open up possibilities for students to explore not only what is communicatively appropriate within the English-speaking society but also desirable uses of English by second language groups within that society. Using the example of People's English in South Africa, Peirce argues that students of English should not be limited to appropriate usage of English within the English-speaking ruling minority of South Africa, but should be encouraged to challenge norms by asking why certain rules for appropriateness exist, whose interests are being served by adhering to these rules, and what other sorts of rules may be more desirable within and for second language groups. People's English in South Africa is concerned less with achieving a prescribed set of communicative competencies and more with "how English is to be taught in the schools; who has access to the language, how English is implicated in the power relations dominant in South Africa; and the effect of English on the way speakers of the language perceive themselves, their society, and the possibilities for change in that society" (1989: 141). Thus, Peirce would disagree with Gee, in that while students must gain access to the discourse practices of the dominant society, they should do so not in order to unquestioningly conform to those practices, but in order to reevaluate and, ultimately, reconstruct them to meet their own social, political, economic, and communicative needs. Peirce calls for the teaching and learning of English in South Africa to become less a form of enculturation and more a means of social and political change for the majority Black population.

The status of English in EFL instructional settings

English assumes vastly different roles in non–English-speaking countries around the world. Commonly referred to as the emerging international language, English is seen by some as a form of linguistic and socioeconomic power (Kachru 1986) and by others as a form of cultural intrusion (Cook 1988). The perceived status of English in EFL instructional contexts will most certainly have an impact on how English is taught and learned.

For example, in post-apartheid South Africa, language attitudes among the majority Black population have shifted away from old resentments of English as an ex-colonial language to English as the language of choice. This is largely due to the perceived social, political, and economic status of

English as well as the rejection of government-mandated attempts to enforce Afrikaans, the language of the white minority, as the medium of instruction. Even attempts to educate Blacks in their native languages (the mother tongue principle) have failed because such indigenous languages lack the perceived status of English. Instead, extralinguistic factors having to do with the perceived socioeconomic mobility associated with English continue to have a greater impact on the success of English as the medium of instruction in South Africa (Alexander 1987, 1989).

In Malaysia, another former British colony, English was at one time the predominant medium of instruction. However, while recent nationalistic movements have shifted the language of instruction to Malay, English continues to be officially recognized as a second language and remains a required subject of all students in government-sponsored schools. While the teaching of individual native languages in Malaysia (such as Malay, Mandarin, and Tamil) receives a great deal of attention, the role of English in the educational system remains important. In 1979, the government reaffirmed the importance of English for all Malaysians, declaring it instrumental in facilitating diplomatic and economic relations within the broader international community (Kaur 1990).

However, in Puerto Rico, the majority of the population remains functionally monolingual in Spanish despite a century of government-imposed policies promoting bilingualism (M. C. Resnick 1993). This is mainly due to strong societal feelings of nationalism, political uncertainty, and a dominant societal imperative against learning English. Since the internal needs of Puerto Rico tend to be met with Spanish, the need for communicative competence in English is minimal. However, while most Puerto Ricans express instrumental motivation to learn English, for better economic or educational opportunities, they tend to experience negative social attitudes toward learning English, and therefore acquire only minimal English language skills. Moreover, given the heavy influence of U.S. media and U.S. popular culture in Puerto Rico, most Puerto Ricans acquire stronger oral language skills than literacy skills in English.

In Japan, English is perceived as one of the most important subjects in school, but its importance can be directly linked to the English entrance examinations required for admittance to Japanese high schools and universities. Since all Japanese students take an entrance examination in English at some point in their education (Kamada 1987), the examination itself influences the national English curriculum by restricting the content of English instruction to the content of the entrance examination – primarily grammar-translation and reading comprehension. The overemphasis on English entrance examinations tends to squelch Japanese students' motivation to learn English for any sort of communicative purposes. Thus, the Japanese tend to develop a strong working knowledge of English grammar and vocabulary, but are much less capable of using English in communicative settings (Christensen 1985). Moreover, while English has been associated with economically and technologically advanced countries for generations, and is valued as an important educational area of study, becoming fluent in English is not perceived as a requirement for greater socioeconomic wealth within Japanese society (Wordell 1985).

These examples suggest that the perceived status of English in EFL instructional contexts can have a powerful impact on the ways in which English is taught, as well as the extent to which English is acquired by EFL students. These examples also carry with them the implication that acquiring English within an EFL instructional context may mean overcoming strong social and cultural barriers.

Commercial materials and second language classrooms

Although most second language teachers long for the perfect textbook, one that will be all things to all students, most also realize the futility of such a prospect. However, over the past decade there has been an explosion in the publishing industry of materials for a wide range of second language instructional contexts. Most, if not all, of these commercial materials are designed to present meaning-based content in a progression of level-appropriate activities to a specific group of second language learners. There are a variety of commercial materials currently on the market. Probably the most popular are the commercial language series that incorporate the four skill areas of speaking, listening, reading, and writing into proficiency-level sequenced textbooks. Each textbook is carefully graded, with a gradual progression of teaching items and built-in review activities. Most include a student's book, a teacher's manual, and supplemental workbooks and/or audiocassettes, and are marketed as complete language programs. There are also commercial materials that devote separate textbooks to each of the language skills, so that an entire book covers grammar, writing, reading, pronunciation, or speaking and listening. Such books tend to be designed for only one proficiency level (beginning, intermediate, advanced), for a particular group of second language students (high school, university, adult), and for instructional programs that separate the skill areas into different courses. Finally, there are commercial materials designed to teach English for specific purposes; for example, English for academic purposes, TOEFL (Test of English as a Foreign Language) preparation, and English for business, engineering, or international teaching assistants.

As the presence of commercial materials in second language instructional contexts continues to grow, so too does concern about the ways in which commercial materials may shape what and how teachers teach. In first language elementary-school reading programs, the role of commercial materials has been at the center of much controversy. Basal readers are designed to provide level-appropriate stories, a teacher's manual with directions and supplemental instructional activities, a scope and sequence of appropriate reading skills to be covered, and assessment measures to record students' reading achievement; nevertheless, they have been charged as being an impediment rather than an impetus to better quality reading instruction (Shannon 1983, 1987, 1989). Specifically, Shannon argues that in the Western world, where science and technology are highly valued, teachers and administrators have come to equate commercial materials with a scientific method of teaching reading, thus, they hold strong beliefs in the power of commercial materials. In fact, many assume that the materials themselves are what actually teach children to read. Shannon found that reading teachers believe commercial materials are the technological solution to the problems of reading instruction and, therefore, rely too heavily on commercial materials to guide and sometimes control their instructional practices. This reification of scientific principles causes teachers to unconsciously alienate themselves from their responsibilities as reading teachers, since they become managers of the commercial materials rather than facilitators of the learning process according to individual needs. In fact, elementary reading teachers' overreliance on commercial materials has been found to cause a lack of flexibility in their instructional practices and a lack of creativity during reading instruction (Rosecky 1978; Shake & Allington 1985). Moreover, given increased class size, the need to maintain student records, and external pressures for schools to quantify reading achievement, reading teachers are neither expected nor encouraged to alter commercial materials to suit the specific needs of their students. Instead, teachers' overreliance on commercial reading materials has been found to lead to instructional practices that lack relevant goals, inhibit students' reading comprehension, and reduce the amount of individualized reading instruction (Durkin 1975, 1983).

Evidence of teachers' overreliance on commercial materials, while presumably not limited to elementary-school reading programs, provides some ominous warnings about the ways in which commercial materials shape what and how teachers teach. No published research has examined the impact of commercial materials on second language teachers' instructional practices. However, given the range of second language instructional contexts and the wide variety of commercial materials marketed for these contexts, one can suspect that commercial materials do, in fact, affect what and how teachers teach.

In EFL instructional settings, teachers who are nonnative speakers of English may find commercial materials to be their only source of linguistic and cultural information about English. Thus, EFL teachers may depend heavily on commercial materials for their syllabus design, lesson planning, and instructional activities. The same might be said for EFL students, since in some EFL contexts, access to information about English may be limited to the textbook. Furthermore, ESL textbooks that are used in EFL instructional contexts may not be appropriate for EFL students, since linguistic and cultural information about language usage differs in ESL and EFL contexts.

The recent shift toward more student-centered curricula (Nunan 1988) requires that the selection of instructional materials be based on students' specific language-related needs and goals. However, second language students are sometimes unable to articulate and define those goals, or such goals are established by school administrators or national curriculum committees, not by the students or classroom teachers. Thus, matching the content and instructional design of commercial materials to the specific language-related needs and goals of a particular group of second language students may be difficult for teachers to do.

This is not to say that commercial materials should be banned from second language classrooms or that their presence there will inhibit effective second language instruction. On the contrary, commercial materials provide a rich source of meaningful content, instructional activities, and important linguistic and cultural information for both teachers and students. However, teachers must be aware that commercial materials possess no scientifically or technologically proven powers to teach second languages; more importantly, teachers must look critically at commercial materials to determine their appropriateness for a particular group of students. In addition, teachers must become skilled at adapting those materials to meet students' needs and goals. Simply put, teachers must be wary of the promises of commercial materials, since the potential to become an impediment to effective second language instruction exists if materials are not selected, implemented, and adapted carefully.

Not all second language teachers have the luxury of selecting their own instructional materials. Instead, many are required to implement curricula that are mandated by school administrators or national curriculum committees. In Malaysia, for example, the implementation of the national English language curriculum has been criticized because EFL teachers' need to fulfill the demands of the national curriculum has been found to take precedence over the individual language-related needs of their students (Kaur 1993). Likewise, in Japan, the preoccupation with preparing for English entrance examinations has led to English curricula that essentially cover the content of the entrance examinations (Christensen 1985). Moreover, most Japanese English teachers feel compelled to prepare their students for these examinations; as a result, they tend not to go beyond direct instruction in grammar rules and vocabulary (Steinberg 1985). Thus, mandated curricula can act as a dominant force in determining how second languages are taught and learned. Commercial materials and national curricula can act as a double-edged sword, in that they can enrich as well as stifle what and how language teachers teach.

The classroom experience

The classroom has been described by Duffy (1982) as a place where teachers are consumed with maintaining a productive flow of activities while faced with a variety of implicit and explicit mandates that define and limit their instructional options. Teachers play a variety of personal and professional roles as they manage the complex social environment in their classrooms:

In short, the classroom is an incredibly complex and restrictive environment. Teachers have limited amounts of freedom and flexibility; they must routinely work within resource shortages, deal with complex (and often unconsciously created) social relations and fend off multiple and conflicting expectations while simultaneously putting forward the image of a cool professional who has the classroom and the children's learning under control. (Duffy 1982: 361)

This caricature of classroom life suggests classrooms are not always easy places to be, and that there are certain conditions that seem to be inherent in classrooms. In fact, Duffy identifies four conditions of classroom life that tend to dominate teacher thinking and can, in effect, limit teachers' instructional practices.

Since teaching, and schooling in general, is largely a social phenomenon, the first condition is the social forces within the classroom itself. Successful classroom communication and learning is contingent upon the social relationships that are established between teachers and students (Doyle 1979). Without mutually established trust, respect, and understanding between teachers and students, negative social forces will conspire against the effectiveness of teachers' instructional practices as well as students' willingness to learn (McDermott 1979).

Duffy's second condition is the drive for activity flow. In fact, he describes activity flow as "survival" (1982: 360), claiming that without the ability to maintain a productive flow of activities, teachers lose control over what is, and is not, supposed to happen in classrooms. Maintaining activity flow during classroom instruction is generally found to be more difficult for novice teachers than experienced teachers. This may be due, in part, to the fact that experienced teachers tend to possess a well-organized knowledge base regarding the students and the classroom environment that enables them to simplify, differentiate, and transform information during instruction, and make alternative choices without disrupting the flow of instruction (Calderhead 1981, 1983; Doyle 1977; Morine & Vallance 1975). Novice teachers, on the other hand, lack a schema for interpreting and coping with what goes on during instruction, and have a limited repertoire of instructional strategies upon which they can rely; thus, they tend to focus on maintaining the activity flow during instruction (Calderhead 1981; Doyle 1977; Fogarty, Wang, & Creek 1983; Morine & Vallance 1975).

For example, in a study of preservice ESL teachers' instructional actions and decisions during the practicum, K. E. Johnson (1992b) found that preservice teachers perceived unsolicited student initiations as off-task behavior and a threat to instructional management. They were more likely to ignore student initiations in favor of maintaining the activity flow. In fact, in most instances, preservice teachers did not respond to or utilize the student's comments, but instead continued with the instructional activity as planned. Focusing on maintaining the activity flow not only consumed the attention of these preservice teachers, but actually limited second language students' opportunities for authentic and self-selected use of the target language during classroom instruction.

Duffy's third classroom condition reflects the mandates placed on teachers from outside the classroom. Besides being required to use commercial materials, teachers are also held accountable to school administrators and parents to demonstrate student achievement. Such pressures can lead teachers to feel compelled to "teach for the test" in order to demonstrate the effectiveness of their instructional practices through student achievement. Moreover, teachers may feel pressure to maintain strict order in their classrooms based on expectations held by themselves and others about appropriate classroom behavior.

Finally, Duffy's fourth condition of classroom life is defined as "role strain" (1982: 361). Role strain implies that teachers are expected to play a multitude of roles: as parents, as counselors, as managers of the curriculum, and, of course, as teachers. These multiple roles place extra strains on teachers, since teachers must contend with students' physical and emotional well-being if they hope to have any sort of impact on students' academic achievement.

Given the social dynamics, managerial concerns, outside mandates, and role expectations inherent in classroom life, it becomes clear how the classroom itself can place constraints on what and how teachers teach. Only when we place what happens inside classrooms within the context of the constraints imposed from outside classrooms can we fully understand the dynamics of classroom communication.

Conclusion

This chapter has shown that second language classroom communication exists within a broader social context than the classroom. A range of social, historical, and political forces that are embedded within the societies in which second language classrooms exist can, and do, impact upon what goes on inside classrooms. Also, a range of school-based issues, such as commercial materials and the classroom experience, influence what and how teachers teach. What goes on inside second language classrooms may be influenced more by larger societal forces imposed upon classrooms than by the interactions that take place between teachers and students within those classrooms.

PART III
PROMOTING COMMUNICATION IN SECOND LANGUAGE CLASSROOMS

9 *Expanding the patterns of classroom communication*

It should be evident at this point that the way in which the patterns of communication are established and maintained in second language classrooms is not random. Teachers, by virtue of the status they hold and the ways they use language, have the authority to retain control over both the content and structure of classroom communication. At times, teachers tightly control the topic of discussion, what counts as relevant to that topic, who may participate, and when. At other times, teachers grant varying degrees of control to their students by allowing them to select the topic of discussion, contribute to what counts as relevant to that topic, and self-select when and how they will participate. Thus, the patterns of classroom communication depend largely on how teachers use language to control the structure and content of classroom events.

Teachers have a variety of reasons, some conscious and others more subconscious, for why they organize classroom communication as they do. It may depend on the pedagogical purpose of their lessons or the assumptions and expectations they hold about their own and their students' communicative behavior. These assumptions and expectations are closely tied to who they are as teachers and as people.

Of course, the same can be said for second language students, in that they too hold assumptions and expectations about their own and their teachers' communicative behavior, which are closely tied to who they are as students. Moreover, the extent to which second language students are willing to contribute to and participate in classroom events depends on what they perceive as their role in those events. Their perceptions are shaped, in turn, by learned ways of talking and communicating that are deemed appropriate within their linguistic/culture group. Thus, establishing and maintaining the patterns of classroom communication is, to a greater or lesser degree, a joint venture between teachers, as they control the content and structure of classroom communication, and students, as they interpret and respond to what teachers say and do.

If teachers wish to promote communication in second language classrooms, they need to allow for greater variability in the patterns of communication so as to maximize students' linguistic and interactional competencies and create more opportunities for students to participate in classroom events. Ultimately, the patterns of classroom communication will determine the ways in which second language students use language for classroom learning and second language acquisition.

This chapter examines a range of issues that teachers must consider if they wish to promote communication in second language classrooms. In addition, it explores the ways in which teachers can extend the patterns of communication so as to foster students' use of language for classroom learning and second language acquisition.

Allowing for variability in the patterns of classroom communication

As previously mentioned, promoting communication in second language classrooms means allowing for greater variability in the patterns of communication so as to maximize second language students' linguistic and interactional competencies and create more opportunities for them to participate in and learn from classroom events. Trueba (1989) claims it is the teachers' responsibility to adjust their instructional practices to the competencies of their students in order to provide appropriate and effective classroom instruction:

[Teachers'] primary obligation is not the strict observance of prescribed curricula and teaching methodologies, but the consistent search for ways to involve students actively in conscious efforts to comprehend and generate texts through culturally meaningful and appropriate methods. Implied is the realization that teachers must have an increased degree of freedom in determining specific needs of linguistic minority populations. The teaching of reading and writing must be grounded in the cultural and social contexts of students, their relevant cultural experiences, and their stage of social integration and acculturation rather than by assuming a universal effectiveness of either the instructional content or method. (1989: 127)

For teachers to adjust their instructional practices as Trueba suggests, they must look closely at their assumptions and expectations about their own and their students' communicative behavior. This means bringing to the surface their own frames of reference, particularly their cultural beliefs, assumptions, and expectations about who they are as teachers, what role they believe teachers should play in second language instruction, what they expect of their students, and the ways in which they judge the appropriateness of their own and their students' communicative behavior in classrooms. Teachers must also identify the linguistic and interactional demands that are embedded in their instructional practices. This means analyzing classroom events and identifying the linguistic and interactional prerequisites that are necessary for students to participate in those events. In addition, teachers must recognize that second language students enter classrooms with a range of linguistic and interactional competencies and that discontinuities may exist between students' competencies and those embedded in classroom events. More importantly, however, teachers must view these discontinuities not as deficiencies, but as culturally appropriate ways of talking and communicating within different linguistic/cultural communities. With the accumulation of these insights, teachers can then begin to adapt, adjust, and extend the patterns of classroom communication so as to maximize students' opportunities to participate in classroom events, which will in turn promote communication in second language classrooms.

Examining cultural assumptions and expectations

If teachers wish to promote communication in second language classrooms, they must become aware of their own cultural assumptions and expectations about what is and is not appropriate in classrooms. One way for teachers to do this is to participate in a process known as *reflective cultural analysis* (Spindler & Spindler 1982). Based on a series of ethnographic research techniques established by Spindler & Spindler (1982, 1987a), Trueba claims:

The purpose of RCA [reflective cultural analysis] is not necessarily to change teachers or students, but to help them understand the cultural differences and the judgments made on the basis of cultural values. If the teacher misunderstands the child's home environment, the teacher cannot assist this child in the acquisition of missing instrumental competencies. The nature of cultural conflict and of the means necessary to resolve it requires RCA. (1989: 45)

Trueba outlines several techniques that can be used to enable teachers to become conscious of their own cultural assumptions and to recognize how these assumptions may conflict with those held by their students. The first technique, *reflective cross-cultural interviewing* (Spindler & Spindler 1987b), asks teachers from one cultural setting to view videos, films, and pictures from their own as well as a different cultural setting. For example, using this technique to compare the underlying educational assumptions of teachers in an American and a Japanese daycare center, Fujita and Sano (1988) videotaped specific activities at both centers and asked both groups of teachers to explain their own instructional activities, as well as those of their cultural counterparts. Their analysis of the ensuing dialogues revealed that both American and Japanese teachers interpreted the other's instructional practices through their own cultural frames of reference. More importantly, however, each held different underlying educational assumptions about the concepts of instructional time and space, and the roles of teachers and children. Specifically, the Japanese teachers viewed the flow of their instructional activities over the course of an entire day, whereas the American teachers viewed such activities within separate instructional moments. The Japanese teachers viewed children as existing in a world separate from that of adults, and thus were willing to offer more direct assistance to them over a longer period of time. The American teachers also viewed children as distinct from adults, but instead believed it was in the children's best interest to acquire the rules of adults as quickly as possible. Therefore, the American teachers encouraged their children to become self-sufficient much earlier than the Japanese teachers. Finally, the American teachers viewed themselves as supervisors and controllers of the children's behavior, whereas the Japanese teachers viewed themselves as facilitators or navigators through the flow of instructional activities. The reflective cross-cultural interviewing technique identified some interesting differences between the educational assumptions of American and Japanese daycare teachers, enabled both groups of teachers to bring their own cultural assumptions to the surface, and allowed them to recognize their assumptions as being distinctly different.

A second technique used to enable teachers to become aware of their own cultural assumptions is the *instrumental activities inventory* (Spindler & Spindler 1987b). The inventory attempts to show contrasts between cultural values and possible discontinuities as cultures modernize and change, or as an individual moves from one culture to another. Using a series of pictures that depict scenarios of activities in the home, school, and community, teachers and students are asked to select preferred scenarios and provide an explanation for their choices. These explanations are then examined to uncover similarities and differences in teachers' and students' cultural values and expectations.

For example, Spindler and Spindler (1987b) used this technique to explore and compare the cultural values and underlying educational assumptions held by teachers in a German and an American school. Overall, they found that the teachers' instructional practices and classroom management styles differed according to their cultural frames of reference. For example, whereas the German teachers believed they represented an external authority, responsible for imposing control and order over their students' behavior, the American teachers assumed the students themselves were responsible for controlling their own behavior. Although both groups of teachers recognized the importance of their students' individual needs, the German teachers viewed individual students as members of groups who were to work competitively but uniformly. The American teachers, on the other hand, saw individual students' needs as the end goal of teaching and learning, and the group as only a means of achieving that goal. Finally, the German teachers assumed full responsibility for student learning, and therefore organized and maintained control over all instructional activities, whereas the American teachers viewed their role as merely reinforcing students' attempts to learn on their own, and thus merely coordinated various instructional activities.

The instrumental activities inventory can be useful in identifying differences in teachers' and students' cultural and educational assumptions, but it is even more important as a means of encouraging them to understand their own cultural assumptions and expectations in comparison to others'. This technique can be adapted to any cross-cultural or multicultural instructional setting, but to do so requires cultural knowledge and information from native-speaker informants from the cultures being compared. This technique can also be used with teachers and students in order to help them recognize each other's the cultural assumptions, expectations, and frames of reference.

One means of enabling teachers to become aware of their own cultural assumptions and expectations is by asking them to participate in a variety of activities in which they reflect on their own teaching. *Personal journal writing* has long been used as a means of enabling teachers to become more reflective about their own classroom practices, as well as to take note of the academic and social progress of their students. Trueba boasts of the benefits:

The insights teachers get from writing about their daily teaching activities are most valuable. Indeed, teachers learn to think critically about their teaching only when they begin to write reflectively, on a regular basis, about their teaching. Writing a personal ethnographic journal also has a healing effect. Teachers working with culturally different children are subject to many pressures and frustrations. Learning to bring these feelings to the surface and articulate them is, for some teachers, not only a learning experience but a matter of psychological survival. (1987: 47)

Establishing *teacher support groups* can also help teachers reflect on their own cultural assumptions and how these assumptions shape their instructional practices. Trueba recommends that teachers in similar teaching environments who hold similar educational philosophies and teaching goals meet regularly to observe and discuss aspects of each others' instructional practices, to examine differences in how students participate in classroom activities, and to evaluate the appropriateness of curricular materials and educational goals for language minority students.

Another type of reflective activity, known as *the stimulated recall technique* (Shavelson 1983), requires videotaping classroom instruction and then asking teachers to provide a running commentary of their thoughts and decisions as they watch themselves teach (K. E. Johnson 1992c). Specifically, teachers are asked to describe why they were doing what they were doing, what they recall thinking about as they were teaching, and what they feel was influencing their instructional decisions. Their comments are audiotaped and then used for personal reflection or for discussion with peer support groups, or with a mentor or supervisor. This type of reflective experience enables teachers to recognize how they interpret and respond to what occurs in their classrooms. It also helps teachers understand their own instructional decision making, specifically, why they choose to act and talk as they do, as well as how they interpret and respond to their students.

Each of the techniques outlined here offers different means by which teachers can begin to look closely and critically at their own cultural assumptions and expectations about classroom communication. Teachers who truly wish to promote communication in second language classrooms must begin by looking inward, at who they are as teachers and how they make sense of their teaching experiences, as well as outward, at why they do what they do in second language classrooms.

Parental involvement

Proportionally, second language students spend much less time in school than at home; therefore, what they learn at home and in their primary social communities greatly influences how they learn, talk, act, and interact. Thus, if teachers wish to promote communication in second language classrooms, they must make a concerted effort to learn about the home culture and social communities of their second language students. By working closely with parents and/or community members, teachers can find out about culturally acceptable ways of acting and interacting, or about culturally bound understandings that are an essential part of who their students are. Unfortunately, encouraging parental involvement in the affairs of the school tends to be ignored or perceived by teachers as a threat to their authority. In a longitudinal study of parent–teacher relationships in three ethnically and socioeconomically different elementary schools, Warren (1988) found that parents were overwhelmingly perceived as potential threats to teachers' authority, and most teachers wished to be insulated from parental intrusions. In general, parent–teacher relations were found to be tentative and stressful for both parents and teachers.

Despite these discouraging findings, parents can provide insightful information about their children's interests, aspirations, and competencies. Furthermore, parents can create a link between the home and school, if they are encouraged to participate in the daily life of the classroom, and if they are made aware of the knowledge and competencies that their children need to be successful in school.

Parents can also play a critical role in providing a home environment that supports the goals of the school. In an ethnographic study of three Mexican immigrant families, Delgado-Gaitan (1987b) found that while parents wanted their children to maintain their cultural values and native language, they also perceived their children's success as directly linked to learning English and acquiring the competencies associated with the U.S. educational system. Unfortunately, these parents were unaware of what was required of their children to succeed in mainstream U.S. schools. Delgado-Gaitan concluded that because of this, they were unable to create a supportive home environment that might help their children adjust to and succeed in school. Ultimately, teachers must recognize parents as a critical link between the home and the school, encourage parental involvement in the school, and view parents as valuable resources for providing culturally responsive education for second language students.

Examining the linguistic and interactional demands of classroom events

In order to promote communication in second language classrooms, teachers must also identify the linguistic and interactional demands that are embedded in classroom events. This means identifying both the academic task structures and the social participation structures. It also means identifying both the linguistic and interactional competencies that are required of students if they are to participate in these events.

In Excerpt 3.1, two students, Kim and Petr, struggled to fit their communicative behavior into the structure of a grammar lesson on negative constructions and personal pronoun usage. The linguistic demands embedded in that classroom event required that Kim and Petr know how to construct negative sentences with "not" and use personal pronouns correctly. The interactional demands required that they fit their talk into the structure of a substitution drill, and thus wait for a direct nomination from the teacher, confine their responses to information given in the textbook, and use specific linguistic constructions to complete the drill. However, both Kim and Petr were confused by the interactional demands of this event, particularly when the teacher shifted from literal questions about the students themselves to questions based on illustrations in the textbook without making these shifts explicit.

In Excerpt 3.2, very different linguistic and interactional demands were embedded in the small group activity in which three students, Jay, Alex, and Sungsu, were asked to generate questions to ask a visiting police officer. The students were allowed to use more exploratory language to generate ideas; at the same time, they participated in the negotiation of meaning as they reached a consensus about the specific question they wanted to ask. Moreover, they were allowed to select the topic of discussion, overlap talk, control the direction of the discussion, and self-select when and how to participate. The linguistic and interactional requirements of this activity allowed for greater variability in the patterns of communication; therefore, these three students were able to successfully carry out the linguistic and interactional demands of this classroom event. Teachers can begin to identify the linguistic and interactional demands that are embedded in classroom events by asking themselves: (a) What is the information to be covered and how is it logically organized? (b) How will students be expected to talk and act? (c) What language-related skills and knowledge will students need to know to participate? and (d) What interactional skills will students need to know to participate? Thus, for all classroom events, teachers must begin to examine the linguistic and interactional demands embedded in classroom events by recognizing what information will be covered and how is it logically organized, how students will be expected to talk and act, and what linguistic and interactional skills students will need in order to participate.

Recognizing competencies and mitigating discontinuities

To promote communication in second language classrooms, teachers must also recognize students' linguistic and interactional competencies, identify discontinuities that may exist between students' competencies and those embedded in classroom events, and then mitigate those discontinuities by adjusting, adapting, and extending the patterns of classroom communication. In Chapter 4, several educational programs that do this were reviewed. For example, the teachers in the Papago Early Childhood Head Start program maintained a high tolerance for nonparticipation, created instructional activities that required both doing and talking, encouraged students to talk in small groups, and were careful not to single out individual students unless they volunteered. Thus, as these teachers recognized their students' linguistic and interactional competencies and identified possible discontinuities, they were able to mitigate those discontinuities by adjusting the patterns of classroom communication so as to maximize their students' opportunities to participate in classroom events.

However, Carrasco (1981) warns that a major obstacle facing teachers' ability to recognize and mitigate discontinuities in second language classrooms is that most teachers hold extremely limited views of their second language students' competencies. This is due, in large part, to the fact that second language students tend to have few opportunities to demonstrate their competencies. For example, when teachers tightly control the patterns of classroom communication, they are in turn restricting second language students' opportunities to demonstrate their competencies and, therefore, are also limiting their own perceptions of their students' competencies. To increase teachers' awareness of their students' competencies, Carrasco asks teachers to "look and listen in" on what their second language students do and say in a variety of social and instructional contexts. By doing so, teachers can make more accurate assessments of their students' competencies, and can be better able to adapt and adjust their own instructional practices and the learning environment to maximize those competencies. Moreover, Carrasco asserts that expanding teachers' awareness of students' competencies tends to raise teachers' overall expectations for their second language students.

In line with Carrasco, Hymes (1981) claims that effective second language instruction starts where the student is; however, to know where a student is requires knowledge of the social/cultural group from which the student has come. Furthermore, starting where the student is means gathering systematic knowledge about the student's linguistic and interactional competencies in relation to the linguistic and interactional competencies of his or her social/cultural group. Through a process known as *ethnographic monitoring,* Hymes (1981) claims that systematic observation of what members of a particular social/cultural group believe, know, say, and do can help teachers recognize the range of their students' linguistic and interactional competencies. Teachers can gain access to this information by taking note of the social and instructional contexts in which second language students' engagement and participation is both high and low, as well as the form or structure of that participation. Teachers can also gain access to information about students' linguistic and interactional competencies by working closely with native-speaker informants, such as parents or community members. Establishing contacts with and gaining information from native-speaker informants may be particularly useful in ESL instructional contexts where teachers work with students from a wide range of linguistic and cultural backgrounds.

To recognize students' competencies and mitigate discontinuities, teachers must also be sensitive to differences in students' cognitive styles, that is, their preferred modes of perceiving, remembering, and thinking (Kogan 1971). Cazden and Leggett (1981) claim that preferences in students' cognitive styles – whether they favor visual, auditory, or tactile-kinesthetic sensory modalities – differ among cultural groups. For example, Chicano mothers were more likely to teach their children through demonstration and modeling, whereas Anglo-American mothers relied more heavily on verbal praise and questioning as a teaching strategy (Laosa 1981). Since children acquire learned ways of talking and interaction within their primary social group, differences in sensory modalities used within these groups will more than likely produce differences in students' preferred learning styles. This is not to say, as Cazden and Leggett (1981) warn, that children who prefer one sensory modality cannot or do not learn through another. However, it does imply that teachers will be less likely to maximize students' competencies if they limit their instructional practices to a single sensory modality. Since children from different linguistic and cultural backgrounds have been found to have different sensory modality strengths, Cazden and Leggett (1981) encourage teachers to vary their instructional practices so as to incorporate more multisensory instructional activities.

Finally, to recognize students' competencies and mitigate discontinuities, teachers must also recognize differences in second language students' orientation toward cooperation versus competition in both social and instructional contexts (Scarcella 1990). Kagan (1989) claims that many cultural groups value cooperativeness over competitiveness – an orientation that is in sharp contrast to the traditional Anglo-American educational system. Delgado-Gaitan (1987a) found that while Mexican students possessed competencies in collaboration, cooperation, and independent decision making, these competencies were not recognized or encouraged in Anglo-American schools. Likewise, Clancy (1986) characterized the Japanese communicative style as being indirect, context dependent, and upholding the needs of the group over those of the individual, which directly conflicts with the Anglo-American communicative style of directness and orientation toward individualism. Teachers must not only recognize the more cooperative learning styles of their second language students, but also incorporate those styles into their classroom instruction. Chapter 7 offers various cooperative learning activities that can act as a means of increasing student motivation and involvement, and create greater opportunities for second language students to participate in classroom events.

Ultimately, for teachers to promote communication in second language classrooms, they must become aware of how their own cultural assumptions and expectations shape their perceptions of classroom communication. They must identify the linguistic and interactional demands that are embedded in classroom events, recognize their students' linguistic, interactional, and cognitive competencies, and determine the extent to which discontinuities may exist. Then they can begin to extend the patterns of communication so as to promote communication in second language classrooms.

Extending the patterns of classroom communication

To promote communication in second language classrooms, teachers must establish an atmosphere in the classroom that is encouraging, supportive, and accepting of any and all student contributions. This means accepting student contributions not as right or wrong answers but, as Hymes (1981) suggests, as an indication of where students are, what students understand, and how they have made sense of what they are learning. Using Hymes's suggestion as a starting point, the focus now turns to the ways in which teachers can extend the patterns of communication in second language classrooms.

Enacting verbal and instructional scaffolds

One way teachers can extend the patterns of communication in second language classrooms is by enacting verbal and instructional scaffolds. Verbal scaffolds (Bruner 1978) represent the ways in which caregivers, teachers, or more experienced peers make it possible for learners to participate in social interactions that are beyond their current linguistic ability level. Verbal scaffolds also represent an important source of comprehensible input for second language acquisition in that they provide language that is adjusted to students' current level of language proficiency and enable them to participate in meaningful interaction before they have acquired the necessary linguistic skills to do so on their own. Instructional scaffolds (Applebee & Langer 1983) operate under the same premise by enabling students to participate in an instructional task without having to assume full responsibility for the task; at the same time, they create opportunities for students to acquire the skills that are necessary to complete the task on their own.

When teachers enact verbal and instructional scaffolds, they assume joint responsibility with students for the interaction and/or task, support students as they make sense of the new information, adapt that support to match students' linguistic and interactional competencies, provide opportunities for students to acquire the necessary skills before actually having to perform, and gradually withdraw that support once students are able to assume more responsibility for the task. Verbal and instructional scaffolds encourage students to use more exploratory language as a means of learning and, as mentioned previously, provide emotional support for students by accepting and building upon what students already know, what they can say, and what they can do. Enacting verbal and instructional scaffolds helps extend the patterns of communication by ensuring that students receive input and support at the appropriate time and level, and as a result, they tend to foster greater student participation.

Making classroom events predictable

Teachers can also extend the patterns of classroom communication by making classroom events predictable. When students know exactly what is expected of them and have ample opportunity to prepare, they are more willing and able to participate in classroom events. To build predictability into classroom events, teachers can provide students with models that demonstrate exactly what they are expected to do within the context of full performance. Suppose, for example, that you are teaching a public speaking class in which you are preparing your students to create and carry out a speech that demonstrates a process. You might start the unit by giving an actual process speech and then using your model speech to help the class generate the critical components of a process speech and appropriate topics for this type of speech. In addition, you might describe how you prepared to give this speech. Thus, your model demonstrates exactly what you expect of your students within the context of full performance, and lets you break down that model into manageable steps so that your students can see how to prepare for and carry out a similar speech.

Making classroom events predictable also means giving students ample opportunity to prepare for what you expect them to say and do. If teachers create opportunities for students to use exploratory language to come to understand new ideas, and then allow students to rehearse those ideas in private rather than in public, they not only foster student learning but also encourage student participation. For example, in my own university-level courses, students write weekly papers (one to two pages) about the required readings. The written style of these papers is very informal, more expressive than academic, and is designed to give students an opportunity to use writing as a means of coming to understand what they are reading. During class discussions, students are much more willing to participate because they have had the opportunity to use exploratory language to make sense of the readings; more importantly, they have had ample opportunity to formulate and rehearse their ideas prior to making those ideas public. I have found that using reaction papers makes even the most reticent students feel more comfortable contributing to our class discussions.

Making classroom events predictable also helps minimize the risk second language students may experience as they attempt to participate in classroom events. Teachers need to show, not just tell, their students exactly what is expected of them, encourage them to use exploratory language to make sense of what they are learning, and create ample opportunities for them to rehearse what they are expected to say and do.

Setting up small groups

Teachers can also extend the patterns of classroom communication by allowing students to work in small groups. Barnes (1976) proposes that small group activities are more conducive to using language for learning since they tend to distance teachers' control over the patterns of communication. In addition, small group activities enable students to take a more active role in what they are learning, as well as have more opportunities to contribute to and help formulate the information that is generated and learned.

However, for small groups to be an effective means of encouraging student participation and fostering student learning, several factors must be taken into consideration. Barnes begins with the importance of *students' feelings of competence*. He claims that the extent to which students are willing to participate in and contribute to small group activities depends on how they think their contributions will be received. To some extent, these perceptions are linked to the perceived status and/or abilities of individual group members. For example, if a student is perceived by his or her peers as more competent, group members may be more likely to defer to this student, thus limiting their own opportunities for interaction and influence in the group. However, teachers can bolster students' feelings of competence by consistently accepting their contributions and showing that they value those contributions by making them part of the instructional content.

A second requirement for successful small group participation and learning is establishing *common ground*. Students need opportunities to make the information that their teachers put before them their own. However, students can do this only if they are given the opportunity to filter this new information through what they already know and have experienced. Small groups are conducive to this, since students are freer to reinterpret and reorganize new information with one another than when directed by the teacher. Barnes warns that if teachers do not allow students to establish common ground, students will merely learn to imitate and memorize teacher-directed information instead of making sense of it on their own.

Third, *focusing students' attention* on specific ideas, concepts, or elements of the instructional content is critical for successful small group participation and learning. Teachers must focus students' attention on features of the information they feel is important, while at the same time encouraging students to generate their own questions about what they think and understand. Focusing students' attention, like establishing common ground, encourages students to make sense of new information in terms of what they already know.

Fourth, *pace*, in Barnes's mind, has less to do with actual time and more to do with the kind of language students are encouraged to use during small group learning. If teachers move too quickly to asking students to demonstrate their learning by performing in front of the class, there will be little time for students to use more exploratory language to come to terms with new information and make it their own. Thus, ample time must be allotted for students to use exploratory language as a vehicle for learning before being asked to make that learning public.

Finally, Barnes suggests that teachers need to encourage students to *use exploratory talk* as preparation for public discussion. While small groups encourage exploration, incompleteness, and low levels of explicitness, making learning public requires knowledge of the needs and expectations of the audience, and the ability to present information in sufficiently explicit and organized ways. Students' success in making learning public depends on the extent to which they have the opportunity to use exploratory talk to sort out and come to terms with new information, as well as their knowledge of and ability to adapt to their audience.

Overall, Barnes characterizes effective small group learning as moving from a focusing stage, in which teachers focus students' attention on new information and what they already know about this new information; to an exploratory stage, in which students are encouraged to come to terms with and make sense of that new information; to a reorganizing stage, in which the teacher informs groups of how they will be expected to demonstrate their learning; and, finally, to a public stage, in which students present their findings to one another and participate in further discussions. Setting up effective small groups along these lines is an important way in which teachers can extend the patterns of classroom communication.

Promoting students' use of language for classroom learning

Extending the patterns of classroom communication also promotes students' use of language for classroom learning. In Excerpt 5.1, the teacher created verbal scaffolds that enabled Tanzi and Yuko to participate in the discussion about the symbolic meaning of the Star of David without assuming full responsibility for the entire dialogue. She did this by receiving what Tanzi and Yuko offered, recasting those offers in terms of the content of the lesson, encouraging Tanzi and Yuko to use language to express their personal understandings, and then connecting those understandings to the content of the lesson. This, in turn, encouraged Tanzi and Yuko to formulate new understandings of what they were learning, while at the same time it created opportunities for them to acquire the skills they will need to eventually carry out such a dialogue on their own. Once Tanzi and Yuko were able to assume more responsibility for their dialogue, the teacher gradually removed her verbal scaffolds.

Excerpt 6.2 was another example of extending the patterns of classroom communication. The teacher accomplished this by encouraging three students, Stan, Rosa, and Zhang, to discuss the observance of Gay Pride Week at an American university. The students were encouraged to initiate questions, control the topic of discussion, and self-select when to participate. Students' contributions were accepted by the teacher and integrated into the content of the lesson. The teacher–student interaction was spontaneous, adaptive, and meaning-focused. The students carried out a variety of language functions, ranging from requesting information to voicing an opinion, all within the context of meaning-focused communication. Overall, such variability in the patterns of communication not only promoted communication but also created greater opportunities for Stan, Rosa, and Zhang to use language for classroom learning.

Promoting students' use of language for second language acquisition

Extending the patterns of classroom communication also promotes students' use of language for second language acquisition. In both Excerpt 5.1 and Excerpt 6.2, the teachers lowered the complexity of their classroom language by reformulating their own language to make it comprehensible for their students. Yuko and Tanzi, as well as Stan, Rosa, and Zhang, were given ample opportunities to initiate, to control the topic of discussion, and to self-select when to participate. They were also given extensive opportunities to use language for meaning-focused communication and to contribute knowledge to the content of the lesson. They were challenged to use language that was beyond their current proficiency level, and their attempts to do so were supported by their teachers' verbal and instructional scaffolds. They had opportunities to participate in a range of language functions and used language in both planned and unplanned discourse. Overall, such variability in the patterns of communication not only promoted classroom communication but also created greater opportunities for each of these students to use language for second language acquisition.

Conclusion

This chapter has examined a range of issues that teachers must consider if they wish to promote communication in second language classrooms. If teachers wish to promote classroom communication, they must be willing to look within themselves, to understand why they do what they do; to look and listen to their students to see what they are capable of; to alter, adjust, and extend what they do, so as to maximize their students' competencies and, in turn, allow students to use language in a way that encourages classroom learning and fosters second language acquisition. Moreover, they must begin to understand how the patterns of communication are established and maintained; come to terms with their own frames of reference; recognize their students' linguistic, interactional, and cognitive competencies; and allow for greater variability in the patterns of communication.

10 *Classroom communicative competence*

Throughout this book, the goal has been to examine how the patterns of communication are organized in second language classrooms, the effect these patterns have on how students participate in classroom events, and how such participation shapes the ways in which students use language for classroom learning and their opportunities for second language acquisition. To summarize, the classroom is a unique communication context, one in which the meanings being communicated and the structure of that communication are shaped by the actions and perceptions of both teachers and students, as well as by the social, cultural, and institutional contexts within which classrooms exist. Teachers' and students' perceptions of the classroom context are shaped by their own frames of reference, and differences in their perceptions can lead to differing interpretations of and participation in classroom events. The nature of classroom communication as it exists between teachers and students, and among students themselves, is variable. Finally, promoting communication in second language classrooms requires that teachers allow for greater variability in the patterns of communication so as to maximize second language students' linguistic and interactional competencies and create more opportunities for them to participate in and learn from classroom events. Such participation can help create opportunities for students to use language for classroom learning and second language acquisition.

All of these factors contribute to the dynamics of communication in second language classrooms. Another contributing factor is classroom communicative competence, or the knowledge and competencies that second language students need in order to participate in, learn from, and acquire a second language in the classroom. In this chapter, classroom communicative competence is defined in terms of students' knowledge of and competence in the structural, functional, social, and interactional norms that govern classroom communication. Thus, the chapter examines the ways in which teachers can define, establish, and extend students' classroom communicative competence. Finally, classroom communicative competence is recognized as contributing to successful classroom participation, productive classroom learning, opportunities for second language acquisition, and, of greatest importance, the development of overall communicative competence in a second language.

Defining classroom communicative competence

Classroom communicative competence is essential in order for second language students to participate in and learn from their classroom experiences. Of course, it should be evident by now that the norms that regulate classroom communication will vary depending on differences among teachers, students, classroom events, and the sociocultural contexts within which classrooms exist. For teachers to define classroom communicative competence, they must recognize the structural and functional norms that govern classroom communication, the social and interactional norms that regulate participation in classroom events, and the sociocultural contexts within which classrooms exist.

Underlying the structural and functional norms that govern classroom communication are the ways in which information is organized in a lesson and the range of purposes for which the language is to be used during the lesson. As we have seen, when the structural and functional norms are rigidly structured and students are expected to fit their communicative behavior into those structures, they end up having limited opportunities to use language for meaningful communication. In Excerpt 6.1, Peersak, Milo, and Suchada were able to recite the correct information from the clearance sale advertisement within the structure established by the teacher; however, the nature of their participation was limited to one- or two-word "right" answers. Of course, we have also seen excerpts in which teachers allow for considerable variation in the structural and functional norms that govern classroom communication, and thus create a range of ways in which students can participate in and use language within a lesson. In Excerpt 5.1, the teacher's construction of verbal scaffolds enabled both Tanzi and Yuko to not only express their emerging understandings of Anne Frank's experiences, but also reconceptualize those understandings in terms of their own lives. Both students had multiple opportunities to initiate topics, state opinions, and/or request information. Thus, the structural and functional norms that govern classroom communication will shape the ways in which students participate in a lesson and what language functions they will use.

Underlying the social and interactional norms that regulate classroom communication is the social organization of participation, or what Erickson (1982) defines as the allocation of interactional rights and obligations of participants, which regulates who talks and when. Social participation structures can range from highly ritualized to highly spontaneous speech events – once again, depending on the ways in which teachers choose to control how, when, why, and with whom students are to use language in classroom events. In Excerpt 3.2, the teacher granted Jay, Alex, and Sung-su considerable freedom as they generated a question to ask the visiting police officer. This freedom encouraged overlapping, self-selected talk that was directed to other students instead of the teacher.

Finally, there is a range of historical, social, cultural, and political factors that shape the ways in which second language students perceive and respond to their classroom experiences. These factors can be: externally imposed constraints that exist within the students' sociocultural community and affect how teachers perceive their students as well as how students perceive themselves, the language they are learning, and their classroom experiences. Moreover, students may view second language learning as a form of enculturation that forces them into cultural perspectives that may differ from or directly oppose their own.

Besides these factors, there can also be internally imposed constraints within the classroom that affect how students perceive and respond to their classroom experiences. Commercial and/or mandated curricula can not only impact upon what teachers teach, but how they teach. Moreover, the complexities of the classroom experience itself can create difficulties for both teachers and students. As Doyle (1977) suggests, successful classroom communication and learning is contingent upon the social relationships that are established between teachers and students. Without mutual trust, respect, and understanding, second language students may learn little from their classroom experiences.

Hence, since no two second language classrooms are identical, teachers must define classroom communicative competence within their own second language classrooms, for their own second language students, and in the sociocultural contexts within which their own second language classrooms exist. Teachers can begin to recognize how and why they organize classroom communication as they do by examining their own cultural assumptions and expectations about appropriate classroom behavior (see Chapter 9). Teachers can examine the linguistic and interactional demands that are embedded in their classroom events by identifying the prerequisite knowledge and competencies that their students will need in order to participate in and learn from specific classroom events. Teachers can also identify their students' unique linguistic, interactional, and cognitive competencies by ensuring that they have ample opportunity to demonstrate their competencies within a range of academic and social contexts. Finally, teachers can mitigate discontinuities that may exist within their classrooms by altering, adjusting, and extending the patterns of classroom communication so as to maximize their students' competencies and create opportunities for them to use language for classroom learning and second language acquisition.

To summarize, defining classroom communicative competence requires that teachers recognize the norms that govern classroom communication, identify the knowledge and competencies that are necessary for students to participate in classroom events, and be cognizant of the social and contextual issues surrounding classrooms. Defining classroom communicative competence will enable teachers to adjust the patterns of communication so as to maximize students' linguistic and interactional competencies, and create opportunities for students to begin to acquire a repertoire of competencies so that they can participate in a wider range of classroom events.

Establishing classroom communicative competence

As previously mentioned, for teachers to enable their second language students to establish classroom communicative competence, they must allow for patterns of communication that maximize students' linguistic and interactional competencies, which will in turn create opportunities for second language students to participate in and learn from classroom events. One way to help students establish classroom communicative competence is to make the norms that govern classroom communication both explicit and predictable. This can be done by demonstrating and labeling the linguistic, social, and interactional norms that regulate student participation in classroom events. For example, using the class meetings as a way to teach small group interaction skills, Enright and McCloskey (1988) suggest that teachers "be explicit":

Label actions that you are performing. *I'm trying to make sure everyone has a chance to talk. I'm summarizing what has been said.* Explain that students should use these same actions when they have their own small groups. (pp. 245–6)

Explicit directions and concrete explanations can help second language students recognize the implicit norms that regulate how they are expected to act and interact in classroom events. Without such explicitness, second language students can become confused about what is expected of them, or how they should participate. This sort of confusion was exemplified in the experiences of a preservice teacher who complained about her inability to get a group of university-level ESL students (predominately Japanese) to participate in small group discussion activities:

I'm about to give up on this group work stuff. It just doesn't seem to work with this class. I put them in groups, give them the assignment, and they just sit there! I feel like I have to cattle prod them to get them to talk.

After observing her teaching, it appeared that one reason these students were having difficulty participating in small group activities was because the teacher never explicitly stated what she expected them to do. For example, in preparation for a small group activity, she simply stated, "Do numbers 3, 5, and 9 in the book and talk about your answers." By neglecting to make explicit what the students were expected to get out of this activity, how they were expected to proceed, or what they would be expected to do once they were finished, the teacher left the students staring uncomfortably at the floor. Like many preservice teachers, this teacher assumed that her students implicitly knew what she expected of them.

Teachers can also help second language students establish classroom communicative competence by making the norms that govern classroom communication predictable. When students know exactly what is expected of them and have ample opportunity to prepare, they are much more willing and able to participate in classroom events. Moreover, making the norms that govern classroom communication predictable helps minimize the risks of participating in classroom events. Teachers can do this by providing for students concrete models of what they are expected to do, and by breaking down new tasks into manageable steps, while at the same time demonstrating each step within the context of full performance. Finally, teachers can also create opportunities for students to practice instructional tasks using more exploratory language before being expected to perform in front of the entire class.

A classroom scenario

Consider the following classroom scenario as an example of how a teacher can make the norms that govern classroom communication explicit and predictable, recognize students' linguistic and interactional competencies, provide plenty of instructional support, and create opportunities for students to use the language within the context of full performance.

Imagine you are planning a lesson for an intermediate-level English conversation class on polite ways of making and accepting invitations. The goal of the lesson is to enable your students to recognize and perform the appropriate linguistic, social, and interactional norms for accepting and making invitations in informal, semiformal, and formal social contexts. Your textbook provides a unit on making and accepting invitations that contains lists of appropriate linguistic phrases along with three audiotaped dialogues that illustrate making and accepting invitations in three different social contexts.

While planning your lesson, you recall that your students become much more engaged in classroom events when they are given opportunities to relate what they are learning to their own experiences. Therefore, you plan to begin the lesson with a large group discussion in which you will ask students to share their own personal experiences of having to make and/or accept invitations. However, you also recall that your previous attempts at large group discussions have not been very successful. You have noticed that one or two students tend to dominate while the others sit quietly and seem uncomfortable when called on to speak in front of the entire class. To enable your students to feel more prepared to participate in the large group discussion, you plan to ask them to complete a journal assignment (prior to class) in which they will write about their own personal experiences either making and/or accepting invitations. You hope they will be more willing to participate in the large group discussion after they have had an opportunity to rehearse what they have to say in writing.

Besides preparing students for the large group discussion, you want your students to know exactly what is expected of them, so you plan to begin by sharing your own personal example of when you reluctantly accepted an invitation for a blind date. Your model will contain some background information about the social situation and the status of the speakers, and illustrate how you accepted the invitation. You also plan to focus your students' attention on both the meaning of the interaction as well as the linguistic form of your acceptance.

On the day of the lesson, you begin by placing students in pairs and asking them to share their journal assignments with one another. You hope this activity will give them an opportunity to rehearse telling their personal experiences before speaking in front of the entire class. You also plan to make explicit your expectations for this activity, by explaining that this activity will give them an opportunity to rehearse telling their experiences. In addition, you plan to suggest that they read their journal assignments first, elaborate if they can, and then retell the experience in a story format. You also plan to encourage students to use comprehension checks, ask questions, and request further elaboration from their partners if some aspect of the story is unclear. Finally, you will explain that when they are finished they will be expected to retell their partner's story to the class. You have selected a retelling activity because you have found that your students seem to feel more comfortable participating in co-narration than speaking alone in front of the entire class. You have also found that co-narration gives students an opportunity to do much more than narrate a story: It encourages them to ask for clarification and confirmation, and share in jointly constructed dialogue. Moreover, you feel that retellings generate more authentic language use than simple narration. Once the pairs begin to retell their partner's stories to the class, you plan to encourage other students to ask questions and/or make comments if they wish, and to intervene yourself only if there is communication breakdown or if the pairs ask for assistance.

After the group retelling activity, you plan to play the audiotaped dialogues and discuss how the level of formality in each social context determines the linguistic, social, and interactional norms that are followed by the speakers. Since you know that your students' listening comprehension skills are weak, you plan to break the listening task into smaller parts that you feel they can handle. You plan to assign individual students the task of listening for one specific piece of information in the dialogue. For example, you will ask one student to listen for how the speaker introduces the invitation, a second student to listen for the how the actual invitation is made, and a third student to listen for how the listener accepts the invitation. Before you play the dialogue, you will provide some background information about the social context within which the invitation is made and the social status of the speakers. You will also play the dialogue twice, to ensure comprehension.

Next, you plan to begin the discussion of the dialogues by asking individual students to share their assigned information. You will also ask more open-ended questions about the entire dialogue to see if other students wish to contribute to the discussion. For each dialogue, you plan to focus the students' attention on what the speakers say, how they say it, and the level of formality within each social context. You also plan to ask students to provide alternative ways of making and accepting invitations that could fit into each dialogue.

As a final activity for this lesson, you plan to place the students in pairs and ask them to create a scenario in which they have to make and accept an invitation. Since, once again, you feel it is important for your students to see a model of what they will be expected to do, you plan to ask for a student volunteer to help you model this activity for the class. With the help of the student volunteer, you will describe the social context and the status of the speakers, create the invitation, and determine an appropriate acceptance. You and the volunteer will practice and then perform the scenario for the entire class. Then you plan to provide ample time for the pairs to create and practice their own scenarios. Before the pairs begin, you will once again provide directions that will make your expectations for this activity as explicit and predictable as possible. As the pairs are working, you will circulate around the room providing assistance and giving suggestions as needed.

In preparation for the performance activity, you will place two pairs together in a group of four, and ask each pair to perform their scenario for the other. You will then ask the pairs to switch and, once again, perform their scenario for a new pair. Once the pairs have rehearsed their scenarios several times, you will ask for volunteers to perform their scenarios in front of the entire class. During the performance activity, you plan to ask the rest of the class to listen for the specific linguistic, social, and interactional norms for making and accepting invitations in each scenario.

While this classroom scenario is fictitious, it does illustrate the ways in which teachers can use what they know about their students' linguistic and interactional competencies to adjust the structure of classroom events so as to maximize those competencies. It also illustrates how teachers can make the norms that govern classroom communication explicit and predictable, provide plenty of instructional support, and create opportunities for students to use the language within the context of full performance. Making the norms of classroom events explicit and predictable is a critical step in enabling second language students to establish classroom communicative competence.

Extending classroom communicative competence

Extending classroom communicative competence means enabling second language students to develop a broader repertoire of linguistic and interactional competencies so that they can successfully participate in a wider range of classroom events. We have already seen examples of educational programs that attempt to do this. For example, the Kamehameha teachers used "talk-story" to develop students' reading comprehension skills so that they could successfully participate in mainstream reading instruction (Chapter 4). Teachers in this program recognized discontinuities between their students' linguistic and interactional competencies and those expected in mainstream classrooms, and therefore adjusted the norms that regulate the patterns of communication during reading instruction so as to enable their students to acquire the prerequisite competencies needed to eventually participate in mainstream reading instruction.

Thus, expanding students' classroom communicative competence means allowing for patterns of classroom communication that encourage the use of a wider range of linguistic and interactional competencies. This means allowing for more spontaneous, adaptive patterns of communication in which the structure and content of the interaction can be constructed and controlled as much by the students as the teacher. It means allowing for more extended discourse, more meaning-focused interactions, and self-initiated participation. It requires combining both meaning and form-focused instruction so as to create opportunities for students to use language for learning, to perform a range of language functions, and to reflect on the structure and organization of the language. It means providing instructional support so students can participate in classroom events that are beyond their current proficiency levels. It entails creating verbal and instructional scaffolds that support active participation in classroom events. Combining all of these enhances students' opportunities to use language for classroom learning and second language acquisition.

Expanding students' classroom communicative competence may also require that teachers identify the educational, professional, or communicative contexts in which their second language students will eventually be expected to participate. This requires that teachers be aware of their students' academic and/or job-related needs as well as their personal and/or professional goals. Robinson (1991) characterizes the needs of second language learners as including goal-oriented needs, which focus on academic or job requirements that are expected at the end of a language course; individual-oriented needs, or what students themselves wish to gain from the second language course; institutional-oriented needs, or what broader social institutions regard as necessary outcomes from second language instruction; and, finally, process-oriented needs, which reflect what students need to do in order to actually acquire the language.

Students' needs and/or goals will depend on their age and the context of their second language instruction. For second language students in elementary and/or secondary schools, the goal of instruction may be to move students into the mainstream curriculum of the school. Thus, teachers will need to find out what linguistic, interactional, and cognitive competencies students need in order to be successful in mainstream classrooms. To do this, teachers of second language students must work closely with teachers of mainstream students to ensure that the skills they are teaching match the skills their students will eventually need in the mainstream classroom. With university-level and/or adult second language students, teachers can survey their students to determine what they hope to get out of their second language courses and what they plan to do once their courses are complete. For many university-level students, passing a required university entrance exam or the TOEFL may be their primary goal-oriented need. For many adults, survival or conversational English may be their immediate individual-oriented need. Once teachers recognize the full range of their students' needs and the contexts they hope to eventually participate in, they can begin to identify the linguistic and interactional competencies that will be required of their students once they leave the second language classroom.

Ultimately, the greater the range of students' linguistic and interactional competencies, the greater their opportunities to participate in and learn from experiences they encounter both inside and beyond the second language classroom. Therefore, while classroom communicative competence is essential for students to successfully participate in classroom events, it may also contribute to the development of overall communicative competence in a second language.

Conclusion

Classroom communicative competence represents students' knowledge of and competence in the structural, functional, social, and interactional norms that govern classroom communication. Without such competence, second language students may learn little from their classroom experiences. Classroom communicative competence can contribute to successful classroom participation, productive classroom learning, increased opportunities for second language acquisition, and the development of second language competence both inside and beyond the classroom.

Differences among teachers, students, and classroom contexts will inevitably influence how, when, where, and why teachers and students communicate and what students learn from their classroom experiences. This book has proposed an integrated view of classroom communication by acknowledging that the dynamics of classroom communication are shaped as much by the teachers and students who come together in the second language classroom as they are by the face-to-face interactions that occur within second language classrooms. The challenge set before teachers is to recognize both the obvious in their classrooms and the not so obvious within themselves and their students, to understand how both of these dimensions shape the dynamics of classroom communication, and to equip their second language students with the competencies they need to get the most out of their second language classroom experiences, so they can, in turn, get the most out of their experiences with the second language.

References

Adamson, H. D. (1993). *Academic competence: Theory and classroom practice: Preparing ESL students for content courses.* New York: Longman.

Alexander, N. (1987). Fundamentals of a pedagogy of liberation for South Africa/Azania in the eighties. *CEAPA, 2* (1), 12–15. Johannesburg: Centre for Enrichment in African Political Affairs.

Alexander, N. (1989). *Language policy and national unity in South Africa/Azania.* Cape Town: Buchu Books.

Allwright, D. (1984). The importance of interaction in classroom language learning. *Applied Linguistics, 5,* 156–71.

Andersen, E. S. (1986). The acquisition of register variation of Anglo-American children. In B. Schieffelin & E. Ochs (Eds.), *Language socialization across cultures* (pp. 153–61). New York: Cambridge University Press.

Anderson, J. (1980). *Cognitive psychology and its implications.* San Francisco: Freeman.

Anderson, J. (1981). Short-term student responses to classroom instruction. *Elementary School Journal, 82,* 97–108.

Anderson, J. (1983). *The architecture of cognition.* Cambridge: Harvard University Press.

Anderson, J. (1985). *Cognitive psychology and its implications* (2nd ed.). New York: Freeman.

Applebee, A. N., & Langer, J. A. (1983). Instructional scaffolding: Reading and writing as natural language activities. *Language Arts, 60,* 168–75.

Aronson, E.; Blaney, N.; Spikes, J.; & Snapp, P. (1978). *The jigsaw classroom.* Beverly Hills, CA: Sage.

Au, K. H-P. (1980). Participation structures in a reading lesson with Hawaiian children: Analysis of a culturally appropriate instructional event. *Anthropology and Education Quarterly, 11,* 91–115.

Au, K. H-P., & Jordan, C. (1981). Teaching reading to Hawaiian children: Finding a culturally appropriate solution. In H. T. Trueba, G. P. Guthrie, & K. H-P. Au (Eds.), *Culture and the bilingual classroom: Studies in classroom ethnography* (pp. 139–52). Rowley, MA: Newbury House.

Barker, L. L. (1982). An introduction to classroom communication. In L. L. Barker (Ed.), *Communication in the classroom* (pp. 1–15). Englewood Cliffs, NJ: Prentice-Hall.

171

Barnes, D. (1976). *From communication to curriculum.* Middlesex: Penguin.

Barnlund, D. C. (1973). *Public and private self in Japan and the United States.* Toyko: Simul Press.

Beam, K. J., & Horvat, R. E. (1975). Differences among teachers' and students' perceptions of science classroom behaviors and actual classroom behaviors. *Science Education, 59,* 333–4.

Belleck, A. A.; Kliebard, H.; Hyman, R.; & Smith, F. (1966). *The language of the classroom.* New York: Teachers College Press.

Berliner, D. C. (1988). *The development of expertise in pedagogy.* New Orleans: American Association of College Teacher Education.

Beyer, L. (1987). What knowledge is of most worth in teacher education. In J. Smyth (Ed.), *Educating teachers: Changing the nature of pedagogical knowledge* (pp. 19–34). New York: Falmer Press.

Bialystok, E. (1988). Psycholinguistic dimensions of second language proficiency. In W. Rutherford & M. Sharwood-Smith (Eds.), *Grammar and second language teaching* (pp. 31–50). Rowley, MA: Newbury House.

Boggs, S. T. (1972). The meaning of questions and narratives to Hawaiian children. In C. B. Cazden (Ed.), *Functions of language in the classroom* (pp. 299–327). New York: Teachers College Press.

Boggs, S. T. (1985). *Speaking, relating and learning: A study of Hawaiian children at home and at school.* Norwood, NJ: Ablex.

Britton, J. (1970). *Language and learning.* London: Penguin.

Brophy, J. E. (1981). Teacher praise: A functional analysis. *Review of Educational Research, 51,* 5–32.

Brown, R., & Bellugi, U. (1964). Three processes in the child's acquisition of syntax. *Harvard Educational Review, 34,* 133–51.

Bruner, J. (1978). The role of dialogue in language acquisition. In A. Sinclair, R. Javella, & W. Levelt (Eds.), *The child's conception of language* (pp. 241–56). New York: Springer-Verlag.

Bruner, J. (1983). *Child's talk: Learning to use language.* New York: Norton.

Calderhead, J. (1981). A psychological approach to research on teachers' classroom decision making. *British Educational Research Journal, 7,* 51–7.

Calderhead, J. (1983). Research into teachers' and student teachers' cognitions: Exploring the nature of classroom practices. Paper presented at the annual meeting of the American Educational Research Association, April, Montreal, Canada.

Calderhead, J., & Robson, M. (1991). Images of teaching: Student teachers' early conceptions of classroom practice. *Teaching and Teacher Education, 7,* 1–8.

Campbell, N. J. (1978). The relationship between students' and teachers' perceptions of teacher behaviors in the junior high classroom. *Journal of Instructional Psychology, 5,* 16–20.

Canale, M., & Swain, M. (1980). Theoretical bases of communicative approaches to second langauge teaching and testing. *Applied Linguistics, 1,* 1–47.

Carrasco, R. L. (1981). Expanding awareness of student performance: A case study in applied ethnographic monitoring in a bilingual classroom. In H. T. Trueba, G. P. Guthrie, & K. H-P. Au (Eds.), *Culture and the bilingual classroom: Studies in classroom ethnography* (pp. 153–77). Rowley, MA: Newbury House.

Carroll, J. A. (1981). Talking through the writing process. *English Journal,* November, 110–120.

Cazden, C. B. (1986). Classroom discourse. In M. C. Wittrock (Ed.), *Handbook of research on teaching* (pp. 432–63). New York: Macmillan.

Cazden, C. B. (1988). *Classroom discourse: The language of teaching and learning.* Portsmouth, NH: Heinemann.

Cazden, C., & Leggett, E. L. (1981). Culturally responsive education: Recommendations for achieving Lau Remedies II. In H. T. Trueba, G. P. Guthrie, & K. H-P. Au (Eds.), *Culture and the bilingual classroom: Studies in classroom ethnography* (pp. 69–86). Rowley, MA: Newbury House.

Chaudron, C. (1988). *Second language classrooms: Research on teaching and learning.* New York: Cambridge University Press.

Christensen, T. (1985). University entrance examinations and English teaching in Japanese high schools: A non-Japanese evaluation. *Speech Evaluation, 12,* 12–20.

Clancy, P. M. (1986). The acquisition of communicative style in Japanese. In B. Schieffelin & E. Ochs (Eds.), *Language socialization across cultures* (pp. 213–50). New York: Cambridge University Press.

Clark, C. M., & Creswell, J. L. (1979). Participants' versus nonparticipants' perceptions of teacher nonverbal behavior. *Journal of Classroom Interaction, 14,* 28–36.

Cole, M., & Scribner, S. (1974). *Culture and thought: A psychological introduction.* New York: Wiley.

Coleman, J. S.; Campbell, E. Q.; Hobsob, C. J.; McPartland, J.; Mood, A. A.; Weinfeld, F. S.; & York, R. L. (1966). *Equality of educational opportunity.* Report from the Office of Education. Washington, DC: U.S. Government Printing Office.

Connelly, F. M., & Clandinin, D. J. (1988). *Teachers as curriculum planners: Narratives of experience.* New York: Teachers College Press.

Cook, D. (1988). Ties that constrict: English as a Trojan hourse. In A. Cummings, A. Gagne, & J. Dawson (Eds.), *Awareness: Proceedings of the 1987 TESL Ontario Conference* (pp. 56–62). Toronto: TESL Ontario.

Cook-Gumperz, J., & Gumperz, J. J. (1982). Communicative competence in educational perspective. In L. C. Wilkinson (Ed.), *Communicating in the classroom* (pp. 13–24). New York: Academic Press.

Cooper, H. M., & Good, T. L. (1982). *Pygmalion grows up: Studies in the expectation communication process.* New York: Longman.

Cummins, J. (1982). Academic acheivement of minority students: Fitting the facts to the policies. Working draft: A report (on bilingual education) prepared for The Ford Foundation. Unpublished manuscript, Ontario Institute for Studies in Education.

deCharms, R. (1972). Personal causation training in the schools. *Journal of Applied Psychology, 2,* 95–113.

Deford, D. (1985). Validating the construct of theoretical orientation in reading instruction. *Reading Research Quarterly, 20,* 351–67.

Delgado-Gaitan, C. (1987a). Traditions and transitions in the learning process of Mexican children: An ethnographic view. In G. Spindler & L. Spindler (Eds.), *Interpretive ethnography of education: At home and abroad* (pp. 333–59). Hillsdale, NJ: Erlbaum.

Delgado-Gaitan, C. (1987b). Parents' perceptions of school: Supportive environments for children. In H. T. Trueba (Ed.), *Success or failure? Learning and the language minority student* (pp. 131–55). New York: Newbury House.

DeVries, D. L., & Slavin, R. E. (1978). Teams-Games-Tournament: A research review. *Journal of Research and Development in Education, 12,* 28–38.

Doyle, W. (1977). Learning the classroom environment: An ecological analysis. *Journal of Teacher Education, 28* (6), 51–5.

Duff, P. (1986). Another look at interlanguage talk: Taking task to task. In R. Day (Ed.), *Talking to learn: Conversation in second language acquisition* (pp. 147–81). Rowley, MA: Newbury House.

Duffy, G. (1982). Fighting off the alligators: What research in real classrooms has to say about reading instruction. *Journal of Reading Behavior, 14,* 357–73.

Duffy, G., & Ball, D. (1986). Instructional decision making and reading teacher effectiveness. In J. Hoffman (Ed.), *Effective teaching of reading: Research and practice* (pp. 163–80). Newark, DE: International Reading Association.

Durkin, D. (1975). The importance of goals for reading instruction. *The Reading Teacher, 28,* 380–83.

Durkin, D. (1983). Is there a match between what elementary teachers do and what basal reader manuals recommend? *The Reading Teacher, 37,* 734–44.

Edwards, D., & Mercer, N. (1986). Context and continuity: Classroom discourse and the development of shared knowledge. In K. Durkin (Ed.), *Language development in the school years* (pp. 172–202). London: Croon Helm.

Elbaz, F. (1983). *Teacher thinking: A study of practical knowledge.* London: Croon Helm.

Ellis, R. (1984). *Classroom second language development.* Oxford: Pergamon.

Ellis, R. (1990). *Instructed second language acquisition.* Oxford: Blackwell.

Enright, D. S. & McCloskey, M. L. (1988). *Integrating English: Developing English language and literacy in the multicultrual classroom.* Reading, MA: Addison-Wesley.

Erickson, F. (1982). Classroom discourse as improvisation: Relationships between academic task structure and social participation structure in lessons. In L. C. Wilkinson (Ed.), *Communicating in the classroom* (pp. 153–81). New York: Academic Press.

Faerch, C., & Kasper, G. (1986). The role of comprehension in second language learning. *Applied Linguistics, 7,* 257–74.

Fillmore, L. W. (1982). Instructional language as linguistic input: Second-language learning in classrooms. In L. C. Wilkinson (Ed.), *Communicating in the classroom* (pp. 283–96). New York: Academic Press.

Finnan, C. R. (1987). The influence of the ethnic community on the adjustment of Vietnamese refugees. In G. Spindler & L. Spindler (Eds.), *Interpretive ethnography of education: At home and abroad* (pp. 313–30). Hillsdale, NJ: Erlbaum.

Finnan, C. R. (1988). Effects of Southeast Asian refugees on schools and school districts. In H. Trueba & C. Delgado-Gaitan (Eds.), *School and society: Learning content through culture* (pp. 119–35). New York: Praeger.

Florio, S., & Schultz, J. (1979). Social competence at home and at school. *Theory into Practice, 18,* 234–43.

Fogarty, J. L.; Wang, M. C.; & Creek, R. (1983). A descriptive study of experienced and novice teachers' interactive thoughts and actions. *Journal of Educational Research, 77,* 22–32.

Forman, E. A., & Cazden, C. B. (1985). Exploring Vygotskian perspectives in education: The cognitive value of peer interaction. In J. V. Wertsch (Ed.), *Culture, communication and cognition: Vygotskian perspectives* (pp. 332–47). New York: Cambridge University Press.

Freeman, D. (1989). Teacher training, development, and decision making: A model of teaching and related strategies for language teacher education. *TESOL Quarterly, 32,* 27–45.

Freeman, D. (1990). "Thoughtful work": Reconceptualizing the research literature on teacher thinking. Plenary paper presented at the annual Washington Area TESOL Conference, October, Washington, DC.

French, P., & Woll, B. (1981). Context, meaning and strategy in parent-child conversation. In G. Wells (Ed.), *Learning through interaction: The study of language development* (pp. 157–82). Cambridge: Cambridge University Press.

Fujita, M., & Sano, T. (1988). Children in American and Japanese day-care centers: Ethnography and reflective cross-cultural interviewing. In H. Trueba & C. Delgado-Gaitan (Eds.), *School and Society: Learning content through culture* (pp. 73–97). New York: Praeger.

Gage, N. (1978). *The scientific basis of the art of teaching.* New York: Teachers College Press.

Gass, S. (1979). Language transfer and universal grammatical relations. *Language Learning, 27,* 327–44.

Gee, J. P. (1986). Orality and literacy: From *The savage mind* to *Ways with words. TESOL Quarterly, 20* (4), 719–46.

Gee, J. P. (1988). Dracula, the Vampire Lestat, and TESOL. *TESOL Quarterly, 22* (2), 201–25.

Gee, J. P. (1990). *Social linguistics and literacies: Ideology in discourses.* London: Falmer Press.

George, D. (1984). Working with peer groups in the composition classroom. *College Composition and Communication, 35* (3), 320–26.

Gere, A. R., & Abbott, R. D. (1985). Talking about writing: The language of writing groups. *Research in the Teaching of English, 19* (4), 362–81.

Gibson, M. A. (1987). The school performance of immigrant minorities: A comparative view. *Anthropology and Education Quarterly, 18,* 262–75.

Givon, R. (1979). *On understanding grammar.* New York: Academic Press.

Gregg, K. (1984). Krashen's monitor and Occam's razor. *Applied Linguistics, 5,* 79–100.

Grimm, N. (1986). Improving students' responses to their peer's essays. *College Composition and Communication, 37* (1), 91–4.

Grossman, P. (1990). *The making of a teacher: Teacher knowledge and teacher education.* New York: Teachers College Press.

Grossman, P. L.; Wilson, S. M.; & Shulman, L. S. (1989). Teachers of substance: Subject matter knowledge for teaching. In M. Reynolds (Ed.), *Knowledge base for the beginning teacher* (pp. 23–36). New York: Pergamon.

Gumperz, J. J. (1977). Sociocultural knowledge in conversational inference. In M. Saville-Troike (Ed.), *Linguistics and Anthropology* (pp. 191–211). Georgetown University Roundtable on Langauges and Linguistics. Washington, DC: Georgetown University Press.

Halliday, M. A. K. (1973). *Exploring the functions of language.* London: Edward Arnold.

Harris, M. (1986). *Teaching one-to-one: The writing conference.* Urbana, IL: National Council of Teachers of English.

Harris, S. (1980). *Culture and learning: Tradition and education in northeastern Amhen Land.* Darwin: North Territory Department of Education.

Harste, J. C., & Burke, C. L. (1977). A new hypothesis for reading teacher research: Both the teaching and learning of reading is theoretically based. In P. D. Pearson (Ed.), *Reading: Theory, research and practice* (pp. 32–40). New York: Mason.

Hatch, E. (1978). *Second language acquisition.* Rowley, MA: Newbury House.

Heath, S. B. (1982). Questioning at home and at school: A comparison study. In G. Spindler (Ed.), *Doing the ethnography of schooling: Educational anthropology in action* (pp. 103–31). New York: Holt, Rinehart, & Winston.

Heath, S. B. (1983). *Ways with words: Language, life and work in communities and classrooms.* Cambridge: Cambridge University Press.

Hoffman, D. M. (1988). Cross-cultural adaptation and learning: Iranians and Americans at school. In H. Trueba & C. Delgado-Gaitan (Eds.), *School and society: Learning content through culture* (pp. 163–80). New York: Praeger.

Hymes, D. (1972). On communicative competence. In J. B. Pride & J. Holmes (Eds.), *Sociolinguistics: Selected readings* (pp. 269–93). Harmondsworth: Penguin.

Hymes, D. (1974). *Foundations in sociolinguistics.* Philadelphia: University of Pennsylvania Press.

Hymes, D. (1981). Ethnographic monitoring. In H. T. Trueba, G. P. Guthrie, & K. H-P. Au (Eds.), *Culture and the bilingual classroom: Studies in classroom ethnography* (pp. 56–8). Rowley, MA: Newbury House.

Johnson, D. W. (1981). Student-student interaction: The neglected variable in education. *Educational Researcher, 10* (1), 5–10.

Johnson, D. W., & Johnson, R. T. (1979). Conflict in the classroom: Controversy and learning. *Review of Educational Research, 49,* 51–70.

Johnson, K. E. (1992a). The relationship between teachers' beliefs and practices during literacy instruction for non-native speakers of English. *Journal of Reading Behavior, 24* (1), 83–108.

Johnson, K. E. (1992b). Learning to teach: Instructional actions and decisions of preservice ESL teachers. *TESOL Quarterly, 26* (3), 507–35.

Johnson, K. E. (1992c). Tapping experienced teachers' knowledge during the TESOL practicum. *Guidelines, 14* (2), 43–53.

Johnson, K. E. (1994). The emerging beliefs and instructional practices of preservice English as a second language teachers. *Teaching and Teacher Education, 10* (4): 439–52.

Johnson, K. E. (1996). The vision vs. the reality: The tensions of the TESOL practicum. In D. Freeman & J. Richards (Eds.), *Teacher Learning in Language Teaching* (pp. 30–49). New York: Cambridge University Press.

Jordan, C. (1981). The selection of culturally-compatible classroom practices. *Educational Perspectives, 20,* 16–19.

Kachru, B. J. (1986). *The alchemy of English: The spread, functions and models of non-native Englishes.* Oxford: Pergamon Press.

Kagan, S. (1989). *Cooperative learning: Resources for teachers.* San Juan Capistrano: Resources for Teachers.

Kamada, L. D. (1987). Intrinsic and extrinsic motivation learning processes: Why Japanese can't speak English. Paper presented at the Japan Association of Language Teachers International Conference on Language Teaching, October, Seirei Gakuen, Hamamatsu, Japan.

Kamler, B. (1980). One child, one teacher, one classroom: The story of one piece of writing. *Language Arts, 57,* 680–93.

Kaur, K. (1990). Students' and teachers' perceptions of goals, tasks, and evaluation in ESL classrooms in Malaysia. Unpublished master's thesis, Syracuse University.

Kaur, K. (1993). Knowing is not doing: Constraints to implementing a student-centered curriculum. Paper presented at the 27th Annual TESOL Convention, April, Atlanta, GA.

Kerr, D. H. (1981). Teaching competence and teacher education in the United States. *Teachers College Record, 84* (3), 540–52.

Kinzer, C. K., & Carrick, D. A. (1986). Teacher beliefs as instructional influences. In J. Niles & R. Lalik (Eds.), *Solving problems in literacy: Learners, teachers, & researchers* (pp. 127–34). 35th Yearbook of the National Reading Conference. Rochester, NY: National Reading Conference.

Kitade, R. (1990). Non-verbal communication. In K. Kamakura (Ed.), *Cross-cultural communication of the Japanese* (pp. 97–117). Tokyo: Hokuju-Shuppan.

Kogan, N. (1971). Educational implications of cognitive styles. In G. S. Lesser (Ed.), *Psychology and educational practice* (pp. 242–92). Glenview, IL: Scott, Foresman.

Koike, I. (1990). *A general survey of English language teaching in Japan.* Toyko: Sangodo.

Krashen, S. (1981). *Second language acquisition and second language learning.* Oxford: Pergamon.

Krashen, S. (1982). *Principles and practice in second language acquisition.* Oxford: Pergamon.

Krashen, S. (1985). *The Input Hypothesis: Issues and implications.* New York: Longman.

LaForge, P. G. (1983). *Counseling and culture in second language acquisition.* New York: Pergamon Institute of English.

Lampert, M. (1985). How do teachers manage to teach? Perspectives on problems in practice. *Harvard Educational Review, 55* (2), 178–94.

Laosa, L. M. (1981). Maternal behavior: Sociocultural diversity in modes of family interaction. In R. W. Henderson (Ed.), *Parent-child interaction: Theory, research, and prospects* (pp. 125–67). New York: Academic Press.

Lemke, J. L. (1985). *Using language in the classroom.* London: Oxford University Press.

Lemke, J. L. (1989). The language of classroom science. In C. Emihovich (Ed.), *Locating learning across the curriculum* (pp. 216–39). Norwood, NJ: Ablex.

LeVine, R. A. (1978). *Women's education and maternal behavior in the Third World: A report to the Ford Foundation.* Laboratory of Human Development, Harvard Graduate School of Education.

Lewis, A. (1981). Minority education in Sharonia, Israel, and Stockton, California: A comparative analysis. *Anthropology and Education Quarterly, 12,* 30–50.

Littlewood, W. (1981). *Communicative language teaching: An introduction.* Cambridge: Cambridge University Press.

Long, M. (1981). Input, interaction and second language acquisition. In H. Winitz (Ed.), *Native language and foreign language learning and teaching* (pp. 379–94). New York: Annals of the New York Academy of Sciences.

Long, M. (1983). Native speaker/non-native speaker conversation and the negotiation of meaning. *Applied Linguistics, 4,* 126–41.

Long, M. (1985). Input and second language acquisition theory. In S. Gass & C. Madden (Eds.), *Input in second language acquisition* (pp. 377–93). Rowley, MA: Newbury House.

Long, M., & Sato, C. (1984). Methodological issues in interlanguage studies:

An interactionist perspective. In A. Davies, C. Criper, & A. Howatt (Eds.), *Interlanguage* (pp. 253–79). Edinburgh: Edinburgh University Press.

Lortie, D. (1975). *Schoolteacher: A sociological study.* Chicago: University of Chicago Press.

Macias, J. (1987). The hidden curriculum of Papago teachers: American Indian strategies for mitigating cultural discontinuity in early schooling. In G. Spindler & L. Spindler (Eds.), *Interpretive ethnography of education: At home and abroad* (pp. 363–80). Hillsdale, NJ: Erlbaum.

MacLure, M., & French, P. (1980). A comparison of talk at home and at school. In G. Wells (Ed.), *Learning through interaction: The study of language development* (pp. 205–39). Cambridge: Cambridge University Press.

Malcolm, I. (1979). The West Australian Aboriginal child and classroom interaction: A sociolinguistic approach. *Journal of Pragmatics, 3,* 305–20.

Malcolm, I. (1982). Speech events of the Aboriginal classroom. *International Journal of Sociology of Language, 36,* 115–34.

Mangano, N., & Allen, J. (1986). Teachers' beliefs about language arts and their effects on students' beliefs and instruction. In J. Niles & R. Lalik (Eds.), *Solving problems in literacy: Learners, teachers, & researchers* (pp. 136–42). 35th Yearbook of the National Reading Conference. Rochester, NY: National Reading Conference.

McDermott, R. P. (1977). Social relations as contexts for learning in school. *Harvard Educational Review, 47* (2), 198–213.

McLaughlin, B. (1987). *Theories of second language acquisition.* London: Edward Arnold.

McLaughlin, M. W. (1991). The Rand Change Agent Study revisited: Macroperspectives and microrealities. *Educational Researcher, 19* (9), 11–16.

Mehan, H. (1979). *Learning lessons: Social organization in the classroom.* Cambridge, MA: Harvard University Press.

Mendonca, C. O., & Johnson, K. E. (In press). Peer review negotiations: Revision activities in ESL writing instruction. *TESOL Quarterly.*

Morine, G., & Vallance, E. (1975). *Special study B: A study of teacher and pupil perceptions of classroom interaction.* Technical Report No. 75–11–6. San Francisco: Far West Laboratory.

Morine-Dershimer, G. (1982). Pupil perceptions of teacher praise. *Elementary School Journal, 82,* 421–34.

Ninio, A., & Bruner, J. (1978). The achievement and antecedents of labeling. *Journal of Child Language, 5,* 1–15.

Nisbett, R., & Ross, L. (1980). *Human inferences: Strategies and shortcomings of social judgment.* Englewood Cliffs, NJ: Prentice-Hall.

Nowicki, S., Jr., & Strickland, B. R. (1973). A locus of control scale for children. *Journal of Consulting and Clinical Psychology, 40,* 148–54.

Nunan, D. (1988). *The learner-centred curriculum.* Cambridge: Cambridge University Press.

Ogbu, J. U. (1982). Cultural discontinuities and schooling. *Anthropology and Education Quarterly, 13* (4), 290–307.

Ogbu, J. U. (1987). Variability in minority responses to schooling: Nonimmigrants vs. immigrants. In G. Spindler & L. Spindler (Eds.), *Interpretive ethnography of education: At home and abroad* (pp. 255–78). Hillsdale, NJ: Erlbaum.

O'Malley, J.; Chamot, A.; & Walker, C. (1987). Some applications of cognitive theory to second language acquisition. *Studies in second language acquisition, 9,* 287–306.

Pajares, M. F. (1992). Teachers' beliefs and educational research: Cleaning up a messy construct. *Review of Educational Research, 62* (3), 307–32.

Palincsar, A. S. (1986). The role of dialogue in providing scaffolded instruction. *Educational Psychologist, 21,* 73–98.

Peirce, B. N. (1989). Toward a pedagogy of possibility in the teaching of English internationally: People's English in South Africa. *TESOL Quarterly, 23* (3), 401–20.

Perret-Clermont, A. N. (1980). *Social interaction and cognitive development in children.* New York: Academic Press.

Peters, A. M., & Boggs, S. T. (1986). Interactional routines as cultural influences upon language acquisition. In B. Schieffelin & E. Ochs (Eds.), *Language socialization across cultures* (pp. 80–96). New York: Cambridge University Press.

Philips, S. (1972). Participant structures and communicative competence: Warm Springs children in community and classroom. In C. B. Cazden (Ed.), *Functions of language in the classroom* (pp. 370–94). New York: Teachers College Press.

Philips, S. (1983). *The invisible culture: Communication in the classroom and community on the Warm Springs Indian Reservation.* White Plains, NY: Longman.

Piaget, J. (1957). *The language and thought of the child.* London: Routledge & Kegan Paul.

Pienemann, M. (1988). Psychological constraints on the teachability of language. In W. Rutherford & M. Sharwood-Smith (Eds.), *Grammar and second language teaching* (pp. 85–106). Rowley, MA: Newbury House.

Pintrich, P. R.; Cross, D. R.; Kozma, R. B.; & McKeachie, W. J. (1986). Instructional psychology. *Annual Review of Psychology, 37,* 611–51.

Ratner, N., & Bruner, J. (1978). Games, social exchange and the acquisition of language. *Journal of Child Language, 5,* 391–401.

Reid, I., & Croucher, A. (1980). The Crandall Intellectual Achievement Responsibility Questionnaire: A British validation study. *Educational and Psychological Measurement, 40,* 255–8.

Resnick, L. B. (1985). Cognition and instruction: Recent theories of human competence. In B. L. Hammond (Ed.), *Psychology and learning: The masters lecture series, vol. 4* (pp. 127–86). Washington, DC: American Psychological Association.

Resnick, M. C. (1993). ESL and language planning in Puerto Rican education. *TESOL Quarterly, 27* (2), 259–75.

Richards, J. C., and Crookes, G. (1988). The practicum in TESOL. *TESOL Quarterly, 22,* 9–27.

Robinson, P. (1991). *ESP today: A practitioner's guide.* Englewood Cliffs, NJ: Prentice-Hall.

Rosecky, M. (1978). Are teachers selective when using basal guidebooks? *The Reading Teacher, 31,* 381–5.

Samson, B. (1980). *The camp at Wallaby Cross.* Canberra: Australia Institute for Aboriginal Studies.

Sato, C. (1982). Ethnic styles in classroom discourse. In M. Hines & W. Rutherford (Eds.), *On TESOL '81* (pp. 11–24). Washington, DC: TESOL.

Scarcella, R. (1990). *Teaching language minority students in the multicultural classroom.* Englewood Cliffs, NJ: Prentice-Hall.

Schon, D. (1983). *The reflective practitioner: How professionals think in action.* New York: Basic Books.

Schon, D. (1987). *Educating the reflective practitioner.* San Francisco: Jossey-Bass.

Schunk, D. H. (1992). Theory and research on student preceptions in the classroom. In D. H. Schunk & J. L. Meece (Eds.), *Student perceptions in the classroom* (pp. 4–23). Hillsdale, NJ: Erlbaum.

Scollon, P., & Scollon, S. W. (1990). Some cultural aspects of teaching English to Asian adults. Unpublished manuscript, Dept. of Anthropology, Harvard University.

Scribner, S., & Cole, M. (1981). *The psychology of language.* Cambridge: Harvard University Press.

Selinker, L. (1974). Interlanguage. In J. Richards (Ed.), *Error analysis* (pp. 31–54). Essex: Longman.

Shake, M., & Allington, R. (1985). Where do teachers' questions come from? *The Reading Teacher, 38,* 432–9.

Shannon, P. (1983). The use of commercial reading materials in American elementary schools. *Reading Research Quarterly, 19,* 68–85.

Shannon, P. (1987). Commercial reading materials, a technological ideology and the deskilling of teachers. *Elementary School Journal, 87,* 307–29.

Shannon, P. (1989). Class size, reading instruction, and commercial materials. *Reading Research and Instruction, 28,* 18–29.

Sharan, S. (1980). Cooperative learning in small groups: Recent methods and effects on achievement, attitudes, and ethnic relations. *Review of Educational Research, 50,* 241–72.

Sharan, S., & Lazarowitz, R. (1978). *Cooperation and communication in school.* Tel-Aviv and Jerusalem: Shocken.

Shavelson, R. J. (1983). Review of research on teachers' pedagogical judgment, plans, and decisions. *Elementary School Journal, 83,* 392–413.

Shavelson, R. J., & Stern, P. (1981). Research on teachers' pedagogical thoughts, judgments, decisions, and behavior. *Review of Educational Research, 51,* 455–98.

Shulman, L. S. (1986). Those who understand: Knowledge growth in teaching. *Educational Researcher, 15* (2), 4–14.

Shulman, L. S. (1987). Knowledge and teaching: Foundations of the new reform. *Harvard Educational Review, 57,* 114–35.

Shulman, L. S., & Grossman, P. L. (1987). Final report to the Spencer Foundation. Technical Report of the Knowledge Growth in a Profession Research Project. Stanford, CA: School of Education, Stanford University.

Sinclair, J. McH., & Coulthard, R. M. (1975). *Towards an analysis of discourse: The English used by teachers and pupils.* London: Oxford University Press.

Slade, M. (1982). Aptitude, intelligence or what? *The New York Times,* October 24, pp. 22–3.

Slavin, R. E. (1978). Student teams and achievement divisons. *Journal of Research and Development in Education, 12,* 39–49.

Slavin, R. E. (1980). Cooperative learning. *Review of Educational Research, 50,* 315–42.

Spindler, G. D. (1974). The transmission of culture. In G. D. Spindler (Ed.), *Education and cultural process* (pp. 303–34). New York: Holt, Rinehart, & Winston.

Spindler, G., & Spindler, L. (1982). Roger Harker and Schoenhausen: From the familiar to the strange and back again. In G. Spindler (Ed.), *Doing the ethnography of schooling: Educational anthropology in action* (pp. 20–47). New York: Holt, Rinehart, & Winston.

Spindler, G., & Spindler, L. (1987a). Teaching and learning how to do the ethnography of education. In G. Spindler & L. Spindler (Eds.), *Interpretive ethnography of education: At home and abroad* (pp. 17–33). Hillsdale, NJ: Erlbaum.

Spindler, G., & Spindler, L. (1987b). Cultural dialogue and schooling in Schoenhausen and Roseville: A comparative analysis. *Anthropology and Education Quarterly, 18* (1), 3–16.

Steinberg, M. T. (1985). English instruction in Japanese junior high schools. In C. B. Wordell (Ed.), *A guide to teaching English in Japan* (pp. 95–124). Tokyo, Japan: Japan Times.

Suarez-Orozco, M. M. (1987). Towards a psychological understanding of Hispanic adaptation to American schooling. In H. T. Trueba (Ed.), *Success or failure? Learning and the language minority student* (pp. 156–69). New York: Newbury House.

Swain, M. (1985). Communicative competence: Some roles of comprehensible input and comprehensible output in its development. In S. Gass & C. Madden (Eds.), *Input in second language acquisition* (pp. 235–53). Rowley, MA: Newbury House.

Tharp, R. (1982). The effective instruction of comprehension: Results and description of the Kamehameha Early Education Program. *Reading Research Quarterly, 17,* 503–27.

Trueba, H. T. (1987). The ethnography of schooling. In H. T. Trueba (Ed.), *Success or failure? Learning and the language minority student* (pp. 1–14). New York: Newbury House.

Trueba, H. T. (1989). *Raising silent voices: Educating the linguistic minority for the 21st century.* New York: Newbury House.

van Lier, L. A. W. (1991). Inside the classroom: Learning processes and teaching procedures. *Applied Language Learning, 2* (1), 29–68.

Vygotsky, L. (1978). *Mind in society.* Cambridge: Harvard University Press.

Wagner-Gough, J. (1975). Comparative studies in second language learning. *CALERIC/CLL Series on Language and Linguistics, 26.*

Warren, R. L. (1988). Cooperation and conflict between parents and teachers: A comparative study of three elementary schools. In H. Trueba & C. Delgado-Gaitan (Eds.), *School and society: Learning content through culture* (pp. 137–60). New York: Praeger.

Watson, K. A. (1972). The rhetoric of narrative structure: A sociolinguistic analysis of stories told by part-Hawaiian children. Doctoral dissertation, University of Hawaii.

Webb, N. M. (1982). Student interaction and learning in small groups. *Review of Educational Research, 52* (3), 421–45.

Weinstein, C. S. (1983). Students' perceptions of schooling. *Elementary School Journal, 83,* 288–312.

Weinstein, C. S. (1990). Prospective elementary teachers' beliefs about teaching: Implications for teacher education. *Teaching and Teacher Education, 6,* 279–90.

Weinstein, R. S.; Marshall, H. H.; Brattesani, K. A.; & Middlestadt, S. E. (1982). Student perceptions of differential teacher treatment in open and traditional classrooms. *Journal of Educational Psychology, 74,* 678–92.

Weinstein, R. S., & Middlestadt, S. E. (1979). Student perceptions of teacher interactions with male high and low achievers. *Journal of Educational Psychology, 71,* 421–31.

Wertsch, J. V. (1979). From social interaction to higher psychological processes: A clarification and application of Vygotsky's theory. *Human Development, 22,* 1–22.

Wertsch, J. V. (1984). The zone of proximal development: Some conceptual issues. In B. Rogoff & J. Wertsch (Eds.), *Children's learning in the "zone of proximal development"* (pp. 7–18). New Directions in Child Development, no. 23. San Francisco: Jossey-Bass.

White, L. (1987). Against comprehensible input: The input hypothesis and the development of second-language competence. *Applied Linguistics, 8,* 95–110.

Whorf, B. L. (1956). *Language, thought and reality: Selected writings.* Cambridge: MIT Press.

Widdowson, H. G. (1978). *Teaching language as communication.* Oxford: Oxford University Press.

Wigdor, A. K., & Garner, W. R. (Eds.). (1982). *Ability testing: Uses, consequences, and controversies.* Part I: Report of the Committee. Washington, DC: National Academy Press.

Wilcox, K. (1982). Differential socialization in the classroom: Implications for equal opportunity. In G. Spindler (Ed.), *Doing the ethnography of schooling: Educational anthropology in action* (pp. 269–309). New York: Holt, Rinehart, & Winston.

Wilkinson, L. C. (1982). Introduction: A sociolinguistic approach to communicating in the classroom. In L. C. Wilkinson (Ed.), *Communicating in the classroom* (pp. 3–12). New York: Academic Press.

Willett, J. (1987). Contrasting acculturation patterns of two non-English speaking pre-schoolers. In H. T. Trueba (Ed.), *Success or failure? Learning and the language minority student* (pp. 69–84). New York: Newbury House.

Wilson, S. M., & Wineburg, S. S. (1988). Peering at history through different lenses: The role of disciplinary perspectives in teaching history. *Teachers College Record, 89,* 525–39.

Winne, P. H. (1980). *Matching students' cognitive processing to text with instructional objectives or adjunct questions.* Instructional Psychology Research Group Report No. 80–02. Burnaby, BC: Simon Fraser University.

Winne, P. H., & Marx, R. W. (1980). Matching students' cognitive responses to teaching skills. *Journal of Educational Psychology, 72,* 257–64.

Wittrock, M. C. (1986). Students' thought processes. In M. C. Wittrock (Ed.), *Handbook of research on teaching* (pp. 297–314). New York: Macmillan.

Woods, P. (1987). Life histories and teacher knowledge. In J. Smyth (Ed.), *Educating teachers: Changing the nature of pedagogical knowledge* (pp. 121–36). New York: Falmer Press.

Wordell, C. B. (1985). Diverse perspectives on English teaching in Japan. In C. B. Wordell (Ed.), *A guide to teaching English in Japan* (pp. 3–19). Tokyo: Japan Times.

Yates, P. D. (1987). A case of mistaken identity: Interethnic images in multicultural England. In G. Spindler & L. Spindler (Eds.), *Interpretive ethnography of education: At home and abroad* (pp. 195–218). New York: Erlbaum.

Index

academically oriented language use, 80

acculturation patterns, 62, 146; accommodation without assimilation, 131; adaption, 131; forced, 131–2

classroom communication: definition of, 7–9; dynamics of, 39, 160; integrated view of, 3, 9; norms that govern, 161–4, 166; structure of, 4–5, 9–10, 25–6

classroom communicative competence, 5–6, 10, 15, 161–2; definition of, 160; establishing, 163–7

classroom events: fitting into, 42–7; interactional demands of, 146, 151–2; linguistic demands of, 151–2; opportunities to participate in, 146; predictability of, 155–6; structure of, 40–2; students' perception of, 39, 40; variability in, 47–51

classroom learning, 7; optimal conditions for, 87–9, 100, 120; students' use of language for, 14, 73–6, 76–81, 158

classroom norms: cultural differences in, 5, 51, 52–3

classroom settings: adult level, 63; elementary level, 9, 48, 150; preschool level, 62, 66, 147; secondary level, 18, 23, 43, 76, 93; TESOL practicum, 32, 36; university level, 101, 121, 125, 163

cognitive learning theory, 88

cognitive style (students'), 153

communication context (*see also classroom communicative competence*): classroom as a, 4–5, 39, 76; communicative competence, 13, 67; expanded definition of, 134

communicative style, 59–63; Anglo-American, 60, 154; Australian Aboriginal, 60–1; definition of, 59; Japanese, 59–60, 154; Mexican, 61, 154

community-based issues, 129, 132; cultural

discontinuities, 65–6, 130–1; parent–teacher relationships, 132; perceived status of English, 134–6; variability in response to schooling, 130–2

competencies (students'): linguistic and interactional, 56–7, 70–1, 145–7, 152–3, 160, 162–4, 166–7

comprehensible input, 86, 88

contextualization cues, 42

control over classroom communication: interactional control, 21–2; thematic control, 21

conventionalized language, 10–1, 22, 106

cooperative learning techniques, 112, 114–5; group investigation, 115, 120–4; Jigsaw Method, 114; peer-tutoring model, 114–5, 117–20; Student Teams and Academic Divisions, 114; Teams-Games-Tournament, 114

cultural discontinuity hypothesis, 65–6; primary discontinuities, 65; secondary discontinuities, 65–6; universal discontinuities, 65

cultural groups (students): African-American, 130, 166; Asian-American, 115, 130, 132; Australian Aboriginal, 60–1, 115; Brazilian, 62; Chicano, 66; Chinese, 115; French Canadian, 130; German, 132; Hispanic-American, 131; Iranian, 131; Japanese, 63, 115, 147, 154, 163; Korean, 57, 64; Malaysian, 93; Mexican-American, 47, 130, 131, 132, 150, 154; Native American, 57–8, 66–7, 69, 115; Patidar, 132; Polynesian (in Hawaii), 68; Puerto Rican, 57–8, 66–7, 69, 115; Punjabi, 64, 131; Russian, 63; South African, 134; Taiwanese, 53; Vietnamese, 52, 64; West Indian, 130, 132

cultural groups (teachers): American, 61, 148–9, 154; German, 148–9; Japanese, 138; Malaysian, 93, 138

101483